C000009737

The Landscape of Humanity

ST ANDREWS STUDIES
IN PHILOSOPHY AND PUBLIC AFFAIRS

Founding and General Editor:
John Haldane, University of St Andrews

Values, Education and the Human World
edited by John Haldane

Philosophy and its Public Role
edited by William Aiken and John Haldane

Relativism and the Foundations of Liberalism
by Graham Long

Human Life, Action and Ethics:
Essays by G.E.M. Anscombe
edited by Mary Geach and Luke Gormally

The Institution of Intellectual Values:
Realism and Idealism in Higher Education
by Gordon Graham

Life, Liberty and the Pursuit of Utility
by Anthony Kenny and Charles Kenny

Distributing Healthcare:
Principles, Practices and Politics
edited by Niall Maclean

Liberalism, Education and Schooling:
Essays by T.M. Mclaughlin
edited by David Carr, Mark Halstead and Richard Pring

The Landscape of Humanity: Art, Culture & Society
by Anthony O'Hear

Faith in a Hard Ground:
Essays on Religion, Philosophy and Ethics by G.E.M. Anscombe
edited by Mary Geach and Luke Gormally

Subjectivity and Being Somebody
by Grant Gillett

The Landscape of Humanity

Art, Culture and Society

Anthony O'Hear

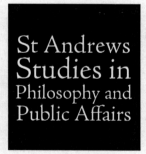

St Andrews
Studies in
Philosophy and
Public Affairs

ia

IMPRINT ACADEMIC

Copyright © Anthony O'Hear, 2008

The moral rights of the author have been asserted.
No part of this publication may be reproduced in any form
without permission, except for the quotation of brief passages
in criticism and discussion.

Published in the UK by Imprint Academic
PO Box 200, Exeter EX5 5YX, UK

Published in the USA by Imprint Academic
Philosophy Documentation Center
PO Box 7147, Charlottesville, VA 22906-7147, USA

ISBN 9781845401122 (paper)
ISBN 9781845401450 (cloth)

A CIP catalogue record for this book is available from the
British Library and US Library of Congress

Cover Photograph:
St Salvator's Quadrangle, St Andrews by Peter Adamson
from the University of St Andrews collection

Contents

To Tricia, Natasha, Jacob and Thea

ad familiam meam amandam amatamque

Preface

The fifteen essays in this book have been written over a period of years, from the early 1990s to the time of publication (2008). Most have already been published in some form, though all have been revised to a greater or lesser extent for this volume. This is to reduce repetition and inconsistency as far as possible, and also to take account of developments in my thinking where these bear on the topics under discussion.

In the order in which they appear in this volume, the original places of publication are as follows:

'Evolution and Aesthetics'
   in *Biology, Evolution and Life*, edited by A. O'Hear, Cambridge University Press, 2005, pp 155–76.

'Historicism and Architectural Knowledge'
   in *Philosophy, 68, 1993*, pp 127–44.

'Prospects for Beauty'
   in *Philosophy at the New Millennium*, edited by A. O'Hear, Cambridge University Press, pp 175–91.

'Kantian Disinterestedness'
   not previously published; part of a paper on the approaches of Dürer and Cranach to the illustration of the Book of Revelation, written jointly with Natasha O'Hear, and presented to the D Society at the University of Cambridge in February 2007.

'The real or the Real? Chardin or Rothko?'
   in *Philosophy, Religion and the Spiritual Life* edited by Michael McGhee, Cambridge University Press, 1992, pp 47–58.

'Two Cultures Revisited'
   in *Verstehen and Humane Understanding*, edited by A.O'Hear, Cambridge University Press, 1997, pp 1–17.

'Art and Censorship'
   in *Philosophy, 66, 1991*, pp 512–16.

'To Swim with Strong Strokes in the Lake of Antique Poetry'
lecture given at the Prince of Wales' Educational Summer School, Buxton, Derbyshire, June 27th, 2004, and published in a slightly different version as the Epilogue to the author's *The Great Books*, Icon Books, Thriplow, Cambridge, 2007, pp 433–49.

'Art and Technology: an Old Tension'
in *Philosophy and Technology*, edited by Roger Fellows, Cambridge University Press, 1995, pp 143–58.

'Science and Religion'
in *The British Journal for the Philosophy of Science, 44, 1993*, pp 505–16.

'Democracy and Openness'
in *Political Philosophy*, edited by A. O'Hear, Cambridge University Press, 2006, pp 39–56.

'Hayek and Popper: *The Road to Serfdom* and *The Open Society*'
in *The Cambridge Companion to Hayek*, edited by Edward Feser, Cambridge University Press, 2006, pp 123–47.

'Criticism and Tradition in Popper, Oakeshott and Hayek'
in *The Journal of Applied Philosophy, 9, 1992*, pp 65–75.

'*The Open Society* Revisited'
in *Karl Popper: Critical Appraisals*, edited by Philip Catton and Graham Macdonald, Routledge, Abingdon, 2004, pp 65–75.

'Britain and Europe: an Oakeshottian Meditation'
not previously published.

I would like to thank the various publishers concerned for permission to reprint previously published material in this volume.

I would also like to thank Professor John Haldane, General Editor of the *St Andrews Studies in Philosophy and Public Affairs*, whose idea the volume was, both for his faith in the project and also for our many conversations over the years.

Anthony O'Hear
April 2008

Introduction

The Landscape of Humanity

The fifteen essays in this book collectively develop a conception of human culture, which is humane and traditionalist, and which also sees within human experience pointers to a world beyond the material. The first five essays focus on the aesthetic in general and on beauty in particular, in an attempt to uncover what is involved in both notions, and how on the one hand they relate to our embodied existence, and how on the other they evoke intimations of transcendence. The second set of five essays all touch on human culture in a broader sense, by exploring within culture the specific places of science, of religion, and of what we might think of as the expressive arts. We look at the place within a culture of a tradition of great books and also of technology in relation to artistic expression, as well as considering reasons why censorship might be seen as necessary in relation to art. The final selection of five essays focuses on politics, and particularly on the potential tensions between calls for democratic openness in a society and the need in any viable society for a settled background of tradition. These tensions are explored in relation to multi-culturalism and to the European federalist project.

Art

In the first chapter, I consider the relation between biological evolution and our aesthetic sense. As suggested at various points in this collection, one of the tasks of human existence is precisely to experience the world through our sense and sensibility, to articulate and reflect on that experience, giving voice and expression to what we perceive and experience. Our embodiment is the starting point of all our aesthetic endeavours, and the point to which they will always return. As integral to our embodiment, we have a nature which we share in part with animals, and this includes responding favourably, perhaps even aesthetically to certain types of stimuli. Some of this may be due to events and adaptations way back in our evolutionary history. But examining the attempts of Darwin and others to find continuities between our aesthetic sense and animal responses leads us to see that human aesthetic responses go far beyond anything discernible in the animal kingdom. We appreciate beauty for its own sake, and we characteristically see in it intimations of a world beyond the material.

If our aesthetic sense and the works which are produced by us in response to it transcend the biological, are they free of historical and sociological determinism. As works of the human spirit, we should not see artistic activity and creation in deterministic terms, any more than the rest of history, or so I argue in the second chapter. We should resist attempts of art theorists to insist that as history is moving in a particular direction and progress has its own ineluctable demands, only one style or approach is valid at a particular time. Artists and architects are as free as anyone else to stand out against historical trends. Nevertheless all our creativity is rooted in tradition and in what has emerged from tradition, so we should be cautious about radical breaks with the past (especially when 'progress' is invoked to justify them). This tendency is, as I argue in the chapter, particularly dangerous in architecture, which has widespread and long-lasting effects, and if it goes wrong, these can be deeply de-humanising.

Chapters 3 and 4 address the topic of beauty. Much modern art is deliberately unbeautiful, and modern writers on art are reluctant to speak of beauty at all. The reasons for this are examined, but more important than the analysis of the cause is the need to re-assert the centrality of beauty to the aesthetic endeavour. Beauty should be one of the main aims of artistic endeavour, if not the main aim. It is through the pursuit of beauty as something to be sought for its own sake that art and the aesthetic evince their strongest intimations of transcendence. As these intimations spread out over the whole of human life, including the moral, the religious and the true, art cannot be confined in a purely 'aesthetic' realm, as Kant would have it with his doctrine of disinterestedness as a requirement of 'pure' beauty. Taking the depictions of the Book of Revelation by Dürer and Cranach respectively as examples, Chapter 4 is a critique of the Kantian thesis.

In the fifth and final chapter in the section on art, I argue that if our particular vocation as human beings is to articulate and respond to the world in our own particular way, then the best artists will include those who attend to human experience and the things which frame that experience and among which we live. Following Proust, I take Chardin to be a paradigm case here, one who quietly and meditatively explores the small things of the human world. By contrast, wiping away all the detail of our experience in an attempt to gain pure, immaterial expression, as Mark Rothko appeared to do, may be a human and artistic cul-de-sac. There are analogies here with theological attempts to cut loose from the symbolism and dogma of particular religions to set sail on the sea of undifferentiated ecumenical agreement, as I suggest, a point to which we return from a different angle at the end of the next section.

Culture

In the first chapter of the second part (Chapter 6), a distinction is drawn between science and culture more generally. Science prescinds from the subjective and the human, which is precisely where its strength derives. But the subjective and the human are the very areas which are at the heart of culture. They are at the core of the human world, what the phenomenologists refer to as the life world (*Lebenswelt*); they are the focus of *Verstehen* or of our understanding ourselves and the world from within. While deploring the suggestion that there are *two* cultures, science being at most one part of culture in the wider sense, I consider the extent to which culture in this sense is specific to a particular tradition or community. This is a contrast with science, which in aim anyway, is not specific to particular cultures, but, as we argue, there are also ways in which we can, culturally, reach out beyond the confines of our particular cultural traditions and inheritance.

The seventh chapter focuses on a specific and controversial aspect of the relation between art and the wider culture, that which leads to political and populist calls for censorship. Without defending censorship, I argue that the advocates of censorship may have a more lively sense of the power and impact of art than those who argue for an artistic realm insulated from political, moral and religious interference. Looking at the relation between the arts and culture in a wider sense, Chapter 8 argues for the importance of the notion of a corpus of great books, works which have stood the test of time, and which should be taken on their own terms if they are to benefit us. Then in the ninth chapter we return to the idea that works of art are essentially works of the creative human spirit and imagination, produced by beings living within a culture. As such, if they are to succeed, they cannot be mechanical or produced by a computer or any other device not endowed with humanity; in the essay we show in detail, and against much of the spirit of our age, why this is so.

Chapter 10 considers the role of science and religion within the human world by means of a comparison of the two activities. Both seem committed to going beyond everyday experience. At a very general level, and taking up themes from Chapter 6, this does not appear to be a problem for science, though it still leaves us with problems in verifying and even understanding the parts of science which go beyond the empirically testable. But the transcendence of experience must pose a critical problem for religion which has to maintain an internal link to human experience, or so I argue. How can religion be both transcendent and rooted in human experience? Beyond saying that it must be both, however, in the essay I am unable to do more than point to the problem, while insisting that the religious — like the aesthetic and the moral — remains an irreducible and unavoidable element of human experience.

Politics

The final five chapters develop an analysis of the political realm which gives due weight to tradition and the traditional. A connecting thread here is the political philosophy of Karl Popper, whose work in this area had already been invoked in Chapter 4, in applying his anti-historicist arguments in the aesthetic realm. Central to Popper's political philosophy is the notion of what he calls the open society. From the perspective from which these essays are written — one which stresses the significance of human freedom and creativity — there is much to be praised in Popper's politics. As well as his attack on historicism, there is his anti-collectivism and individualism, all promulgated at a time (the 1940s) when state socialism seemed intellectually irresistible. Popper provided a telling critique of certain forms of political closure at a critical time in our history. However, as emerges in the course of the essays, more is needed to keep a society together than Popperian openness.

The first essay (Chapter 11) examines the connection between democracy and openness in a very general sense, showing that democracy on its own will not necessarily safeguard basic human freedoms and that it has its own collectivist tendencies, which must be resisted as far as possible. For a democracy to operate in a humane and open way, as Aristotle urged, society needs a strong and settled middle class; I suggest here and in Chapter 14 that this middle group needs to be committed to traditions of liberty and humanity, and that this puts certain limits on the possibility of exporting western democracy to places without these traditions, or indeed of maintaining it at home in the face of large groups acknowledging no allegiance to these traditions.

The next two chapters (12 and 13) analyse and compare the political philosophy of Popper with those of Hayek and Oakeshott. Chapter 12 contrasts Hayek's *The Road to Serfdom* with Popper's *The Open Society and Its Enemies*. Despite considerable agreement on the key point of the limits to planning, there are quite significant differences between Popper and Hayek in these books, particularly on the matter of rationality, differences which became more pronounced in the later writings of Hayek in particular. In Chapter 13 Hayek's evolutionary and irrationalist approach to human institutions is contrasted with Popper's critical rationalism and with Oakeshott's conception of the significance within a political realm of intimations, a non-rational, but not irrational sense of what at any given time is acceptable. The suggestion is that the sort of allegiance a political realm needs for its successful maintenance is best seen in terms of Oakeshottian intimations, deriving from a shared sense of tradition, than either in a purely formal commitment to critical rationalism and openness (or democracy) or in a fundamentally irrational evolution of norms and institutions.

Chapter 14 tackles head on and in greater depth the limitations of Popperian openness. A society needs more than openness to hold together, as will be seen all too clearly if and when an open society is threatened from within by significant groups which do not share its basic or core values. Popper was aware of this problem, and suggested measures to be taken in such a case, but I argue that, despite post-*Open Society* developments in his own thinking on the importance of tradition to a liberal society, his political philosophy needs filling out with a far sturdier account of tradition than he was able to give. These reflections seem particularly timely, given that for the first time in decades politicians from all sides are beginning to turn their attention to just what is meant by being British (or whatever). But, as I suggest in the final essay, the national allegiances necessary to keep a people together are not threatened only from within. The European project is an example of the type of rationalism in politics Oakeshott inveighed against throughout his career; not only that, it seems predicated on dissolving the ties by which peoples and societies are held together. In this context it is time for a renewed appreciation of the role benign traditions of liberty and individualism have played and still play in our common histories.

Chapter 1

Evolution and Aesthetics

I want to begin with four quotations, fairly typical of their type, and germane to our topic because they encapsulate what many artists and art lovers feel about art and music. These feelings are often inchoate, to be sure, and in the cold light of analytical day they may look extravagant and exaggerated. But they do capture something of the experience people often have of art and beauty, and for that reason alone must be given some phenomenological plausibility at least.

First quotation:

> It is reserved to art to salvage the kernel of religion, inasmuch as the mythical images which religion would wish to be believed as true are apprehended in art for their symbolic value, and through ideal representation of those symbols art reveals the concealed deep truth within them.

Second quotation:

> (In art) for a brief moment we really become the primal essence itself, and feel its unbounded lust for existence, and delight in existence. Now we see the struggles, the torment, the destruction of phenomena as necessary. For all our pity and terror we are happy to be alive, not as individuals but as *the* single living thing, merged with its creative delight ...

Something of what we experience in, say, *Tristan und Isolde* may be alluded to by these two extracts. In this context, we might also think of the experience of some of Titian's late paintings, *The Flaying of Marsyas*, (Archiepiscopal Palace, Kromeriz), for example, or of the exuberance of some of Rubens, his hunting scenes, say, or of the implacability of Homer and of Aeschylus, of the mystical vision in John Cowper Powys's *A Glastonbury Romance*, or of some of D.H. Lawrence, and of the serious vein underlying the silvery brilliance of Ovid's *Metamorphoses*. And we could think of the evocation of the sublime in so many of Turner's canvasses. Mention of

Turner might remind us that many people have analogous experiences in observing aspects of the natural world and feeling themselves a part of nature.

But leaving nature aside for the moment, our third quotation, taking up some of the theme of the first, says

> Good art, thought of as symbolic force, rather than statement provides a stirring image of a pure, transcendent value, a steadily visible enduring human good ... in an unreligious age ... the clearest expression of something grasped as separate and precious and beneficial.

And finally, 'our highest dignity lies in the meaning given to us by works of art; it is only as an aesthetic phenomenon that existence and the world are eternally justified.'

Notice that Nietzsche (for it is, of course, Nietzsche's notorious claim on art's behalf in *The Birth of Tragedy*) does not say that the world is justified (or not) as an evolutionary process, or as chains of survival and reproduction, or as blind drive to procreate, or as random variation and selective retention. It is justified as an aesthetic phenomenon, and at least in *The Birth of Tragedy*, it actually is justified. Notice, too, in our third quotation Iris Murdoch — for it is she — speaks of an enduring human good, but also of a transcendent value. And analogous, non-naturalistic remarks could be made of quotation one (Wagner) and of quotation two (Nietzsche again).[1]

I am not going to discuss these quotations directly, beyond insisting that they do represent aspects of a vision of art and beauty, with a long history and still resonating — if beneath the surface — with many today. Nevertheless, examining what might be called the evolutionary account of art and beauty, as given by Darwin and his followers, may throw some indirect light on them, as I will suggest at the end of this paper. However, even at this stage, it will be obvious that the sentiments underlying my quotations will be in no little tension with what many take to be the message of orthodox Darwinism.

In so far as Darwinism is a doctrine of causal meaninglessness — indeed, in the hands of authors such as Jacques Monod and Richard Dawkins, perhaps *the* doctrine of causal meaninglessness — anyone in the least degree affected by any of the four quotations will

---

[1] The first quotation is from Richard Wagner, 'Religion und Kunst' in his *Gesammelte Schriften und Dichtungen*, 2nd edn (Leipzig: 1888), vol. 10., p. 211; the second is from Friedrich Nietzsche, *The Birth of Tragedy* (1871), section 17 (in the Penguin Classics edition, Harmondsworth, 1993, trans. Shaun Whiteside); the third from Iris Murdoch, *The Fire and the Sun* (Oxford: Oxford University Press, 1977), pp. 76–7; and the fourth from Nietzsche's *The Birth of Tragedy*, section 5.

have to treat a wholly Darwinian account of art and of our sense of the beautiful with suspicion. At the very best, it will be radically incomplete. For, without any supplementation, Darwinism explains phenomena, to the extent that it does explain them, in terms of a blind, unconscious and unintelligent nature populated with creatures driven for no purpose to survive for a time, if they are lucky, to reproduce themselves, again given good fortune, and then to die; and all this for no other reason than the fact that they have these drives and enough physiological and behavioural adaptations to survive and reproduce; and with no result other than that with luck and the cunning of the randomly produced adaptiveness some of them do actually succeed in reproducing themselves, and in some cases producing offspring actually better fitted to their environments than their parents.

We should not be so impressed by the rhetoric of creationists or of their polar opposites, evolutionary atheologians like Monod and Dawkins into thinking that Darwinism is formally incompatible with religious belief or meaning. Nevertheless it cannot be denied that Darwinism has been a major weapon in the hands of those concerned to deny any meaning to our existence or that of the universe as a whole. It has been such a weapon precisely because, on its surface at least, Darwinism analyses life, including human life, in terms of five billion years of processes of random variation and selective retention. We, as every other living thing, are products of chance, mutations in the genetic structure of earlier creatures, as are all our traits and dispositions, which, directly or indirectly, have been selected because of their contribution to survival and reproduction. According to Darwin, all living things strive to reproduce themselves at a geometrical ratio, and according to what he called the 'law of natural selection', according to which any variations in the 'least degree injurious' will be 'rigidly destroyed'.[2] This picture is not, as has just been noted, formally incompatible with meaning, religious or otherwise, but any such meaning will have to be added to it.

So, maybe there are aspects to our existence which do point beyond the blind drive to survive and reproduce. And maybe, if there is anything in our initial quotations, our intimations of beauty and other aesthetic properties are such aspects. In any case we do seem to spend an awful lot of time and effort in pursuing aesthetic ends. We beautify and decorate our environments, public and private, we create and appreciate works of art, and we seek and

---

[2]   Charles Darwin, *The Origin of Species* (1859), first para of chapter 4, (Harmondsworth: Penguin Books, 1882), p. 131.

appreciate the aesthetic aspects of nature. And we do all these things in a way which seems to have little to do with survival and reproduction, and which may at times interfere with survival and reproduction, as when artists starve in garrets or when opera fanatics spend their fortunes and ruin their marriages in pursuing their passion or when young girls devote all their time and energy to ballet training, all in apparent violation of Darwin's law of natural selection and without any indication of the types in question dying out. So even at the crudest level, does not aesthetic interest provide a counter-example to the theory of evolution?

Darwin was himself worried by the threat aesthetics posed for his theory for at least two reasons. In the first place, if aesthetic sensibility were confined to human beings, it would — against his theory — suggest a radical discontinuity between humans and other animals. Then, secondly, even in the animal kingdom there are aesthetic contrivances, such as the tails of peacocks and the plumage of humming birds. These contrivances seem to contribute nothing to survival and reproduction, but they are costly to produce, and in the case of peacocks' tails they may actually be injurious to their possessors in preventing or impeding flight.

In *The Descent of Man* Darwin tackled both these questions. His strategy was to show that both the appearance of beauty, as in the peacocks' tails, and the taste for it, as in the case of peahens' choices, go hand in hand as mutually supporting and demanding players in the struggle for existence. And, insofar peahens and the like have an aesthetic sensibility, there is no discontinuity between us and the rest of the animal kingdom, even if our aesthetic tastes are more developed than those of most other animals.

What Darwin argued was that the elaborate displays found among animals and birds, particularly during mating, could be explained only on the assumption that birds and animals were capable of appreciating beauty. That is the only way in which we could explain why so much effort, metabolic and behavioural, went into producing these things, as beyond certain in-built preferences for regularity and symmetry, 'why certain bright colours should excite pleasure cannot be explained'.[3]

Darwin was concerned to demonstrate continuity between humans and other animals, so if he could show that there was in animals a genuine aesthetic sense, one large ostensible discontinuity

[3] Charles Darwin, *The Descent of Man* (1871), quoted from the 2nd edn, 1874, vol.1, p. 141.

would have been eliminated. The tails of male peacocks and the songs and plumage of many other birds are, in Darwin's own terms, elaborate, graceful, splendid, beautiful and highly ornamented. That the females of the species in question appreciate these things cannot be denied, says Darwin, and in just the same way that human females do, who deck themselves out with the same plumes of the same birds. And in the animal kingdom, it is the most splendid and beautiful males who succeed in getting the most and best females — as, in the case of peahens selecting the peacocks with the most luxuriant tails, has more recently been confirmed systematically by experiment and observation.

But do the peahens who chose the peacocks with the best tails do so because they admire their beauty? That they might not be choosing on aesthetic grounds was actually the subject of an early dispute between Darwin and Alfred Russel Wallace. Wallace was in general somewhat un-Darwinian in emphasising differences between humans and other animals, a point to which we will return. But in the matter of female choice of mates, Wallace was more Darwinian than Darwin himself in denying that there was anything functionless or purely aesthetic in behaviour which played so significant a role in the development of a species.

Darwin himself argued that selection pressures alone, building on some initially inexplicable caprice or aesthetic preference could have been enough to explain the apparent admiration female birds had for the extravagance of their mates, and for the development within a species of males with ever more elaborate tails, songs and plumage. In the development of the species in question, females initially had preferences for males with the attributes in question. The resultant pairings produced off-spring with similar tastes and attributes. The most splendid of the new males are then, in their turn chosen by the ever more choosy females descended from the original choosers, and one more twist is given to the evolutionary spiral, which will go on developing until checked by some countervailing pressure.

The evolutionary potential of this sort of selection pressure and its trajectory moving far from its original starting point was well demonstrated by R.A. Fisher in 1930.[4] Fisher showed that once a preference gets embedded in a population, it will tend to move forward with ever increasing rapidity under its own momentum. It may even, as is the case with peacock's tails, produce unwieldy and, from

---

[4]   See R.A. Fisher, *The Genetical Theory of Natural Selection* (Oxford: Clarendon Press, 1930).

the point of view of simple survival, potentially injurious adaptations. After all, peacocks with splendid tails are pretty poor flyers, and so more vulnerable to predators than they would be were their tails more modest. Does this example refute Darwin's principle about the the inevitable eradication of variations in the least degree injurious? Darwin thought not, because what the luxuriantly tailed peacocks may have lost in terms of sheer survival, they more than made up for in reproductive advantage over their less well endowed competitors. Injury and advantage in evolutionary terms are many faceted, and cannot be read off from a creature's performance on just one dimension. Evolution is a theory of reproduction, as well as of survival.

Darwin, supplemented by Fisher, provides a convincing enough account of how in a particular species, the development of what is, for us, aesthetically pleasing characteristics can occur as a result of female choice (and specifically as a result of what Darwin somewhat ungallantly refers to as the initially inexplicable operation of female caprice). But what he does not show is that either in the beginning of the evolutionary trajectory or at its end the females are choosing for aesthetic reasons. And it was on precisely this point that Wallace parted company with Darwin. Wallace insisted that in the human realm aesthetic response is part of our 'spiritual nature' — which we did not share with animals—whereas what looks to us like an aesthetic response in the animal realm is actually no such thing. For big tails, fine plumage and vibrant songs presuppose in their owners health, strength and vitality; ornamental display can also be a sign of territorial dominance, which also indicates general strength and superiority.

How does Darwin know that the females are not choosing their beautiful males because what we see as their beauty is symptomatic of other more utilitarian qualities? Could nature ever endow its creatures with properties and tastes which were not, in Wallace's terms, 'sensible'?[5] Evolution is a process powered by the drives individuals have to survive and reproduce and shaped by the environmental response to the means by which different creatures seek to satisfy those drives. Could evolution ever allow its creatures to waste time and effort on drives and properties which are literally useless? Wallace, more selectionist here than Darwin, thought not. Every trait of any significance had to endow its possessor with direct adap-

---

[5]   On Wallace and aesthetics, see Helena Cronin, *The Ant and the Peacock* (Cambridge: Cambridge University Press, 1993), pp. 186–91

tive advantage in survival and reproduction. Caprice alone and aesthetic sense could play no significant role in a domain governed by the iron logic of natural selection, and certainly not to the extent envisaged by Darwin and Fisher.

How, then, might it be possible to decide between the view that aesthetic preference in animals is really aesthetic and the view that what looks to us to be aesthetic preference, on the part of peahens say, is really a preference for other qualities which go along with the aesthetic, and which are not chosen via aesthetic appreciation? The problem is that there is no direct way of deciding. All we have is broad brush behaviour, which is susceptible of several interpretations. What we cannot do is ask a peahen why she makes the choices she does, or what precisely it is she admires in her mates. Nevertheless, if we compare what we see of peahens and other animals in this area with what seems to be crucial in human aesthetic judgements, that animals have a genuine aesthetic sense can come to seem highly doubtful.

We can usefully begin this enquiry by considering some of the things Kant says about aesthetic judgements.[6] In the first place, they are seen by Kant as both disinterested and universal, and right at the start we have a difference. For, whatever else the peahen is doing when she chooses the peacock with the best tail, she is judging neither disinterestedly nor universally.

In speaking of aesthetic appreciation as disinterested, part of what Kant means (the true part—see Chapter 4) is that we are not interested in consuming or possessing the object we are reacting to. We are interested in its 'real existence' and contemplate it for its own sake, rather than as something which we could consume or sell or use. Of course, one might have both an aesthetic interest in something and some other interest. An art dealer might admire a painting for aesthetic reasons and for its monetary value to him; a landowner might appreciate his estate both for its beauty and for the lustre it added to his reputation. But in each case, it is possible, theoretically at least, to distinguish the aesthetic from the other interest.

The disinterestedness of the aesthetic judgement can be characterised in terms of the object in question being contemplated rather than used, and this goes even for cases where one admires something aesthetically for its fittedness to function. That is to say, we can speak of a beautiful car or aeroplane, and part of what we are admiring here may be the way the design refers to what it is intended to do,

---

[6]   In Immanuel Kant, *The Critique of Judgement* (1790), sections 1– 60.

and, by its sleek lines or whatever, symbolises that. But in saying that, say, the racing cars of the 1950s were beautiful in comparison to today's F1 monstrosities, we will be standing back from actually using the cars, even if the contemplation does eventually issue is use (though in this case, today's Ferrari would undoubtedly outperform its 1950s predecessor). Aesthetic enjoyment is, in Kant's terms, a 'reflective' rather than an 'organic' or 'appetitive' pleasure.

Matters may seem more complicated when we turn to sexual beauty. In admiring a beautiful woman is the man disinterested? Or is he looking at her as a potential or even an actual lover? This is a question which takes us back to Plato. In *Phaedrus* (250ff) Plato had argued that our first perception of beauty comes when we fall in love with a beautiful youth. The lover shudders with awe and reverence, as at the sight of a god. He is seized by a strange sweating and by fever. Warmth enters the soul through the beauty coming in through the eyes. The soul grows wing and aches, as when a child is teething. When he is parted from the loved one, he is maddened, and will suffer any shame to get back in the presence of the beloved.

In his discussion of the power of sexual attraction, Plato undoubtedly touches on aspects of our emotive life which Kant would rather we forgot. In Plato's descriptions any reflective enjoyment is intermingled with the appetitive and the organic. In this Plato may be telling us something about the genesis of our aesthetic sense which Kant overlooks, and which points more in the direction of Darwinian accounts of beauty. For many people a strong and particular feeling for beauty and for the aesthetic does seem to accompany adolescence and sexual awakening. But not the only or necessarily the earliest intimation of the aesthetic. Even quite young children are often moved by the beauties of nature, in a purely contemplative way.

In any case, even if there are experiences of sexual beauty which are, in a sense, mixed, and which might point to some of our experience of beauty as being rooted in our physical nature, as Plato points out, the madness and the possession or would be consumption of the lover is only the first stage in the soul's ascent to the beautiful. When sanity returns, the lover will experience beauty in a calm way; his sense of the beautiful diffuses itself over all parts of material creation, where it is to be found, and not just the sexual. He turns from the 'slavish and illiberal' devotion to 'individual loveliness' to set sail on the 'open sea of beauty', before eventually finding rest in Beauty itself, something wholly abstract and non-material. (See *Symposium*, 210–12)

As we shall see, abstract, non-material beauty is a step too far in an aesthetic account of beauty. But what Plato says about the second stage is suggestive, even in the case of the beauty of beautiful bodies. A calm, disinterested appreciation here is not out of the question. There can be a chaste, non-possessive appreciation of female beauty, either in the flesh or in the painted image. Despite the claims of John Berger, not every painted nude is an incitement to male possession or fantasy, even if many are. Titian's *Education of Love* (Borghese Gallery, Rome) is certainly a celebration of female flesh, but it is at the same time a reminder of the poignancy and uncertainty of love and of the pain of the experience (in the painting the achingly beautiful Venus is binding the love-inducing gaze of Cupid). In his later work Rubens continually and, in my view successfully, used female nudity, including exuberant depictions of his own wife's abundant and fleshy beauty, to evoke the blessings of peace and of fertility. Even Titian's *Venus of Urbino* (Uffizi Gallery, Florence) and Velasquez's *Rokeby Venus* (National Gallery, London), though certainly reminders of the most organic pleasures possible and of the processes of reproduction, are reflective reminders, which can and should be viewed aesthetically, that is disinterestedly, reflectively and without engaging desire directly.

What is striking about the reflectiveness which Kant sees in the aesthetic judgement is that there is no obvious analogue in the animal realm. We say that the peahen admires the peacock's tail only because she chooses the cock. The judgement, if such it is, is interested, organic, the manifestation of a very basic desire, which is indeed the only criterion for the existence of any judgement on the hen's part. She is only at the stage of Plato's maddened lover, if indeed she is even that far. We hear no stories of animals admiring some aesthetic feature of their environment reflectively and disinterestedly, or of connoisseurship before depictions of goddesses. And even if we are able to discern rhythm and melody in the song of a bird, it is far from clear that the birds do. Even less do they treat their songs aesthetically, using them as material to be developed musically, as, by contrast, the composer Messaien tried to do (with, in my opinion, rather mixed success).

If disinterested aesthetic judgements are not found in the animal kingdom, nor are universal ones. When the peacock with the most beautiful tail is chosen by a peahen, she is not implying that all observers, or even all peahens, should concur in finding it beautiful. Nor, when I declare a preference for dark over milk chocolate am I implying that every right-minded person should agree. But when I say that Beethoven's late quartets are great works of art, spiritually deep, full of exquisite lyricism, earthy humour and fascinating counterpoint, I am intending that what I say should command general assent. The fact that some of Beethoven's contemporaries failed to appreciate the late quartets means that I am committed to saying that they were in error over them, that for whatever reason (unfamiliarity or surface strangeness, perhaps) there was some failure in their appreciation (or some mistake in my own reactions). I am not simply saying that these contemporaries of Beethoven were unable to see that future generations of listeners would find the quartets deep, humorous, lyrical, and so on.

In my view, the most natural way of explaining the Kantian universality of the aesthetic judgement, to which, it should be stressed, no equivalent can be found in the kingdom of non-linguistic animals, is to say that those who fail to agree with some generally acceptable aesthetic judgement are mis-perceiving something in the work in question. In my view, but not in Kant's. As is well-known, Kant emphasised the universality of the aesthetic judgement, while denying its objectivity. He thought that when I judge something beautiful or ugly or elegant, and so on, I am speaking not about real features of the object in question, objectively present in it. What I am indirectly, but really referring to, are feelings the object conjures up in me, in my breast. Aesthetic judgements are, in Kant's terms, subjective.

Part of the reason for this was that Kant thought that aesthetic judgements were singular. That is to say, an aesthetic judgement is one which is always, on the surface at least, about particular unique properties of the particular object it is (ostensibly) about. Many will agree with Kant here, up to a point. An aesthetic judgement by me about a work of art, say, requires experience by me of that specific object, and its unique combination of properties. A mere description will not suffice if I am interested in making a judgement about its aesthetic value. Nor will it be possible to sum up my grounds for my judgement in any general formula, which does not refer to specific features of the object in question. Thus, you can say that in a good painting a balance of form and detail is needed, but that general principle will not tell us why, let us say Veronese's *Marriage Feast at Cana* (Louvre, Paris) is an aesthetic triumph, while Frith's *Derby Day* (Tate Gallery, London), with much the same amount of form and detail, is hardly a painting at all. To make a judgement of that sort with any degree of confidence, you will have actually to look at the works in question, and experience their precise and singular qualities.

But even if, as Kant rightly implies, aesthetic judgements cannot be usefully captured in terms of general formulae, it is simply prejudice to say—as Kant appears to do—that a non-formalisable judgement cannot be objective, or about real properties of objects. Judgements about the guilt or innocence of an accused person in court are also singular and non-formalisable, in much the same sort of way as aesthetic judgements, but they are certainly about something objective. Nor is their singularity and non-formalisability the main reason for Kant denying objectivity to aesthetic judgements. The deeper reason seems to be due to his realisation of what we might call the 'magnetism' of value. Beauty is something that attracts us, and ugliness repels, and so on with other aesthetic (and ethical) properties. But how can they do this if they are straightforward properties like squareness or redness, which have no necessary affective charge? If the recognition of beauty or of ugliness were due to something happening in us rather than to something outside us, that problem would be quickly solved. But, I think, far too quickly.

For it is not the case that every time I recognise something as beautiful I am then and thereby attracted to it, any more than I am always drawn to do the right thing and never the wrong thing. One could well—in one's youth, perhaps—admit the beauty of the painting of Raphael or the fineness of the poetry of Horace without being particularly attracted to either. The point is that while aesthetic and moral properties characteristically do engage us and are rooted in our genetically given constitution and our psychology, they can and do transcend their origins in such a way as to open a theoretical gap between recognition of a given property and actual responses in particular cases. No such normative gap—a gap which allows us to say that someone *ought* to like or admire some aesthetic feature of an object, even though they don't—exists in the animal case. They just respond or fail to respond. There would just be no sense in arguing that a peahen who failed to respond to the most luxuriant tail in her vicinity was making a mistake in judgement, as opposed to simply lacking a particular behavioural response.

In analysing aesthetic judgements as obliquely referring to the emotions which objects of aesthetic value stir up in us, Kant was, as in so much else, following Hume. For Hume, seeing an object as beautiful or ugly is a matter of 'gilding or staining it with the colours borrowed from internal sentiment'. Nevertheless, like Kant, Hume is also insistent on the universality of the aesthetic:

the same Homer, who pleased at Athens and Rome two thousand years ago, is still admired at Paris and at London. All the changes of climate, government, religion, and language have not been able to obscure his glory. Authority or prejudice may be able to give a temporary vogue to a bad poet or orator; but his reputation will never be durable or general. When his compositions are examined by posterity or foreigners, the enchantment is dissipated and his faults appear in their true colours. On the contrary, a real genius, the longer his works endure, and the more wide they are spread, the more sincere is the admiration which they meet with.[7]

Hume, like Kant, wants to hold both that aesthetic judgements are potentially universal and that their source and ultimate reference is human taste; both, that there is such a thing as good taste, vindicated and manifested through universal assent and the test of time, and that this good taste is not objectively warranted by the objects themselves, but is a matter of those objects attracting our feelings or (in Hume's case) of their being gilded and stained by them. For Hume, as for Kant, the cross-cultural and trans-temporal critical-creative dialogue which elicits the cool, reflective and disinterested judgement that Homer is a poet of great stature, is ultimately a dialogue about what exists (or ought to exist) only in our minds. It is not about anything which is really or objectively there.

But why 'ought to exist' and how universal, if these judgements are not based on something which is actually there, and actually there apart from any feelings I or anyone else happen to have at any time? And what is the dialogue about, if it is not a dialogue about the *Iliad* itself? The attempt of Hume and Kant to subjectivise the aesthetic judgement is hard enough to accept in itself, but is particularly hard in the context of its supposed normativity and universality. It is time to suggest an approach to beauty which maintains its objectivity, but which does not deny its roots in human, and ultimately instinctual responses, nor its valuational — that is magnetizing — nature.

To find the Rokeby Venus beautiful is to make an objective judgement (and one which most people acquainted with the painting would agree with), but it is not to make a judgement which is factual in the scientific sense. It is a judgement which needs a specifically human sensibility to discern, and which will not be captured by the more universally intelligible concepts and theories of natural science. But to deny it objectivity on those grounds alone would sim-

---

[7]   David Hume, 'Of the Standard of Taste' (1757), para 11.

ply be to indulge in a piece of philosophical dogmatism, according to which only the scientifically accessible is granted the title of real. So, on the view being advanced here, aesthetic judgements are indeed *our* judgements, that is judgements made possible only by our biological and cultural traditions, but they nonetheless reveal genuine properties of the objects in question.

When Hume and Kant and their followers deny this, they are in fact saying little more than that beauty is not a formalisable property, nor one which could feature in those types of scientific theory which deliberately prescind from properties which would be intelligible only to creatures with a very specific—in his case human—sensibility. To be sure, as already hinted at by the difficulty of finding rules for beauty, and by its extreme context dependence, there will be no set of physically determinable properties shared by and only by beautiful objects, such as sunsets, sunflowers, pictures of sunflowers and musical evocations of sunsets. But that a Mediterranean sunset, a field of sunflowers, van Gogh's *Sunflowers* and Strauss's *Im Abendrot* are all beautiful is certainly something experienced by most of us as true, as demanded by the objects just mentioned, and as authoritative and compelling as anything in science. They are also judgements on which there is perhaps surprising convergence among different people and at different times, in the making of which people certainly believe themselves to be speaking about qualities of the things they are seeing or hearing, and not about feelings in their own breasts.

Indeed, that beauty is not just a projection or a matter of internal sentiment merely is strongly suggested by the experience most of us have had of learning that something is generally regarded as beautiful, of not initially appreciating it as such, and then, with further acquaintance, care and attention coming to find it beautiful (a phenomenon memorably described by Proust in a number of passages). In other words, what *is* beautiful actually directs, shapes and explains our experience of its being beautiful. It is not as if the feelings in us towards that thing existed prior to our assimilation of standards of true beauty, standards which we take to have an existence and a logic independent of empirically given feelings people have. In other words, whatever its origin may have been in ancestral sensibility, taste and instinct, in the human world as we know it, beauty is something objective and outside of us, commanding our attention and allegiance individually and collectively.

As far as the logic of beauty goes, it is perfectly possible that some aesthetic prophet could demonstrate to a whole people that there was something amiss about its taste — as, with some success and justification, Ruskin and Pugin did in nineteenth-century England. And some might feel there is an even more pressing need for a Ruskin of the present day to reveal the aesthetic of the Disney empire as not so much popular as vulgar, garish and mawkish. (And maybe also we need some person with the authority of a Ruskin or a Carlyle to pull us all up over our connivance in rap and pop music and in the sheer lowness of popular television — though it is arguable that if there were such a person, these appalling phenomena would never have come to play so large a part in national and publicly funded life.) All this aside, though, when we read great criticism — Ruskin on Turner, say, or Nietzsche on Wagner, Eliot on Milton, or Leavis on Eliot — what we have does not have the logical form of mere expression of emotion. These critics are pointing to features of the works they are discussing, and drawing judgements about those works, which we are urged to accept, based on the features they have pointed to. The criticisms demand us to respond to the works in a particular way, in a way we may not previously have realised, because of what they show us about the works; if we disagree — as in possibly three of the cases we probably should — we will have to point to countervailing features which override the original judgement.

Note, incidentally, how discourse of this sort reinforces Kant's views on the universality of the aesthetic judgement, and also on its singularity: that, to stay with our examples, religiosity like Eliot's, but in hands other than his, a neurasthenic sensibility like Wagner's, but without his colossal grasp of structure, or a power of language like Milton's employed for a lesser purpose, might well have had the dire effects Leavis and Nietzsche and Eliot purported to find in the works as a whole. While there are reason which support and must support aesthetic judgements, an aesthetic judgement will always depend on the precise and unique way a particular set of reasons bears on the specific case.

Reflection on the way discussions about beauty actually proceed shows clearly that neurological and evolutionary accounts of the perception of beauty are necessarily incomplete (at best). To take an example of the former, P.W. Atkins has written of the near universal and favourable recognition of the golden section as being 'like the resonance of an electronic circuit to a distant transmitter, when a certain frequency can induce an enhanced power'. Particular circuits in the brain respond to the scanning of golden sections, the brain itself then responds in 'an enhanced manner' and our response is 'the one that normally correlates with perceived "beauty"'.[8] What is perceived as beauty, on this neurological account, is what meshes with our brain circuitry, which is itself a product of our DNA. As our DNA, and the behaviour it provokes, is itself part of our evolutionary history, an account like Atkins' will both fit into and fill out an evolutionary perspective.

The connection is made explicitly by E.O. Wilson. In *Biophilia* he writes that aesthetic contrivances 'play upon the circuitry of the brain's limbic system in a way that ultimately promotes survival and reproduction'.[9] Wilson's idea is that aesthetic interest has been embedded in us because of the general usefulness of curiosity and the search for connexions and similarities. More specifically, because of our ancestral past, we are disposed to find beautiful scenes and bodies which contribute in various ways to survival and reproduction. Thus it has recently been shown that, various allegedly superficial differences in taste aside (as between the large women of Renoir and Rubens, say, and the more gamine figures fashionable in the 1960s), men universally prefer women with figures with the same (low) waist-hip ratio, of about 0.70%, which is constant as between both Renoir's beauties and those of today.[10] Perception of this ratio in a woman is supposed to indicate to the males the woman's potential fertility and absence of actual pregnancy, which in turn is supposed to explain why men find women of this type beautiful. Men also prefer women with other characteristics, such as bright eyes and good complexions, which indicate youth (and hence ability to have healthy children). Wilson himself would explain the near-universal predilection for pictures for what are in effect Claude-type classical landscapes in terms of our ancestors having been disposed to favour landscapes which were conducive to survival on the savannah — that is to say, places where there was good vegetation, a source of water, such as a river or a lake, and also some higher ground to facilitate the perception of prey and predators.[11]

[8]   P.W. Atkins, 'The lion, the rose and the ultimate oyster', in *Modern Painters*, vol. 2, no.4, Winter 1989, pp. 50–5.

[9]   E.O.Wilson, *Biophilia* (Harvard University Press, 1984), p. 61.

[10]   See also Steven Pinker, *How the Mind Works* (London: Allen Lane, 1998), pp. 485–7.

[11]   See also Wilson, *Biophilia*, pp. 109–11.

In fact this idea of the universality of what has been called by Denis Dutton a 'pervasive Pleistocene taste in landscape' has in a sense been confirmed by the researches of two emigré Russian artists, Vitaly Komar and Alexander Melamid, in 1993. Komar and Melamid surveyed people around the world, and found that their taste in landscape was pretty constant, and much as Wilson had suggested, with the addition that there was a marked preference for some famous human figure in the picture. On this basis, and clearly ironically, they then concocted an impossible mélange of these elements, which they called *America's Most Wanted*, a Hudson River School scene, with George Washington standing beside a lake in which a hippo is disporting itself.[12]

I do not want to deny that at some level perception of aesthetic properties, and aesthetic interest more generally, is based in our physical constitution, our brain structure, and hence indirectly in our evolution. It is indeed this grounding in the physical which leads me to reject the Platonic notion of a non-physical aesthetic. Our common biology also provides the start of an explanation as to why there are aesthetic universals, aesthetic preferences common to us all, to the extent that there are such things; though I do not believe that this is a purely physical matter. Aesthetic interest is connected to a wider sense of human flourishing and human potentiality, which though at some level is also common to us all, takes us beyond purely biological imperatives.

But what I do want to question is the view implicit in Atkins, at least, that the perception of beauty is an automatic response to a generalisable stimulus. The same golden section can be made out in many different objects: a prehistoric palace in Mexico, a temple in Greece, a sketch by Le Corbusier, numerous renaissance paintings, the Palazzo della Cancelleria in Rome, and, of course, in a Euclidean textbook. Even if the perceiver saw all of these things as balanced, this is not the same thing as harmonious, let alone as beautiful. It is only the right sort of balance which is harmonious or beautiful, or balance in a particular context. Even if modernist architects and their propagandists have forgotten it, Alberti's adage, that the beauty of ornament must be added to the harmony of proportion, remains true. But what is the right combination of proportion and ornament? And it would be simply absurd to say that the aesthetic interest in

[12] See also Denis Dutton, 'Art and Evolutionary Psychology' in *The Oxford Handbook of Aesthetics*, ed. Jerrold Levinson (Oxford: Oxford University Press, 2002), in which there is a full discussion of Komar and Melamid, and of much else relevant to our present theme.

Raphael's *The Crucified Christ with the Virgin Mary, Saints and Angels*
(National Gallery, London) is somehow explicable in terms of the
geometry underlying the painting. Even if geometry is a necessary
condition to an aesthetic like Raphael's it is not a sufficient condition.
All the humanity and all the religion in the painting would be
overlooked on an account framed in terms like those used by Atkins.
(And it is surely significant in this context that Clement Greenberg
who attempted a similarly reductive aesthetic was also the great
spokesman for abstract painting, arguing heroically — or
quixotically, as the case may be — that the history of painting should
be seen as a history of a drive to the painterly purity of abstraction.
But, for all the persuasive power of critics and others committed to
abstraction, it is hard to see anyone finding the golden section on its
own of even fleeting aesthetic interest.)

What goes for the golden section also goes for waist-hip ratios of
0.70% and for Claudian landscapes. These features would provide at
most a substratum of what is required for true beauty and for real
aesthetic interest. In fact it is doubtful that they do even that. For
many people, including possibly for the painter himself, Rubens's
most touching depiction of female beauty is the painting called *The
Little Fur* (Kunsthistorisches Museum, Vienna), in which Helena
Fourment is precisely not painted as an ideal subject for
evolutionarily determined male admiration, but rather as a real
woman, beautiful and beloved, to be sure, but also with the imperfections of reality, and, as far as one can see, with a waist-hip ratio
which is certainly not 0.70%. In other words, to reduce beauty, even
female beauty to some standard format is just crass, as it simply
ignores the full human context in which the beauty of a person is
actually recognised.

This point becomes even clearer when we turn to landscape.
Whatever Wilson and those polled in public opinion surveys might
say about their preferred scenes, it is noteworthy that Ruskin found
Claude's approach to the subject insipid. Although Claude had a
'fine feeling for beauty of form' and 'considerable tenderness of perception', the overall effect is of a kind of 'feminine charm' and of an
artist 'incapable of enjoying or painting anything energetic or
terrible.'[13] Ruskin had a point. To maintain aesthetic interest, an artist has to do more than give us a formulaic chocolate-box landscape.
But once the task of the landscape painter is seen as, at least in part,

---

[13]   John Ruskin, *Modern Painters* (1860), vol.5, part 9, chapter 5, as in the Cook and
       Wedderburn edn (London, 1903–12), vol.7, p. 319.

showing us things we might not otherwise have noticed or appreciated, it becomes far from clear that he or she has to stick with scenes our savannah roaming ancestors might have found conducive to their survival. And in fact they don't, even on chocolate boxes. Since Turner and Ruskin, at least, mountains and stormy seas have featured hugely in landscape taste, and since Sidney Nolan and Fred Williams, deserts too, all terrains one imagines early man would have done his level best to avoid, and which evolution should therefore have given us a predisposition to find ugly. Post romanticism we do not, of course, have any such predisposition or not in all cases, though we do in some, those too dreary and desolate, perhaps. But how dreary is too dreary? Couldn't a Turner or a Graham Sutherland even change our earlier assumptions about that? We are back with the Kantian insistence on the non-generalisable nature of aesthetic judgements, just as we are when we enquire as to just what degree of roughness might prevent our Claudian sylvan glade (complete with picturesque rocks) from being insipid.

Aesthetic judgements focus on the precise detail of a given work or object, and they are also normative. They are about how this particular thing ought to be, with its full human resonance. They are judgements which are elucidated by giving reasons and how they apply in the particular case, and how the particular thing relates to other aspects of our lives and the human world generally. In this sort of discussion, appeals to brain circuitry or to evolutionary history will be strikingly irrelevant. They may tell us something about the origins of some of our preferences in an entirely general way, but they will tell us nothing about how or why this bit of ornament in a building enhances or destroys its overall harmony, or why *The Little Fur* is so humanly resonant, or why D.H. Lawrence's novels are so much fuller and more convincing than his essays, even when both seem, on the surface, to be conveying the same general messages.

To put this point another way, our experiences of beauty and other aesthetic properties (including negative ones) are not like certain nerves or neurones being stimulated. They are not just a matter of the senses or the brain being appeased. They are not like hunger or thirst or our drives to reproduce being assuaged or aroused. Aesthetic experience always involves reflection and judgement. At the very lowest level it always involves a perception of the beautiful object as an object of such and such a sort, and beautiful in such and such respects. As a result of this intentionality of the aesthetic judgement, critics of a judgement of ours can then point to features of the object we have missed or comparisons we should have made or connexions we should have drawn. We might then be led to revise or refine or reject our original judgement, and so to modify the experience.

There is nothing analogous in sensory stimulation, whether this is pleasurable or painful. Even though selective attention can modify an experience of pure pleasure or pure pain, what is at issue in these cases is an experience unmediated by thought or judgement, and not responsive to reasoning in the way judgements, including aesthetic judgements are. We can have aesthetic or quasi-aesthetic judgements closely tied to or based on sensations, as in the case of wine-tasting perhaps, but even here, in the element of judgement involved, the experience takes on rational and cognitive dimensions transcending the purely sensory. In a positive aesthetic experience, the pleasure in question is not just experienced; it is perceived as having a value, and if Kant is right, as having a universal value, and also as being bound in with all sorts of other attitudes and values we have or ought to have. Art may be for art's sake, but it is never just for art's sake. It is because of the valuational dimension of the aesthetic that aesthetic judgements are open to criticism and refinement, and, for the subject of an aesthetic experience, life is improved cognitively, emotionally and even morally.

The neural circuitry and evolutionary accounts of the experience of beauty overlook the intentionality of aesthetic experience and the role that reason-giving and justification play in refining our sense of the beautiful. They are thus unable to account for the way that far more than the formal properties of things contributes to our sense of what is beautiful and why, in our aesthetic endeavours, the clichés of chocolate box and pin-up will not do. Related criticisms can be made of the recent attempts by writers like Steven Pinker and Geoffrey Miller to account for artistic endeavour in terms of the status and sexual advantage successful artists and owners of art secure as a result of their work and possessions.

Some artists certainly do succeed in this way. Due to the acclaim their work brings them, and seeing artistic motivation in terms of sexual success or status more generally would certainly bring it within the general orbit of evolutionary explanation, where what is done is done for advantage in survival and or reproduction. To this fairly crude notion Miller adds a refinement in his book *The Mating Mind*.[14] What attracts potential mates to successful artists is their

---

[14] Pinker, in *How the Mind Works*, pp. 522–4, Miller in *The Mating Mind: How Sexual Choice Shaped the Evolution of Human Nature* (New York: Doubleday, 2000).

skill in performance, the rarity of great performance, and its consequent expense and difficulty. So, on this view, art is explained in terms of sexual selection, artistic virtuosity being valued by potential mates both for its rarity and as a symbol of other skills in the performer. Again, at one level, this theory is not entirely baseless; one has to think only of the careers of the likes of Liszt, Picasso and Augustus John.

However, in either simplistic or sophisticated versions, the sexual selection view explains at most one side of artistic activity. It explains at some level why the artists might want to be artists, and why some of them might drive themselves beyond the norm. It does not explain why women mob them, if mob them they do, and why the rest of us shower them with wealth and adulation. Leaving aside the obvious point that in mature artistic traditions virtuosity in itself is not the only or indeed the most admired quality in an artist, the sexual selection account fails to explain why it is precisely artistic virtuosity which is so admired, as opposed to virtuosity in, say, arithmetic or coal mining or sheep-shearing. Nor, at a more profound level, does it explain what the artist himself finds worthwhile in his performance, and leads him on to master it in the way he does. Picasso was promiscuous and highly sexed, and artistic success undoubtedly enabled him to satisfy himself in these ways beyond most men's wildest dreams, but this was a by-product of his artistic genius. He had first to succeed artistically, and to do this he had to understand and feel what art was about, and having grasped this, he had both to be able to innovate artistically, and to want to innovate artistically. He, like his admirers, had to be gripped by a sense that art was worth doing for itself and on its own terms — for it is because he and they have this sense that he is admired for his supreme ability at that. He is not admired because of the wealth and riches he gets through art; unlike a business man who is admired because of the riches his work brings, an artist is admired for his work, and logically, admiration for his riches come afterwards. The sexual selection accounts of artistic activity are, in other words, externalist accounts, touching on some of the dynamics of artistic communities and esteem, but they tell us nothing about the meaning or justification of judgements of beauty, about their internal logic or value.

An evolutionary theorist like Miller could grant some of this. He could admit that to see a given behavioural trait as having had a certain function in its evolutionary history is not equivalent to its having that function now. On this view, in prehistory virtuosic artistic performances, by their rarity and skill, demonstrated rarity and skill in their possessors, who were thereby, like peacocks with luxuriant tails, preferred by potential mates; and because of this the taste for art and ability in it got into our genes. But then, this taste having got into our genes, so to speak, we can now value art and artists for other reasons than those to do with mate acquisition. But this concession is not enough. It is not just true (though it is) that artistic motivation nowadays floats free of its evolutionary origins, with a logic and system of values of its own, unconnected to whatever might have been true in the remote past. Even this modified evolutionary account fails to explain why it was *artistic* virtuosity which was admired in the first place. In sum, if there is anything to the 'performance' account of our aesthetic taste and sensibility, the direction of explanation must be exactly the opposite to that postulated by Pinker and Miller. That is, it is because artistic performance is admired for aesthetic reasons, that outstanding performers become attractive to potential mates and gain high status, rather than the other way round.

So, what then is aesthetic experience based in? It involves, at various levels, a delight in appearance, to be sure, a harmony for a time between us and how things appear. But does it take us any further than that? Does it, as our opening quotations suggested, suggest any deeper transcendence of the immediate? Does it intimate to us that we are 'at home' in the universe, as religion at one time preached, and as, in different ways, science and morality might contest (science by telling us that the world is really very different from how it seems, morality — at least on some accounts - by imposing on us duties which we either cannot fulfil or which have to be fulfilled at supreme personal cost)?

This is not the place to attempt an answer to these questions, or even any adequate analysis of their meaning. But our reflections on evolution prompt the following dilemma. Either, as our opening quotations implied, art and aesthetic experience really do point to some transcendence of the material world; in which case, evolution cannot give us a full account of human life and experience. Or, alternatively, art is a purely human creation and aesthetic experience has no transcendent dimension. In which case, something like an evolutionary explanation of these phenomena would in all likelihood be called for, even if we are at the moment far from any such account. At any event, any sense of transcendence aesthetic phenomena evoke would itself be illusory.

Maybe this sense of transcendence—which certainly does attach to many works of art of the past—has in some obscure way helped the species to survive and reproduce. It would be much the same way as, according to Michael Ruse, the (for him) equally illusory belief in an objective moral reality may in the past have helped human communities and individuals to flourish evolutionarily.[15] In both cases, the picture would be of survival devices tricking us into feelings of transcendence and illusions of objectivity for their own devious ends. But then, if this is true and it is generally realised to be true, we will look back on those forms of art which do intimate transcendence of some sort as belonging to a certain primitive and backward stage of humanity, as do the religious traditions out of which so many of them grew. In such circumstances, and in the absence of any transcendent ambition or dimension, art itself is likely to degenerate, as Ruskin predicted as early as 1846, into what he called mere aesthesis, 'mere amusement, ministers to morbid sensibilities, ticklers and fanners of the soul's sleep'—much like what you can see in today's most admired galleries of contemporary art, in fact.[16] Perhaps, too, surveying the cultural scene of the West today, both high and low, we might recall Darwin's own strictures about the 'barbarous races of men', with their 'hideous ornaments and equally hideous music'.[17] Post Darwin, and perhaps in part because of Darwin, the aesthetic wheel would seem to have turned full circle.

---

[15] See also Michael Ruse, in 'Evolution and religion', paper presented at The Royal Institute of Philosophy's schools' conference, Warwick, 1995.

[16] Ruskin, *Modern Painters* (1846), vol. 2, part 3, chapter 1, as in Cook and Wedderburn edn, vol. 4, p. 36.

[17] Charles Darwin, *The Descent of Man*, vol. 1, p. 142.

Chapter 2

Historicism and Architectural Knowledge

Even today, apologists for modernist and post-modernist architecture frequently appeal to what, following Sir Karl Popper, I will call historicist arguments. Such arguments have a particular poignancy when they are used to justify the replacement of some familiar part of an ancient city with some intentionally untraditional structure; as, for example, when a familiar nineteenth century block of offices in a prime city site is swept away to make room for something supposedly more fitting to the 'new millennium', a 'twentieth century contribution to monumental architecture', a building 'of substantial importance of the present age'.[1] Similarly, those architects or consumers of architecture who fail to conform to whatever stylistic demands the age is held to demand are marginalized in many supposedly serious discussions of architecture, and made to feel out of place and out of time.

The fact that assertions and arguments of this sort are thrown around unself-consciously in discussions of planning and architecture makes me think that, despite the pioneering efforts of David Watkin and of Sir Ernst Gombrich,[2] the full implications of the anti-historicist message contained in Popper's book *The Poverty of*

---

[1]   All the phrases quoted are taken from statements made at the time a particularly controversial planning decision was made in London (and are taken from reports of 9 June 1989 in *The Guardian* and *The Daily Telegraph* referring to the acceptance of Lord Palumbo's scheme to redevelop the Bank area of London). But similar thoughts and expressions are commonplace in planning enquiries and applications throughout Europe at least.

[2]   David Watkin, *Morality and Architecture* (The University of Chicago Press, 1984. Originally published in 1977); E.H. Gombrich, 'The logic of Vanity Fair: alternatives to historicism in the study of fashions, style and taste', in *The Philosophy of Karl Popper*, ed. P.A. Schilpp (Illinois: Open Court Publishing Co., 1974), pp. 925–57.

Historicism have not been generally appreciated in the realm of architecture or in aesthetics generally.[3] Part of the aim of this paper is to remedy this lacuna. Having analysed the influence of historicism on thinking about architecture, I will go on to give an account of architectural knowledge which gives due weight to what has been learned in the history of architecture, while eschewing historicism.

Historicism

I will begin by saying what I am taking historicism to be. Historicism is any approach to human affairs which assumes first that there is an inevitable course to human history, and then goes on to insist that the individual must simply submit him or herself to that course. As what I have to say is being applied to architecture, I will at the outset make clear that my use of the term 'historicism' is different from that employed by Sir Nikolaus Pevsner in his well-known *Outline of European Architecture* and elsewhere.[4] For Pevsner, and for many subsequent writers on architecture and aesthetics, a historicist building or work of art is one whose design imitates a style associated with a past age. William Morris is thus commended by Pevsner for not 'disguising' a town hall as a Greek temple. Despite Morris's sources of inspiration in the late Middle ages, he did not imitate:

> He recognised historicism as the danger it was. What he did was to steep himself in the atmosphere and the aesthetic principles of the Middle Ages, and then create something new with a similar flavour and on similar principles. This is why Morris fabrics and wallpapers will live long after all applied art of the generation before his will have lost its significance.[5]

Whatever one might think of this talk of applied art and its significance, as we will shortly see, Pevsner himself is, in Popper's sense, a historicist. His approach to architecture actually makes him an ideal-type historicist.

Popper says in the Introduction to *The Poverty of Historicism* that the historicism he is criticizing is any approach to the social sciences (including history) which assumes that historical prediction is their principal aim, and which assumes that this aim is attainable by discovering the 'rhythms' or 'patterns' or 'laws' or 'trends' which

---

[3]   K.R. Popper, *The Poverty of Historicism* (London: Routledge & Kegan Paul, 1961).

[4]   Nikolaus Pevsner, *An Outline of European Architecture*, 5th edn (Harmondsworth: Penguin Books, 1957).

[5]   Pevsner, *An Outline of European Architecture*, p. 277.

underlie the evolution of history.[6] Although the versions of historicist thought with which we are most familiar in practice are those which see the evolution of history as a progression to some ideal future state, it will be evident that, in Popper's sense, Spengler is a historicist just as much as Marx or Lenin. Nevertheless, if you believe that the world is inevitably progressing towards a revolutionary utopia, and if, despite the supposed inevitability of the progression, the example of actual historicists of a progressivist cast is anything to go by, politically your aim will be to re-fashion the present in the light of the way you think history is going, morally you will regard your opponents and their aspirations as expendable in the light of your superior historical insight, and methodologically you will see human individuals in terms of the historical evolution to which they willy-nilly contribute, and their decisions and activity as the embodied form of history's cunning.

Against the prophetic pretensions of historicism, Popper gives the following argument.[7] The course of human history is strongly influenced by the growth of human knowledge. We cannot predict by rational or scientific methods what this growth will be. If we could, then we could know now that we do not yet know, perhaps how safely to dispose of nuclear waste or how to write a programme for translating natural speech episodes in English into French. We cannot, therefore, predict the future course of human history.

Critics of this argument will point out that, as it stands, it costs only against our ability to predict the future course of history. That course could still be determined; beneath the unpredictable flux there might still be trends operating in a law-like way. God or some super-human intelligence, standing outside the intricacies of human thought might be able to predict our thought patterns and to know our future thoughts and discoveries.

While the objection is valid, I believe its scope to be restricted. Whatever might be the case with super-human intelligences and whether human choice and inventiveness are determined or not, the argument suggests convincingly enough that we will never have the ability to predict our future knowledge states. And this alone should make us wary of the pretensions of Marx, Spengler, Pevsner or anyone else to make historical prophecies or to define the spirit of our age in the light of their supposed knowledge of the trends underlying historical development. For what comes to be called the spirit of

[6]   Popper, *The Poverty of Historicism*, p. 3.
[7]   See also *ibid.*, preface, pp. v–vi.

a given age is always liable to be altered beyond present imagining or predictions by some new discovery or application of a new technology, as the example of the microcomputer in our own lives shows.

It is not, of course, just unpredictable changes in science and technology which change spirits of ages. Both the upsurge of militant Islam as a world force and of free-market economics in Britain and the United States in the late 1970s and early 1980s had seemed highly implausible to commentators and political scientists of the 1960s and early 1970s, commentators who had come to see the development of the world in largely secularist and largely welfarist terms. Islam and Reaganomics were certainly against the spirit of age. Nevertheless, what from a world-historical perspective might have seemed somewhat contingent events (e.g. the vacillations of the Shah of Iran, the unpopularity of Edward Heath as leader of the British Conservative party) enabled resolute individuals (in these cases the Ayatollah Khomeini, Mrs Thatcher) unexpectedly to seize power and to change the spirit of their age. Even if my examples and their interpretation do not command universal assent, the point I am making here is one that would be readily accepted by anyone who has ever been close to the formation of public policy. Along with scientific innovations, political ideas and influences change in unpredictable ways. Leaving aside for a moment the moral implications of attempting to force people to submit to spirits of ages, there is thus no reason from within history for individuals to allow themselves to be dragooned into thinking or acting in a particular way, even when, as I concede sometimes happens, one particular trend of thought or behaviour seems both predominant and likely to predominate. History (like evolution itself, as Stephen Jay Gould never tired of telling us) is full of examples of erstwhile predominant trends and forms of behaviour ceasing to predominate, often initially because of small and to the rationalizing historicist mind unimportant facts, such as the personal foibles of individuals, their health, and even, to take the classic case of Antony and Cleopatra, the shape of a nose. Thus, though, in retrospect we can explain a particular sequence of historical developments, part of the explanation of the sequence will involve an arguably improbable change of direction within the sequence at crucial moments, leading, let us say, to the rise of Augustus rather than the Antony. The significance of these chance-ridden bifurcations in the course of history makes historical *explanation* a far safer enterprise than historical projection.

We need, in fact, to go further in the attack on historicism than does Popper's argument. The unpredictability of human history does not reflect a merely epistemological problem. There is good reason for treating human history and human creativity in evolutionary terms, as involving chance happenings and leaps of imagination, both of which take us beyond what is at any given time in ways which are fundamentally unpredictable. Indeed, even talking of human history as an evolutionary process has fundamentally indeterminist implications, implications which are rarely realized by those who try to combine talk of evolution with historicist overtones. For the whole point of calling a process evolutionary is to assert that in the end it is unpredictable and has no definite direction or directiveness built into it *ab initio*. An evolutionary process involves random leaps beyond what already exists, which are then weeded out or reinforced by the environment. It can thus be seen in terms of a goal or problem-oriented process, but to see it in this way should not blind us to the degree to which the whole process is fuelled by randomness. Moreover, quite small apparently insignificant differences in the circumstances surrounding given random mutations, allowing some initially to prosper and others to be suppressed before they have the chance to show their mettle can affect the way in which one evolutionary line comes to predominate over another. Quite small differences in circumstances can then determine whether in the future a given moment comes to be seen as a crucial one in evolutionary history.

Human history or the history of some human activity is not blind like a biological evolutionary process. It consists in large part of more or less rational responses to perceived problems. Nevertheless there is in some of those responses a high degree of creativity and unpredictability, particularly when — for that very reason — a response is seen as breaking new ground and perhaps even changing the very goal and nature of the practice to which it belongs. And here our inability to predict a genuinely creative response on the basis of existing forms of thought and expression is surely highly significant. Given Beethoven (and a few other factors such as Byron, Shakespeare and the French Revolution), we might just about have been able to foresee the emergence of a phenomenon such as the music of Berlioz, but one hardly begins to understand how even the profoundest knowledge of Haydn, Mozart, Hummel, Cherubinin and the rest could have led to a genuine prediction of the work of Beethoven himself. Talk of revolutionary romanticism here is the merest hand-waving; an innovatory movement like the Romantic movement is brought about by men like Beethoven who are laws unto themselves, geniuses in Kant's terms, which is partly why they have the influence they have. Looked at from the perspective of such men, talk of style or of the spirit of the age is bound to be *ex post facto* rationalization, while prescriptions such as those routinely uttered by Pierre Boulez about composing in the light of historical imperatives, and which would, for example, lead us to pass over tonal compositions written in classical form today, are bound to seem an intolerable restriction on individual creativity.

Thus far my argument against historicism has been partly epistemological and partly ontological. I have argued that *we* cannot *know* the future course of *our* history; and that, above that, human history, like other evolutionary processes, contains elements of indeterminacy. A common response to these lines of thought is to concede that they may be true, but to say that, nevertheless, we can in certain circumstances have justified true beliefs about certain general lines of historical development. Even if some precise aspects of the future may be either or both unpredictable and undetermined, its broad general lines are both knowable and determined. On this basis, and again the argument as so far presented, we would be safe enough in making assertions about the current spirit of the age.

While I think the spirit of the age and the direction of history are more difficult to identify in any precise sense than the objection suggests, I am prepared to concede it for the moment, because my key objection to attempts to apply historicism in the creative sphere is not at first blush either epistemological or ontological. It is, in a broad sense, moral. My point is that even if one has succeeded in identifying the trend of an age, or of a style, that in itself gives no reason whatever for refusing a hearing to works judged in those terms anachronistic. That this reflex response to 'anachronism' is characteristic of our time is, of course, a tribute to the success in our time of historicist thinking in the arts. But so as not to go getting embroiled in disputes about the relative significance in the history of twentieth-century architecture of, say, Le Corbusier and Lutyens, I will here simply point to one incontrovertible example of an artistically significant 'anachronism' from the history of music: the later work of Bach. When the *avant-garde* of Bach's day was busy with melody and line, Bach continued to write fugues. For his pains he was dismissed as a relic of an earlier, less enlightened age (as Glenn

Gould put it).[8] Other than showing a certain calmness of nerve, what do we now think of Bach's refusal of the historicist invitation? From our distance and our perspective, both the debate and the criticism seem so parochial as to be of merely historical curiosity, despite the fact that there was, in fact, something right in the judgement of Bach's younger contemporaries. Eighteenth-century music did begin of show a pre-occupation with melody at the expense of counterpoint. Nevertheless, there was nothing necessary about this, and absolutely no artistic necessity for anyone to follow fashion. And it is quite possible that if more composers had stuck with counterpoint, the history of music might have turned out differently.

Although I believe that the epistemologico-ontological aspect of historicism and its moral aspect are distinct, a strong rejection of the latter (the sense that one *ought* to conform to the spirit of the age) can be helpful in undermining the former (the spirit of the age itself or, perhaps more accurately, what is taken to be the spirit of the age). Conversely, a strong commitment of the former, coupled with a strong sense that one is in tune with the spirit of one's own age, can be a powerful weapon with which to criticise, intimidate or even suppress those not inclined to conform to one's vision. (If they then willingly or unwillingly do conform, one's historicist viewpoint will appear to have been confirmed.)

The close connection between historicism and attempts to curb individual dissent and creativity is not coincidental. Historicists are, as Popper notes, uncomfortably aware of the uncertainty of the human factor. He refers to Karl Mannheim's remark that the political problem is to organize human impulses in such a way as they will direct their energy to the right strategic point, steering the total process of development in the desired direction. Popper points out that this programme implies an admission of failure on the part of the historicist.

For it substitutes for his demand that we build a new society, fit for men and women to live in, the demand that we 'mould' these men and women to fit into his new society. This, clearly, removes any possibility of testing the success or failure of the new society. For those who do not like living in it only admit thereby that they are not yet fit to live in it; that their 'human impulses' need further 'organising'.[9]

---

[8]   Glen Gould, 'Art of the fugue' in *The Glenn Gould Reader*, ed. T. Page (London: Faber & Faber, 1987), p. 15.

[9]   Popper, *The Poverty of Historicism*, p. 7.

This passage shows that historicist doctrines have both built-in untestability and oppressive overtones. The historicism Popper criticises is, in both respects, strikingly similar to what Pevsner advocates in his defence of architectural modernism.

Modernism

Pevsner grants that to many people architectural modernism 'often looks rather forbidding and seems to lack human warmth' but asserts that the same is true of contemporary life: 'Here, too, amenities to which we have been used are being replaced by something more exacting and more elementary.'[10]

We live in a society in which production is not just in the mass as Le Corbusier had it, but also for masses. According to Pevsner, the old days of atomized individualism, which precisely because of this individualism failed to produce an architectural style, are over. The age of mass building and mass style will bring about a removal of all unnecessary ornamentation and a concentration on function. Indeed, 'research into function' will become the central task of the architect and form the keystone of a new and genuine architectural style. The new men who experience the benefits of all this functionalism in the public arena will have their private taste transformed. Even London Transport bus shelters will be instrumental in this renaissance of taste and style: ' Those who have experienced the functional advantage of these shelters, the advantages of so much glass and so little in the way of roof support, will be prepared to welcome something of the same kind at home.'[11]

Those who continue to hanker after the sham ornamentation and individualism of the past simply show the extent to which they are unworthy of the more exacting and more elementary times of which Pevsner would have them be proud.

Modernists such as Le Corbusier and Pevsner, then, revelled in collectivist and totalitarian approaches both to architecture and to society. For them, we had reached an age in which the individual was subordinate to the mass; he and all his activities had to be seen in functional terms, in terms of the contributions the individual he was, was able to make the mass. All this was supposed to motivate an architecture devoted to the pursuit of function, devoid of ornamentation delightful for its own sake. The new architecture was dismiss-

---

[10] Pevsner, *An Outline of European Architecture*, p. 285.

[11] Nicholas Pevsner, *Studies in Art, Architecture and Design* (London: Thames & Hudson, 1968), vol. 1, p. 202.

ive of past architectural authorities which, from its point of view, were simply reflecting the architectural *moeurs* appropriate to bygone ages.

I will not comment here in any detail on the spuriousness of the doctrine of research into function, or on Pevsner's claim that if your job is to design a nursery school what you must first do is to 'find out all about nursery school work'.[12] It is none the less worth making the point that what Pevsner calls 'nursery school work', is not something that stands independent of often unarticulated and tradition-based conceptions about the type of building appropriate to places of learning. In fact, in any building beyond the rudest hut, merely providing shelter from the elements, there is no notion of a function it is to serve that stands in total independence of the feel and the aesthetic meaning the building will have for those who are to use it. Part of what is involved in the transformation from mere building to architecture is precisely the way that structural elements of building are made harmonious or beautiful to look at, and often by a process of serendipity, become features of design regarded as valuable in their own right and able to survive technological changes according to which they no longer serve their original functional role. Nor can it be entirely accidental that school and university building devoid of elegance, historical reference or comfort have gone along with an increasingly utilitarian approach to education, in which initiation into an inheritance of civilized thought and expression is no longer seen as education's primary aim and justification. Nor indeed, is it accidental that many of the most prized examples of 'functional' excellence, such as James Stirling's History Faculty building at Cambridge, have proved to be highly unfunctional for the purpose for which they were designed. As we shall see, traditional modes of building often contain elements of functional importance whose roles becomes apparent only when architectural revolutionaries attempt to design buildings without reference to tradition.

Post-modernism

According to Charles Jencks, though, the 'Modern Age', which sounds as though it would last forever, is 'fast becoming a thing of the past'.[13] If this just means that the austere modernist style of architecture which Pevsner used to advocate is now a taste shared by few

[12]   See also Pevsner, *An Outline of European Architecture*, p. 284.

[13]   Charles Jencks, *What is Post-Modernism?* (London: Academy Editions, 1987), p. 7.

who have any dealing with modernist buildings, one might well agree. However, and this is where Jencks is far closer to Pevsner that it at first seems, it is clear that Jencks, in speaking on behalf of what is called post-modernism, means something far more portentous. He goes on to say

> The Post-Modern Age is a time of incessant choosing. *It's an era when no orthodoxy can be adopted without self-consciousness and irony,* because all traditions seem to have some validity. This is partly a consequence of what is called the information explosion, the advent or organized knowledge, world communication and cybernetics.[14]

And he asserts that it is now impossible to return in a straightforward way to previous cultures and forms.

While there is, doubtless, such a thing as the information explosion and world-wide instant communication, Jencks clearly intends on the basis of this fact to paint a picture of our age and its spirit, and to derive certain moral and aesthetic imperatives therefrom. What he says about self-consciousness and irony would appear — perhaps unfortunately — to be belied by the rise of modern Islam. Aesthetically, Jencks would deploy his historicist analysis of the modern age to disparage the un-ironic classicism of architects such as Quinlan Terry and Robert Adam. In similar vein, Richard Rogers, the architect of the Lloyds Building and of the Pompidou Centre, proclaims that his firm's design policy represents a search for an aesthetic which recognizes that in a modern technological society, such as ours, change is the only constant, again, presumably intending to rule out an aesthetic such as that advocated by the Prince of Wales, which emphasizes stability, tradition and eternal verities.[15] Erecting principles of design on supposed characteristics of the modern age, such as change or choice, is historicism, pure and simple, as objectionable in its own way as an approach to aesthetic and architectural problems as Pevsner's dogmatic and monolithic modernism.

Jencks' view of post-modernism can be briefly stated. Because we live in a world of incessant choosing, there can be no such thing as orthodoxy in any field, and certainly not in art or architecture. Once we realize this, anything becomes possible. We can make our choices from style or place in the world, past or present. But precisely because our choices are weightless, loaded down with neither authority nor seriousness, any reference we make to a style, be it classical or modern, is bound to be self-conscious, ironical, 'doubly coded' as Jencks and his mentor, Umberto Eco, would put it. The Post-Modern architect uses a style in the same way a lover versed in the teachings of Roland Barthes, say, might utter the clichés of love-making to express his love, but in quotation marks, so to speak, to signify his superiority over the man who unconsciously speaks in cliché.

The Jencks-Eco view of post-modernism is echoed in even more portentous terms by Jean Baudrillard. He declares that post-modernism is 'the possibility of resuscitating images at the second level, *ironically of course*' (my italics). He went on to insist that

> one is no longer in a history of art or a history of forms. They have been deconstructed, destroyed. In reality there is no more refer-ence to forms. It has all been done. The extreme limits of these possibilities have been reached. It has destroyed itself ... all that are left are pieces, playing with pieces ... one is in a kind of post-history that is without meaning ...[16]

It is impossible not be struck by the historicism underlying these reflections, the belief that because of our historical situation all that is left to us is irony and fractured images. And certainly this is the way post-modernist architects and artists treat past styles in their own work. Often in the same building they juxtapose motifs from one style or period with motifs from other periods in a way calculated to destroy any sense of unity or harmony in the whole.

But one wonders why this ironical and decontextualized use of past styles should be the only or the best architectural response to the problems of the present age. It is sometimes said that because any reviver of a past style is by definition conscious that he is refer-ring to models from the past, there is bound to be a certain detach-ment in his attitude, leading inevitably to irony. But that this is simply false as it stands is shown by the example of Pugin, whose Gothic revivalism was highly self-conscious, anything but ironical or uncommitted.

It will then, no doubt, be urged that because, unlike Pugin, we do not believe in the doctrines of medieval Christianity, any play-ing with the Gothic form on our part is bound to be not just self-conscious, but also playful and ironical. But this view rests on the

---

[16] Jean Baudrillard, 'Game with vestiges', interview in *On the Beach* (1984), vol. 5, pp. 19–25.

premise that the Gothic arch, say, makes sense only in a context of Christian belief, a premise not the less dubious because it was the basis of Ruskin's condemnation of the use of the Gothic in railway stations. If the premise were true, the attitude I have often heard expressed, that Victorian railway stations replete with Gothic motifs and arches and huge iron vaults provided far more appropriate and exciting settings for the start or finish of journeys than the functional steel and glass structures which replaced them, would be simply unintelligible; whereas the truth is that everyone who has ever made a railway journey knows exactly what is meant.

In this knowledge, the lie is given to one of the fundamental beliefs of many advocates of post-modernism: that architecture is a system of signs with specific meanings, often of a religious or political sort. While it is true that architectural styles have been used to embody religious and political aspirations, the way in which they do this is through the experience a building produces in those who use or perceive it and not through embodying any verbally precise premise or literal statement. The experience of a building is not constrained or exhausted by the precise propositional content associated with it on any particular occasion. In fact, because of the soaring and weightless impression it can give to the perceiver, the Gothic arch is particularly suited to express a yearning for timelessness and transcendence. This is a yearning which is not tied down to the dogmas of medieval Christianity, but is something fundamental to the human condition. I therefore see no reason *a priori* why Gothic arches should not be used in a modern public building, and used without irony.

The ironical posture of post-modernism is an attempt to respond to a quasi-historical analysis of 'social reality' in exactly the same way as the supposed functionalism of Modernism was. With social reality now no longer seen as that of a central party collectivism but as 'irreducibly' pluralistic and plastic, in the absence of deference to standards accepted as objective and transcending individual choice, taste will be dictated by those who have the financial resources to express their whims and dominate the market. This point was not lost on the curators of the 1989 Whitney Biennial who tell us that Capitalism has overtaken contemporary art, quantifying and reducing it to the status commodity. Ours is a system adrift in mortgaged goods and obsessed with accumulation, where the spectacle of art consumption has been laid out in a public forum geared to journalistic hyperbole.[17]

Are these would-be culture critics, who nevertheless promote what they appear to be attacking, for this phenomenon or against it? It is hard to be sure, but then, of course, in this Post-Modernist age, everything is double-coded, and nothing what it seems. What, though, is evident is that in a situation in which the act of choosing itself becomes the criterion and basis of taste and in which everything is designed with a view to its being changed in five years, as Rogers advocates, lasting aesthetic values will be the losers, and work distinguished mainly by its frivolity and novelty is likely to flourish. In their joint tendency to deny the significance of what has been learned in the past, and to repudiate its authority in the light of the supposed requirements of the present drift of history, there is a crucial point of convergence between modernists and post-modernists, between the aesthetics of the utopian revolutionary and that of the free marketeer trumpeting the paramount worth of individual choice, whether that choice be informed or not.[18]

Architecture as practical knowledge

While it is true that in different historical periods different demands have been made on architects, I want to close this paper by suggesting that there are in architecture values which have nothing to do with particular historical moments, and that in the development of architecture, practical architectural knowledge has been gained which deserves to be thought of as authoritative. Many of the failures of twentieth-century architecture have stemmed from the refusal to recognize the validity and authority of this knowledge, a refusal on which modernists and post-modernists are united.

In developing this theme, I am taking architectural knowledge as a species of the genus practical knowledge. Practical knowledge is knowledge of how to act, and by extension, of how to feel. It is knowledge of the responses and feelings which are appropriate in

---

[17] Quoted by Jed Perl, 'The Whitney Biennial', in *Modern Painters*, vol. 2, no. 2, Summer 1982, p. 83.

[18] My criticism of modernism and post-modernism, of course, applies only to one particular type of justification of these approaches to the architecture. Some people may admire the clean lines and bland features of modernistic buildings and the humour and inventiveness of the post-modernists for their own sake, as purely aesthetic phenomena. None the less, it cannot be denied that much of the argument advanced in favour of what is presented as the necessity for both these styles derives from historicist premises.

given circumstances. It is in other words the sort of knowledge which underlies moral activity and aesthetic appreciation. A person who simply responds to circumstance on impulse or at random manifests lack of such knowledge. There would be no room there for application of the concept of appropriateness between stimulus and response: there would be only a causal connection with no room for normativity. But though we are creatures with impulses and animal needs, as human beings we are also endowed with self- consciousness and we cannot avoid reflecting on the rightness or wrongness, appropriateness or inappropriateness of what we do. To the extent that we do this, we separate ourselves from the immediacy of our impulses. We cease to treat them, as they are treated in so much modern moral philosophy and economic theory, as primitive data. We transform our impulses and animal needs into *intelligibilia*; we accord them meaning, we see them as eliciting appropriate or inappropriate reactions, as being reasonable or unreasonable springs into action. And in so doing, we imply an ability to restrain and harness our animal nature.

Practical knowledge, then, is knowledge of appropriate action or feeling in a given situation. As such, it is knowledge which characteristically actually issues in action or feeling. If it was not felt as at least prompting action, one could not be credited with a full understanding of the appropriateness of the action or feeling. The ability to give a theoretical account is neither necessary nor sufficient for practical knowledge in either moral or aesthetic realms. What is required is that one should actually act, should actually respond. Nevertheless, the knowledge of what it will be like to fulfil one's aim is an essential part of practical knowledge in the realm of morality and action, for only in this way will one be able to understand in an effective way why some actions are appropriate, others inappropriate. Similarly, in the field of aesthetic creation, an understanding of the likely response to what one produces on the part of a reasonably well-informed audience is a crucial element in intelligent intentional activity on the part of the artist or architect.

In speaking of the likely response of the audience as being part of what guides the architect's intention in designing a building, I am not claiming that the architect is necessarily interested, subjectively, in the response of any particular audience. Nor am I claiming that an architect may not on occasion wish to shock. He may also believe (rightly or wrongly) that some particular work or effect might transcend the ability of any specific audience to comprehend. All I am claiming is that the intention and design of an architect, as of any artist, must in part be guided by what he takes it the experience of a perceiver of his work will be like as and when the perceiver contemplates the work.[19]

My account of aesthetic experience, then, is in part a psychological one. A major aim of any artist must be to produce in his audience experiences of particular sorts, experiences which will be produced in response to and guided by perceptible features of his work. How, though, does the artist come to have knowledge of future feelings and responses to as yet unseen work? And, conversely, how do audiences come to be aesthetically well-informed, to understand just which feelings and responses the artist intends to evoke by given artistic works and effects?

Our view of what life is like, and how the world is perceived by us, is given partly by biology and partly by the traditions of thought and experience we inherit through upbringing. In morality, commentators often stress social conditioning and the divergences between different moralities, some of which can be explained by reference to historical circumstances. Nevertheless, any viable morality has to build on biological reality: on our naturally given strengths and weaknesses, on our natural capacities for selfishness and altruism, on our natural store of sympathy, on our sense of kin and of kind. In so far as we have a sense of what life is like, and of which reactions and actions are appropriate in given circumstances, much will be given to each individual by our common biology on the one hand, and by cultural inheritance on the other. In so far as one's sense of identity depends on the possession of sets of valuations and of a sense of one's duties, responsibilities and deserts, one's very existence as an individual depends on the prior existence of a community in which such valuations and meanings can be learned through their being given communal recognition. The very possibility of practical knowledge—of the knowledge of how to respond and react—depends on the individual approaching experience with certain feelings, with the sense that some things matter and affect him more than others, and on those initially biologically given feelings being

---

[19] See also Richard Wollheim, *Painting as an Art* (London: Thames & Hudson, 1987), p. 44: 'When [an artist] aims to produce a content or meaning, which is his major aim, he also paints so as to produce a certain experience … the required experience must come about through looking at the picture. It must come about through the way the artist worked.'

transformed through culture into a sense of certain reactions and certain aims being right and appropriate.

Much the same will be true in an analogous way of aesthetic response and reaction. Neither artist nor audience starts afresh. Both intellect and feeling are rooted in the general facts of human biology and the particular facts of culture which have made each what he is. Together, these are the factors yielding the very artistic styles and traditions to which we respond 'naturally' and which have played their part in forming our sensibility and sense of how things are. All this reflects itself in a practical and untheoretical awareness and readiness of perceivers to respond in specific ways. It is on his insight into this untheoretical readiness on the part of his audience that an artist or architect can rationally plan and develop his creations; a readiness which he anticipates by putting himself in the position of audience as and while he creates.[20]

The re-valuer of values, be he moralist or artistic theorizer, is set on changing the expectations engendered by this practical knowledge which we have as members of a particular species and as brought up in a particular tradition or set of traditions. There may be various reasons for such departure from tradition. The aim may be to shock or to jolt out of apathy; it may be because of a sense that a tradition ossified: or it may be to expand the audience's sensibility. The fulfilment of each of these aims, of course, depends on the existence of a tradition of sensibility in order to be fulfilled, in order to produce the shock or the expansion of sensibility, or whatever. There is, moreover, a danger inherent in any departure from tradition, the danger being the greater the more radical the departure.

Thus, one might be moved to agree with the Gavin Stamp's evaluation of Le Corbusier, as the exemplification of the twentieth-century, post Nietzschean modernist. For Stamp, Le Corbusier exemplifies *'all the destructive forces of the twentieth century ... machine-worship, utopianism, collectivism, totalitarianism and megolamania'*; personally, he is inspired by *'colossal vanity and egotism'*.[21] These words are not altogether unjust of one who sets his historicist and technology-dominated conception of how men ought

[20] On the way an artist imaginatively (and actually) puts himself in the position of an audience of his work, see also Wollheim's illuminating remarks, *ibid.*, pp. 39–45.

[21] Gavin Stamp, 'The consequences of Le Corbusier', in *The Daily Telegraph*, 9 March 1987. It is well worth noting that some spokesmen for architectural modernism, including Le Corbusier himself, claim that modernism is a true development of the classical style in that the essence of classicism is the organization of space

to live and perceive their world up against what, as a result of biology and tradition, men have actually come to think and feel what life is and what it could be. In Le Corbusier's own case, this refusal to bend to traditional knowledge or to compromise his mathematically inspired dreams reached extraordinary lengths, even late in his career when, according to the received view, he had softened somewhat his earlier commitment to building apartment blocks of what he was pleased to refer to as *'pitiless'* magnificence. In the building of Chandigarh in the Easter Punjab, not only did he fail in any way to accommodate the inevitable street traders of any Indian town (who came anyway), but he planned a rectilinear city of vast squares and motor roads without any effective shade from the equally pitiless sun, and houses lacking the coolness provided by the traditional courtyard and terrace. Inhuman architecture was here allied to an equally utopian political vision, for Nehru had expressly ordered a 'new town unfettered by the traditions of the past' as palliative for the loss of the beautiful, ancient city of Lahore.

Against both architect and politician we must understand that the traditional always encompasses a vast pool of implicit knowledge, of procedures, customs, styles and designs which have survived because they have initially been found responsive to human needs and desires, and which then in turn became constitutive of the needs and desires of succeeding generations. It is more than likely that until a traditional order is disturbed, one will not know just what the role of any particular element in it has been. Much of what is in any tradition will not have been planned and will not be there because it has been planned, but will have endured through a process resembling biological natural selection, shaped invisibly by its actual responsiveness to some need or desire or receptiveness that people actually have. The conception of tradition being proposed here is of an order emerging spontaneously through the survival of certain innovations and the destruction of others, in terms of their actually answering or failing to answer the needs people actually have, rather than in terms of their initial apparent plausibility or self- evidence or supposed conformity of the spirit of the times. It is a conception which can be applied in many fields:

according to 'rational' proportions. This is surely a misunderstanding of the perennial appeal of classical architecture, which is based on the interplay of order and decoration rather than on order per se. What, indeed, would a Greek temple be without the fluting on its columns, the detail of the capitals and the plinths, its triglyphs and metopes, the movement of the sculptured figures in the pediments, and so on?

scientific theorizing, morality, law and custom, as well as in the realm of art. My central point is that these spontaneously developing traditions are real and influential on individuals; indeed, they provide the framework within which true individuality is possible.[22] By contrast, historical 'spirits of ages' are always either *ex post facto* rationalization or bogus prophesying.

There is, then, in a developed tradition of art or architecture, a body of practical knowledge which enables workers within that tradition to communicate to an audience schooled by and within the tradition, enabling them to respond to its works and to find at times comfort and consolation in them precisely where the works show sensitivity to what the audience has come to regard as the familiar, the fitting and the human. In architecture, of all the arts, there is a key role for the familiar the fitting and the human, precisely because architecture provides us so much with the often only partly consciously perceived setting of our lives and our work. I am not arguing that there can be *no* room for innovation in architecture, even of a radical sort. My point is rather that, of all creative people, architects above all should be aware that the costs and dangers of radical innovation are likely to be high. To put it bluntly, except to the composer, it does not matter much if an incomprehensible piece of music is written, whereas a brutal or inhumane or silly building, once put up, adversely affects everyone who lives in or near it, and usually over a considerable time. The potential damage is the greater, the greater the number of untried and untraditional buildings, and, as we see in so many modern cities, the actual damage wrought by untraditional architecture is manifold. So there is, I say, a key role in architecture for respect for the familiar and the fitting, a role forced on architects because of the way what they do impinges on everyone. Of course, to aim at the familiar, the fitting and the human requires on the part of the architect both a modesty before traditional architectural orders and a recognition of the validity of the practical knowledge which goes with them, neither of which can be found in either the grandiosity of the modernists or the supercilious relativism and deification of change and choice of the post-modernists.

---

[22] Here I depart from the individualism of Popper in *The Poverty of Historicism*. The extreme individualism of that book was later recognized by its author to be exaggerated, if we are to believe what he said about the reality of World 3. It is important, though, to see that one can be an anti-historicist, suspicious of talk of sprits of ages and the like, while at the same time asserting the importance of traditional orders and practices for the creation of individual identities.

Enough has been said here and elsewhere about the hubris of modernists and about their unsubstantiated claims to know the course of history and about their equally questionable claim to have the right to foist the knowledge on an as-yet unfit human material. But just as hubristic and just as objectionable, once the point against historicism has been granted, is the post-modernist claim that in the present age, only ironic reference to past architectural styles and orders may be made. Other than their apparent lack of ease with true classicism, what makes Jencks or Baudrillard think that there has to be something ironic about a reference to the classical orders, say, in our time, that was not equally true for Palladio or Hawksmoor or Schinkel in earlier centuries? After all, none of these men inhabited classical Greece, none of them believed in its myths or sought a society based on slavery or on the wealth of the silver mines at Laurion. And more to the point, none of them applied its lesson in the same way. As will be clear from my earlier remarks on Pugin and Ruskin, nothing I have said here supports a static or purist attitude to a tradition, as opposed to one which allows its spontaneous development through a process of trial and error on the part of workers schooled within it and comfortable with its meanings.

What I want to suggest in conclusion is that as far as human life and work are concerned, many of the problems faced by contemporary architects are not so very different from those faced by architects over most of the last 2000 years or so. We as human beings still need to work and live in buildings which reflect our biological nature in scale and design and which build on the widely shared and often untheoretically possessed knowledge encompassed in traditional architectural styles. It is surely significant that we still use buildings of past centuries with no sense of incongruity or awkwardness or irony, and often for purposes quite different from those for which they were originally designed. Such a thing should be impossible were the historicist analyses offered by modernism and post-modernism true. But these analyses are not true; they rest on a spurious view of history and on an oppressively totalitarian view of the relation of the individual to his age, as I argued in the earlier sections of this paper, and on a false understanding of architectural knowledge as I have been arguing now. Architects should forget about historicist analyses of ages, millennia and their spirits, forget about dragooning everyone to conform to the spirit of the age and, with due modesty, as free individuals attempt to retrieve and re-apply the practical knowledge embodied in traditional architectural styles and so help to create an environment truly responsive to the needs people have actually come to have.[23]

[23] Earlier versions of this paper were given at the London centre for Philosophical Study's series of lectures on philosophy and architecture in 1990, at the first conference of the Centre for Environmental Policy Study in London in 1991, at Petr Oslzly's seminar in Brno, and at the King's College London Philosophy Society. I have benefited from comments made at all these meetings, and particularly from those of Professor Sir Colin St John Wilson.

Chapter 3

Prospects for Beauty

Ruskin said 'Great nations write their autobiographies in three manuscripts, the book of their deeds, the book of their words and the book of their art. Not one of these books can be understood unless we read the two others, but of the three the only trustworthy one is the last.'

Kenneth Clark, who quoted these words at the beginning of his television series *Civilisation,* adds that

> writers and politicians may come out with all sorts of edifying
> sentiments, but they are what is known as declarations of intent.
> If I had to say which was talking the truth about society, a speech
> by a Minister of Housing or the actual buildings put up in his
> time, I should believe the buildings.[1]

Well, his time, the time when he wrote those words was 1968–9. And we all know what the judgement of the early twenty-first century is of the buildings of the 1960's. What, though, of us, now at the turn of the new millennium? What do we read in the book of our art?

We read the blank opacity of the Millennium Dome, the sheer perversity of the proposed extension to the Victoria and Albert Museum, and the minutiae of Tracey Emin's life and bed; we read Chris Ofili's *Madonna* surrounded with elephant dung; we read the scatology of Gilbert and George; in novels squalor, pornographic description and an attitude of weary disillusion are routine; in serious music cacophony and pretension dominate over melody, harmony and grace; in dance the confrontational spirit of much modern choreography and in the theatre, all manner of cruelty and perversion not elevated or redeemed, are all gloried in. And these are only the 'highbrow', publicly lauded and often publicly funded examples. Go lower, go into popular taste, and you will find the unrelieved indignity and coarseness of East Enders and Grange Hill

---

[1] Kenneth Clark, *Civilisation* (1969), from the Penguin edn (Harmondsworth: 1982), pp. 17–18.

(the very programmes highlighted by the BBC's Director-General of the late 1990s in launching his crusade for education); we find pop videos and pop music characterized by crudity, pornographic suggestivity and lack of musicality; and far from any rediscovery of a vernacular architecture in either homes or shops, we find mass produced designs and items assembled without thought or sensitivity to place or history.

The above collection is a very mixed bag. But they do have one thing in common, I think. None could be described as aiming at, or at reaching the beautiful. Indeed, to raise the question of beauty in connection with them would be to miss their point, to criticize them from the wrong point of view. They are aiming at other things, and at things which, by and large, are incompatible with beauty.

To other ages than ours this would have seemed a strange, if not remarkable state of affairs. Art might be about lots of things, but one thing it is certainly about is beauty, at least if not all art, most art, most of the time. This, at any rate is an intuitive pre-reflective thought and a thought which might seem to have some connection or resonance with the experience of the Parthenon or the *Odes* of Horace or St Mark's in Venice or Chartres Cathedral or Botticelli's *Primavera* or Vermeer's *View of Delft* or Shakespeare's *Hamlet* or Mozart's *G minor symphony* (K550) or Constable's *Hadleigh Castle* Schumann's *Dichterliebe* or Renoir's *Boating Party*.

Of course, none of these works is the same or directly aiming at the same sort of thing. But in relation to each them the following words might be appropriately uttered:

> What a piece of work is man! How noble in reason! How infinite in faculty! In form, in moving, how express and admirable! In action how like an angel! In apprehension how like a god! The beauty of the world! The paragon of animals!

Hamlet goes on, 'And yet, to me, what is this quintessence of dust? Man delights me not; no nor woman neither, though by your smiling you seem to say so.'

As a culture, are we stuck in Hamlet's slough of disgust? Do we even remember that there were once moments in our history when we might have believed in the nobility of man and in the potential of his works to uplift, and in which this sense of beauty might have transformed our attitude to the natural world and to fate itself?

I am aware of the very unphilosophical nature of these remarks, prejudices some might think them. So let us turn to philosophy to see if we might find help there. However three fairly representative philosophical quotations suggest that this might be something of a blind alley: 'Despite its ancient aura as one of the supreme values in human life and in the cosmos some philosophers give beauty short shrift.'[2]

> Beauty is a topic of great philosophical interest and one that is relatively unexplored. Few would deny its importance and yet the mere suggestion that it be defined drives intelligent people to witless babble.[3]

> Until the eighteenth century, beauty was the single most important idea in the history of aesthetics ... (but as a consequence of the modern notion of fine art) beauty lost its traditional centrality in aesthetic theory and has never since regained it.[4]

There is a good justifiable reason for this sidelining of beauty in philosophical discourse. It is the Austinian point that describing a work of art or part of nature as beautiful is, in one sense, rather unhelpful. It doesn't point to any precise aspect of a work, and can often be little more than empty gushing (as critics of beauty would have it, not entirely unfairly). Moreover, as Stolnitz goes on to point out in the article just referred to, for some, beauty has become a rather narrow concept, denoting 'pleasure unmixed with pain and the absence of bizarre or discordant elements'. Excluding the sublime and much else, beauty then becomes irrelevant for the evaluation of many admired works of art, maybe even the tragic, and certainly the challenging, as happened when Plato, in his *Philebus* analysed beauty in terms of measure and proportion (64a) and excluded the tragic as a 'mixed' pleasure (50b). On the other hand if, as Janaway suggests, beauty is to serve as a catch-all for absolutely any positive value a work of art can have, 'then beauty really becomes a vacuous ideas for philosophical purposes'.

Against the narrow 'unchallenging' interpretation of beauty, I would simply set Rilke's lines:

> For Beauty's nothing
> but beginning of Terror we're just still able to bear,

[2]   Christopher Janaway, 'Beauty', in *The Oxford Companion to Philosophy* (Oxford: Oxford University Press, 1995), p. 80.

[3]   Mary Mottershill, 'Beauty', in *A Companion to Aesthetics* (Oxford: Blackwell, 1992), p. 44.

[4]   Jerome Stolnitz, 'Beauty', in *The Encyclopedia of Philosophy* (New York: Macmillan Publishers, 1967), vol. 1, p. 262.

and why we adore it so is because it serenely
disdains to destroy us.[5]

Beauty, at least in the sense I want to discuss it, is not a kind of superior prettiness. It can co-exist with discordant and disproportionate elements and even with intimations of terror. It can, as in Homer and in Aeschylean tragedy, co-exist with the absence of pity and the presence of an implacable fate before which we are crushed, and in the face of which the hero sinks to sleep, but not in shame.

Does this, though, mean that in my scheme of things anything can be beautiful? Or that beauty is simply the name given to any aesthetic quality? These two interpretations of the beautiful are not, of course, the same. It may be that anything can be made to look beautiful. Certainly we are familiar with the way in which a Chardin or a Morandi can invest the most commonplace, and even untidy of things with a timeless beauty, a half-eaten fish on a dinner plate or an old jar, for example. Could somebody find beauty in a scene of rape or murder? Here again we have to distinguish: between finding a bit of the scene beautiful (for example, a drop of red blood on a carpet of green grass), and finding the scene itself beautiful. The latter, which cannot be ruled out *a priori,* cannot be ruled out *a posteriori* either — at least not for a culture for whom tragedy is a high point of its art, and for whom the crucifixion is its central religious image. From the crucifixion down to a beggar's lameness, all the tortures and maladies of man were to be made, at least in part, the subjects of art.

The point seems to be that while any subject may become beautiful, it all depends on the way it is treated. I suppose that Titian's *Tarquin and Lucretia* does not glorify the murder and for all its energy has some of the poise and pathos and rightness of judgement of tragedy. But there is also the morally questionable possibility of making the intolerable tolerable through beautifying it, or perhaps more common, of simply reducing its significance simply through making it into a work of art, which is in no sense adequate to the scale of the horror depicted. I am not just thinking of crass entertainment, like the *Titanic* film here: although it has been tried — by Kenneth MacMillan among others — many, including me, would express profound reservations about making a ballet about a rape or a concentration camp or the killing fields of the Somme. The very attempt to use beautiful bodies, inviolate and moving beautifully, in horrific scenes is bound to be deeply problematic.

[5]   R.M. Rilke, *First Duino Elegy* (translated by J.B. Leishman and Stephen Spender, London: Chatto and Windus, 1975), lines 4–7.

While the extent of beautiful subject matter may be unlimited, it is not the case that any evaluation on aesthetic grounds signifies the presence of beauty. After all, ugliness is an aesthetic quality, the opposite of the beautiful. And so are types of dreariness, ungainliness, clumsiness, barbarity, discordance, terror, aggression, sentimentality, exaggeration, irony and grotesquerie. The presence of any of these features in a work of art will militate against its being beautiful, and unless balanced by more positive qualities, may even make it impossible.

It is not my view that any work of art is beautiful. I have already given plenty of examples of works which are not beautiful, and it is not part of my thesis that every work of art ought to be beautiful or to be aiming at beauty. After all, if *Eine Kleine Nachtmusik* (K525) is a work of art, so is its purported companion piece, *Ein Musikalischer Spass* (K522), and for its purpose, an admirable one, described by Alfred Einstein as the negative key to Mozart's whole aesthetic. And indeed over the last couple of centuries many artists have attempted to produce works which are anything but beautiful, precisely in response to various horrors and disasters, and also in an attempt to portray the inhumanity and ignobility of man. One thinks of some of the works of Goya and of Picasso, of Otto Dix, of Georg Grosz, of Leon Golub, of Philip Guston and of Francis Bacon, to take only examples from the visual arts.

I am not claiming that Goya's *Execution of the Third of May* or Picasso's *Guernica* are not considerable works of art. My claim is rather that the repudiation in these works of the beautiful, the refusal in them to gothicize or to prettify is part of what constitutes their power (though prettifying the ugly is not a temptation to which Goya was always immune). If you look at a deliberately unbeautiful work of art, you will begin to see that beauty is associated with such qualities as nobility, grace, balance, harmony, dignity, humanity, sympathy ... not with all of them always and at all times, but overall with what might be called positive and uplifting qualities, rather than with their opposites. It is this positivity of beauty which explains its most obvious, but often un-or under-remarked feature: namely that something or someone beautiful is, for that reason and at least to that extent, attractive. Beauty attracts, but not in any way, because things which are not beautiful can also attract. Beauty attracts in such a way as to inspire love (in Mary Mothersill's helpful phrase) as opposed to the ghoulish fascination or delightful horror evoked by works which glorify violence or are complicit with perversity.

In saying that beauty attracts and that it is a life-enhancing quality, I do not mean to deny the substance of the classical Kantian analysis. Three points from it stand out. The favourable aesthetic judgment, of which the judgement that something is beautiful is the central example, will be disinterested, universal and non-cognitive.

To take disinterestedness first. What this amounts to, or at least the part of Kant's position which is acceptable amounts to, is that in admiring something for its beauty, one is admiring it for what it is, in itself, and not for some other purpose the object might serve. It thus enables us to discriminate between two possible responses to a work of art on the part of its owner, say. The work might be admired aesthetically, but it might also be admired because of what it is worth, or because of the kudos its possession brings. This is obvious enough, and surely acceptable. The disinterestedness of the aesthetic means that in admiring a work's beauty, one is abstracting from the way it might be used for purposes other than simply being admired for what it is.

However, what Kant then goes on to say about disinterestedness is far less satisfactory, and we will consider this more directly in 'Kantian Disinterestedness' (Chapter 4). According to Kant free beauty is when a beautiful object is admired simply for its form. (Kant's example is a flower, as judged beautiful by a non-botanist: non-botanists have no idea what its function is, or what the functions of its parts are, so if we admire it, we admire it simply for its form, its sheer appearance). But in addition to purely formal beauty of this free sort, Kant does go on to admit that we can also find things beautiful because they appear as precisely adapted to their purpose, that is because of their 'dependent' beauty.

So, in admiring a horse or a church because it looks just like a horse or a church ought to look are we admitting a compromising kind of interest in our assessment of its beauty? The answer to this question is surely that we can still admire the church or the horse for what it is, and for its beautiful appropriateness to what it is, quite irrespective of any other way the object might be useful or relevant to other interests or purposes one might have in regard to that thing. For example, even if my horse had just been defeated by Desert Orchid, say, I could still expatiate on the beauty of the victorious horse (as in sport people often do even in defeat).

The admission by Kant of a class of dependent beauty partially rescues his aesthetics from the sterile formalism it is continually prone to, verging on a doctrine of art for art's sake. For, in recognizing dependent beauty as a genuine type of beauty, it means that in making aesthetic judgements we are not barred from taking into account more than the pure form of the object. We can appeal to considerations drawn from the moral, the teleological and the human more generally, as indeed I, as opposed to Kant, think we should. Thus, I might admire the technical and formal qualities of a Kokoschka portrait or a Bacon coupling but be disturbed by the lack of any humanly elevating quality in it; or, to take Kant's own example we might find the adornment of the human body with tattoos of spirals and straight lines unpleasing because it was on the figure of a man.

Nevertheless, although, *pace* Kant in his purist mood, the disinterestedness of beauty does not imply a purely formal attitude to the beautiful, it does mean that in being attracted to something for its beauty we are admiring it for what it is in itself and not because it might be expensive or a good piece of propaganda or a brilliant expression of my current state of mind or a release from some overwhelming sense of guilt or, as much current pop music, a stimulus to sexual license and drug-taking. In other words, it is possible to have a disinterested attitude to a work which is addressed to human interest. We contemplate the work for no purpose other than its contemplation. All this is surely part of what is correctly implied in thinking of something as beautiful, and in this sense our attitude to it is disinterested.

As well as disinterested, the beautiful is also universal. By this Kant means that in judging something to be beautiful we are presupposing that anyone who looks at the object with sufficient care, knowledge and attention will come to the same conclusion. The aesthetic judgement is thus, in Kant's eyes, to be distinguished from a mere preference of taste. Beauty matters, and in our pre-philosophic frame of mind, before we are introduced to the fashionable relativism of the age, we all know this. That is to say, we understand the difference between a preference for dark over milk chocolate (mere taste) and the judgement that almost anything by Beethoven is a superior piece of music to almost anything written by Lord Lloyd Webber or sung by Sir Elton John. This judgement also raises the possibility that it or we or someone else might be mistaken in making it. But these are judgements which can be defended, argued about and justified or criticized in terms of salient features of the works in question: their complexity, musical skill, timeless appeal, intellectual interest, emotional depth, human resonance, and so on.

After disinterestedness and universality, we come to non-cognitiveness. Two connected features of the Kantian analysis here are that these judgements cannot be explicated in terms of general principles, and also that the making of them requires personal acquaintance with the work or works in question. That is to say, there is no rule which could determine whether something is beautiful in advance of the appreciation of the precise character of the work, and we will be in a position to make or defend a judgement of aesthetic quality only when we have actually seen or heard the work. I imagine that most artists and art-lovers would agree with both these points, which taken together constitute the Kantian claim that aesthetic judgements are non-cognitive (or at least the acceptable aspect of that claim); that is, they cannot be justified by appeal to any general rule of principle applied independently of the experience of this particular work of art.

For example, one might judge, as Ruskin did, that in a Veronese painting what would in other hands be a mass of 'trivial or even ludicrous detail' in no way detracts from the nobleness of the whole. (Ruskin was writing of *The Presentation of the Queen of Sheba* in Turin, but the same point could be made of *The Family of Darius before Alexander* in London, and of many other of Veronese's great set pieces.)

But what would be the amount of detail that would have been trivial and ludicrous, even in Veronese's hands? What is it about the composition of a Veronese set piece which preserves balance in the midst of the sort of detail which, in the hands of a Frith, say, might have rendered the painting wholly ununified, a disparate collection of almost randomly assembled elements, in the unpainterly sense a mere narrative, hardly more than a piece of photographic reportage?

There is no general answer to these questions, and the only recourse to the critic is an appeal to precise aspects of the composition of *Derby Day* and how they cumulate in a particular experience, as opposed to *The Presentation of the Queen of Sheba*.

In the same way that I took issue with part of Kant's notion of disinterestedness, I will leave aside the other aspect of Kant's non-cognitivism, the thought that aesthetic judgement 'can be no other than subjective'; I suspect that the implication here that aesthetic judgements are not true or false but merely a part of a subjective reaction arises from Kant's recognition of the non-generalizable nature of aesthetic judgements together with his appreciation of the way that they have to be based in experience. Taken with the belief that only scientific (i.e. measurable and generalizable) judgements can properly be seen as true (or false), aesthetic judgements would then indeed turn out to be neither true nor false. But we need not accede to this implication of the Kantian analysis, which its basic tenets do not, in any case, require. We can simply take from Kant the thought that aesthetic judgements are universal in intent, are disinterested in the sense specified and need to be based on personal direct experience. Taking these claims together will help us to understand why so much contemporary art is not beautiful, and could not be, at least as long as it follows the professed intent of those who create and appreciate it.

As a way into my theme here, I cannot do better than refer to some things Arthur Danto says in a recent essay on the Jewish Museum in New York, entitled 'Post-modern art and concrete selves'.[6] In this essay Danto is discussing whether there could or should be a museum specifically of Jewish art. In an earlier incarnation that museum had adopted what Danto calls a purist attitude to its art: the art exhibited was by Jewish artists (such as Ad Reinhardt and Philip Guston); but there was, as Danto says, nothing particularly Jewish about the art: a pride, no doubt that Jews were up there with the Pollocks and the de Koonings, but the art exhibited could have been exhibited anywhere at that time, and not just in a Jewish gallery.

This all changed in the late 1960's. At that time the museum's trustees began to insist on the art exhibited being specifically Jewish in some sense. Now, while art which reflected a particularly Jewish experience could be universal (just as, perhaps, Spinoza's philosophy) by the time Danto came to write his essay in 1993, this was no longer what was wanted. 'What was wanted were works which, in a way, remained enclosed in their Jewishness, and which would not reach out to or interest non-Jews, except as examples of ethnography.' Connecting what had happened to moral and political philosophy post-Rawls and post-Kant (when pretensions to a universal value system had also been given up) and also to education, with the growth of women's studies, black studies, working-class studies, Chicago studies and so on, where the work reinforces identities, bringing them more and more into consciousness, Danto says this of the art exhibited in the Jewish museum in the 1990s:

[6]   In Arthur C. Danto's *Philosophizing Art* (Berkeley and Los Angeles: University of California Press, 1999), pp. 123–43.

Their conception of art is very much one of interestedness, and is not at all universal. The art, like the museum, speaks in a special way to the group whose art and museum it is. To experience the art is from the start to have an interest ... (an) interest that has as its object the furtherance of the group to which one belongs. The art is there for the sake of that interest.

And, most revealing from my point of view,

It follows that, from this perspective, the primary concern of art (not the art, notice) is not that it be beautiful — or in any case — its being so is secondary. It follows further that artistic experience is not aesthetic either: it is instead political and instrumental ... Needless to say, the art made present to the visitors related to it through interest need not be great art by universal criteria at all.[7]

Danto goes on to comment about the similarly separatist Museum of Women's Art in Washington D.C.: 'critics sometimes noted that the work was not always of the highest quality'. But, as he says, to make a judgement of this sort or at least to regard it as in any way damning or negative is to miss the point: it is to impose an irrelevant conception of art on the art it contains. For this art — be it Jewish, Women's, American/Indian, homosexual or whatever — is precisely not trying to be universal and it is certainly not trying to be disinterested. On the contrary, its whole point is the furtherance of the group to which one belongs.

So, in so far as universality and disinterestedness are part of the conditions of being beautiful, it is hardly surprising if it is mostly not beautiful, or if it is beautiful, it is beautiful only *per accidens,* as it were, through looking at and judging the work against criteria its creators might well reject. Indeed, far from merely being interested, as opposed to disinterested, for Danto whole swathes of contemporary art are what in his 'Bad aesthetic times in the USA?', he calls 'disturbational'. That is to say, it is art which is not just interested and particular, but which intentionally transgresses the aesthetic distance which makes disinterested contemplation possible: 'My concept of disturbation is derived from its natural English rhyme, where images have physical consequences ... and in the main the use of disturbing things is a means to an end.'[8]

He then goes on to say what we will refer to again in 'Art and Censorship' (Chapter 7), that such 'performative' art should be

---

[7]   *Ibid.*, pp. 134–5.

[8]   Arthur C. Danto, 'Bad aesthetic times in the USA?', in *Modern Painters,* vol. 2, no. 2, Summer 1989, pp. 55–9, at p. 55.

aggressive and extreme, subverting expectations about what a work of art should be. It should use shocking means. It is simply not trying to be beautiful or any of the things which traditionally go along with beauty. It is not aiming for a position in the traditional artistic pantheon at which it will characteristically sneer, but rather to transform consciousness. In this quest it is often actually required to be ugly and in other ways aesthetically bad.

Of course, in other contexts many of those Danto is praising would say that in art, political servitude means bad aesthetics; they would probably be thinking of the art of the 1930s produced in accordance with the wishes of the dictatorships of Russia, Germany and Italy. But Danto shows that aesthetics can be subverted by politics of a non-dictatorial, impeccably liberal, impeccably liberational kind. More to the point, precisely by using the Kantian analysis of the judgement of taste Danto shows convincingly enough why politically motivated art and art of ethnic identity is unlikely to be beautiful.

It is unlikely to be beautiful because it is not trying to be beautiful. It has no interest in the universality or disinterestedness characteristic of beautiful things. And nor, of course, does art (in this case primarily music) whose whole aim is to stimulate and impel people into drug use or sexual license. In that case, as in different ways in the others, the art seeks to deny the possibility of being contemplated disinterestedly. It aims to overwhelm the hearer, to take him or her over, to cancel the psychic distance which aesthetic experience requires. It is, in a very direct sense, disturbational. It is in the disturbing sense consciousness-altering, in the same way that political agit-prop aims to be, in the jargon, 'consciousness raising'.

It might, though, be said that similar points could be made about religious art, some at least of which most people would have little hesitation in recognizing as beautiful. Can religious art aspire to the disinterest and universality demanded by Kant? Universality may not be a problem; non-believers clearly have no difficulty in admiring Chartres Cathedral or the *St Matthew Passion*. But are these things disinterested in the relevant sense?

It must be admitted that some religious art is very preacherly, directly and obviously missionary, just like feminist or socialist agit-prop, and that some religious people want art of just this sort (Luther, for example). That would certainly detract from its potential for beauty. But religious art does not have to be didactic or indoctrinatory. It can be, and often is, contemplative, in the sense of being

simply for the glory of God, as would be said. And here there would
be both truth and the disinterestedness characteristic of the beautiful. Things would be portrayed for themselves as they are in themselves. Religious commission and subject-matter do not of
themselves impede an artist in pursuing the virtues of his art: in
using his strength, and muscular precision and skill and insight and
ruthlessness to paint as he sees fit, cutting himself entirely away, as
Ruskin says 'from all love of his fellow creatures'. Indeed a certain
interpretation of the religious impulse — the one which accepted the
world and humanity in all its light and all its shadow, without anxiety or lust or spite or remorse — would actually encourage that type
of disinterested and universalizing artistic impulse (though all this
is a universe away from the 'art for art's sake' of Kantian free beauty,
and points again to the limitations of that concept).

I have dwelt at some length with the ways in which much contemporary art and music repudiates any drive towards disinterestedness and universality, and in so doing makes it hard for it to be
perceived as beautiful, except unintentionally, or by default as it
were. But there is also another way in which beauty can be avoided
by the artist flouting the satisfaction of another of the Kantian conditions for a truly aesthetic experience. In discussing what I called the
non-cognitiveness of the aesthetic experience, I intended to focus on
precisely that: the experience. For aesthetic judgements are
judgements which require experience of the object, and the significance of the experience is not in any straightforward sense the trans-
mission of information. It is because I have heard it that I know that
Mozart's *Jupiter* Symphony is beautiful because of its sublime balance of melody, rhythm, harmony and counterpoint, its
unponderous gravity and its exquisite fusion of learned and gallant
styles. If I had not heard it, I could not know any of these things,
although I might know a great deal about its history, its place in
Mozart's oeuvre, its scoring, and much else besides. A crucial aspect
of the non-cognitive, non-informational nature of the aesthetic experience is that one can hear a work like the *Jupiter* countless times
without its attraction palling, whereas there would be no point in
reading and re-reading a newspaper or a text book, say, once its
informational content had been assimilated.

There are at least two strong tendencies in twentieth-century art
which militate against the experiential requirement. There is first the
assumption, dominant in serialism in music, but not without its
influence and counterparts in architecture and the visual arts, that

what counts in a work is not its perceived or perceivable surface, but its underlying and imperceptible structure (as in later Schoenberg) or more generally its adherence to some abstract blueprint, such as in architecture the doctrine of functionality.

The difficulty with these approaches from the aesthetic point of view, and hence from the perspective of beauty, is that what comes to dominate in the composing of a piece of music or in the designing of a building is not primarily what can be perceived. In the case of the Second Viennese School the innate musicality of a Berg could triumph over theory and dogma. His *Violin Concerto* is, as anyone who has heard it will know, a work of elegaic beauty, as beautiful as anything written in the last century, but this is surely because of how it sounds, not because it adheres to the Schoenbergian dogma. In fact, it does not sound like a piece of serialism, which prompts the conclusion that its conformity to the principles of dodecaphony is irrelevant to the way we hear it, a triumph indeed of Berg's musicality over theoretical constraint.

With much twentieth-century architecture, function took (or was supposed to take) precedence over appearance. It wasn't, as in Kant's dependent beauty, that a building had to look like what it was. It was rather that in it appearance was to be determined by analysis of a set of goals for the building which in themselves dictate no particular appearance, but which are derived from technology and a quasi-scientific account of human need. This doctrine is memorably if rather bathetically expressed in the Pevsnerian injunction that if you want to build a nursery school, you 'must find out all about nursery school work'. This 'research into function' as Pevsner calls it, is all nonsense and should be distinguished from Kant's notion of dependent beauty.

Dependent beauty arises when an object looks as it ought to look when it looks like what it is supposed to be and it is constructed with regard to how it looks. But what Pevsner means by research into function is the view associated with Le Corbusier in his *Unité d'Habitation* phase: that you scientifically determine the optimal amounts of light, air, space, heating and so on for an apartment or a school room. Having discovered these desiderata, you then design your building to fulfil them in the simplest way possible. Aesthetic properties are supposed to play no part in this: ornament is crime, after all; what must be attended to are simply the building's 'practical requirements' not any of the images of enjoyment or entertainment or education or domesticity or worship, which for most people and, one suspects for Kant, would be required by a building looking like what it is for. That is, it would be via its aesthetic properties and its style that it would achieve dependent beauty, not by the elimination of them. Of course, there was actually an aesthetic underlying this twentieth-century functionalism. It was the aesthetic in which anything pertaining to the beautiful or taste of old-fashioned human beings was mere clutter, untidiness to be ruthlessly eliminated by the new rationalism, a rationalism in both its genesis and its effects not surprisingly not unlike that of Schoenberg's musical rationalism.

The upshot was that schools built in the 1960's on reductively functionalist principle are conducive to anything but the education of children, in part one suspects because they lack not just aesthetic qualities in general, but in particular those which might go along with a humane education (such as an architectural style embodying a sense of tradition, some evocation of dignity and authority and a sensitivity to the complexities of light and shade and surface). But then of course, on the doctrine of research into function consideration of aesthetic qualities or effects plays no role at all.

In aiming at theory and function, rather than appearance, art will make the achievement of beauty that much more unlikely. But so it will if the aim is to convey an idea or (as Sir Nicholas Serota likes to put it) to challenge its audience's preconceptions. This 'theory art' reaches its *reductio ad absurduum* in the joke slogans of Jenny Holzer, which once seen do not need to be seen again — or, more accurately, which once heard, do not need to be seen at all. But quasi-philosophical challenge is routinely trotted out as the aim and justification of a host of contemporary works of art, from Damien Hirst's medicine cabinets and pickled animals, to Rachel Whiteread's casts of the underside of chairs, to Gilbert and George's scatology, to Jeff Koons' vacuum cleaners and Robert Mapplethorpe's pornographic photographs.

In these cases, too, there is really no need to see the objects in question, or even if there is an initial visual impact it rapidly diminishes in interest, much as the typical arresting advertisement and for much the same reason. People come into a gallery full of modern installation art and, once they have got the idea, are at a loss to know what to look at: quite the reverse of what happens when people examine a Monet or a Renoir, for example, where fascination with and interest in the surface and what is seen in it appears virtually endless.

I have tried to show that there are aspects of fashion in contemporary art which militate against the achievement of beauty. These are a repudiation of disinterestedness in favour of work which serves some political or therapeutic purpose, an emphasis on art as the embodiment of particular identities, and a focus on non-perceptual properties, such as the underlying imperceptible structure of a work of art, or its satisfaction of functional demands in a utilitarian sense. In all these ways much contemporary art flouts the requirements for the beautiful correctly identified by Kant.

But these, of course, are purely formal requirements. They say nothing about a work's content. A work would in the appropriate sense be disinterested, universal and aiming at what could actually be perceived, and yet still not be beautiful. It could fail to be beautiful because its maker may have wanted it to be ugly and discordant or raucous or unsettling. And he or she may have wanted it to be these or analogous things because of some view the composer or artist had about his and our time or situation. After Auschwitz should we be even aiming at beauty? More profoundly; perhaps, a cultivation of beauty seems to imply that ultimately all is or could be well with the world. Again, this is suggested by Kant's analysis of beauty: that in judging something to be beautiful, we find a harmony between our judgement and it. But how, it would be said, can there be any such harmony except as a temporary and lying diversion, given the lack of any harmony obtaining between the world and us, between us and the rest of our kind, between our deepest yearnings and our inevitable fate, and post-Darwin, within the world itself?

So, in short, even if there are temporary experiences of beauty, these are inevitably tinged with an almost sickly nostalgia and world-weariness — as in the final trio in *Der Rosenkavalier* — and are ultimately no better than a childish avoidance of what we really know (like the elderly Ruskin's advocacy of Kate Greenaway). In other words, we won't have beauty because beauty belongs to our and mankind's infancy.

I cannot say that any of this is wrong. In our post-religious age such an attitude can come to seem all but forced upon us. That so many artists and musicians seem to take this attitude may help to explain why it is that when most of us seek aesthetic delight — or beauty — we do not turn to works of our own time. So, on this view, the prospects for beauty are bleak, and it may go some way towards explaining why it is that art tends these days to be disturbational rather than Kantian.

But there is another possible view, and it is the view associated with Plato. That is, the experience of beauty itself is part of a background which elevates us, which as Nietzsche puts it, justifies our world.

What Plato (or rather Diotima) suggests in *The Symposium* is that the lover of beauty is first captivated by the beauties of individual bodies (a more realistic account of the genesis of a taste for beauty than the rather austere Kantian account). But then, 'by scanning beauty's wide horizon' the aesthete detaches him or herself from the 'slavish and illiberal devotion to the individual loveliness of a single boy', and turns the eye disinterestedly to the 'open sea of beauty'. True aesthetic appreciation has then been reached until it in turn comes to be love for something which is not physical at all.

Now, as far as aesthetics is concerned this non-physical attraction is surely a step too far. However, what is suggestive in the Platonic account is the way a sense for beauty is represented as moving from intense sensual attraction to a sense which diffuses itself over aspects of the whole of creation. But, to come back to our earlier question, does this sense of harmony with things point to anything fundamentally right about the world? To see things in the world, things made by us, and above all to see attempts to confront our fate head on as beautiful, as ultimately redeemable is to show the world as not ultimately alien, and ourselves as not necessarily alienated.

The aesthetic sense points to and presupposes the type of ultimate harmony and meaning in the universe which, in other more direct ways, religions symbolize. Of course, to say *that* is not to say that the religious sense is justified, or that our consolation in aesthetic experience is not, at root, an illusion: in the aesthetic case, wish fulfilment powered by the type of release certain shapes and colours and sounds produce in the chemistry of the brain. So we come back to our age and its lack of care for the beautiful. We lack the type of shared symbolic order which in previous ages sustained artistic styles and forged aesthetic communities. More profoundly, publicly at least we lack the type of vision, religious or otherwise which might have filled out the aesthetic sense into something intimating transcendence and meaning, in Ruskin's terms, transforming *aesthesis* – 'the mere animal consciousness of the pleasantness' – into *theoria* – the sense that beauty has a moral or at least a spiritual core, bearing 'witness to the glory of God'. So, as Ruskin predicted as early as 1846 (long before art for art's sake or the Whistler case), our arts have sunk into 'mere amusement, ministers to morbid sensibilities, ticklers and fanners of the soul's sleep'.[9]

---

[9]   On this aspect of Ruskin's thought, see Peter Fuller's *Theoria* (London: Chatto and Windus, 1988), especially chapter 4.

But this may not be quite the end of the story. The great works of art of the past, those conceived within a transcendent framework, still for many of us have a charge and a vivacity quite missing from the sensations of today. Even as the public culture denies any such thing, many of us have private experiences of *theoria*. And perhaps, as the Kantian system intimates, the aesthetic, or more precisely the experience of the beautiful, does provide a resolution to at least some of our dilemmas; it suggests an approach to life which is neither that of science, with its downgrading of appearance and unattainable thing in itself, nor that of morality with its stern and unfulfillable duties and the endless, apparently pointless suffering to which humanity is subject and demands. For in the experience of beauty we get a sense that, despite the problems of alienation thrown up in different ways by science and morality, we are nevertheless at home in the world.

By 'at home', I mean that the world is not just the blind, random, humanly indifferent entity described by modern science, that it is in some sense responsive to our concerns, that consciousness (our consciousness) does take us to the essence of the world, that meaning and intelligibility are not simply imposed by us on a world which is ultimately meaningless and indifferent. (Even the world of Homer, heartless as it is, does respond to our noblest aspirations: the blood of the heroes, as Ruskin said, though poured out on the ground, rose into hyacinthine flowers; all nature became divine, and 'the gods whom they had never ceased to love, came down to love them ...')

Something of this sort *can* be suggested by aesthetic experience, aesthetic experience intimating a type and a depth of feeling and meaning beyond the everyday. Of course, there may be nothing which corresponds to these feelings, in which case aesthetic experience has no more ultimate significance than a warm bath or Prozac or some other way of affecting the chemistry of the brain. All I can say about that is that this is not how the experience of say, *King Lear,* or Beethoven's *Op.*132 actually *feels;* perhaps in the case of Lear the experience is of an ultimate if heartless justice in which despite the appearance to the world, Lear and Cordelia do not die like dogs, but die with meaning and a certain dignity; or in the case of Beethoven, *Heilige Dankgesang,* praise for the spirit which harmonizes and elevates the universe; and in both cases we are close to Rilke's beginning of Terror, serenely disdaining to destroy us, close though it may come to it.

Dogmatic religion is not implied by these or analogous feelings, nor is traditional theism. Perhaps all that is suggested is something akin to and as vague as William James's 'piecemeal supernaturalism' — that is the belief that there is a power in the universe which works towards the good and helps achieve it, and that in our conscious experience we can somehow link in to that power. The point is that positive aesthetic experience — the experience above all of beauty — will for many people be a pointer to the existence of such a reality, and because of the embodied basis of aesthetic feeling one which, unlike much religious thought, does not seek to play down the reality or significance of the material world.

Of course, for those whose horizons are bounded by a narrow physicalism, none of this will begin to be credible. It may not even make any sense. The point of the last few pages has been to suggest that from such a perspective, both art and beauty may be transformed; more precisely art as a quest for universal and disinterested experiences of beauty will become problematic only if the world can sustain no sense of the beautiful beyond mere *aesthesis*, which will look increasingly like a highly temporary and indulgent retreat from the reality of our condition. So we get instead the shark in formaldehyde or the soiled bed or close ups of the artist's orifices, which at least have the virtue of not suggesting that there is anything more to life than what they show, and are certainly not presented as an escape from an ultimately meaningless existence. What then, are the prospects for beauty? Are we destined to find its most lively expressions *only* in the art of the ever-receding past? Or will the new millennium bring about a renaissance of beauty?

Chapter 4

Kantian Disinterestedness

In a striking remark in *The Reformation of the Image*, Joseph Koerner says that the category 'art' arose only at the end of the Middle Ages 'when religious images, rejected, were remade into objects of disinterested satisfaction'.[1] Koerner also refers to the Hegelian thesis that in 'the golden age of the Late Middle Ages' art fulfilled its 'highest vocation', but that this type of art remains for us a thing of the past; and also to the fairly traditional idea (which he himself rejects) that at the time of the Reformation the art favoured by the reformers became didactic, its aesthetic core retreating and being transformed into an inner and inward spirituality.

In the remark which I have just quoted, Koerner is, of course, referring to the Kantian view that disinterestedness is one of the key elements of the aesthetic attitude. Let me say straightaway that it is a pretty peculiar view of art which would have 'art' in its pure sense appearing only around the time of Luther. Cave paintings, Greek sculpture and tragedy, the Aeneid, Byzantine icons, the mosaics at Ravenna, Gothic cathedrals, the frescoes of Giotto would all not be art on this view, or at least not art in its pure, core-categorial sense. Stipulation aside, we would question the sense of a category which suggests such a degree of rupture in human aesthetic experience at that point. It is also a category that would leave us in a quandary when approaching such towering post-Reformation masterpieces with a profound religious content, such as the Bach Passions, Rubens's Descent from the Cross and the Heiliger Dankgesang from Beethoven's *Op.* 132. Are we to say that in the Magnificat from Monteverdi's Vespers of 1610 we can — for almost the first time in the history of music if Koerner is correct — distinguish a pure aesthetic core from the religious feeling, content and context in which that aesthetic core is clothed, or that in judging and appreciating the

---

[1]   Joseph Koerner, *The Reformation of the Image* (University of Chicago Press, 2003), p. 35.

music we somehow have to prise away the religious varnish from the pure aesthetic canvas? Or is it rather that, even for non-believers, Monteverdi is able to express something of what it is like to feel and believe that in the Incarnation and Mary's obedience, God has indeed magnified the lowly and humbled the proud? And that all this is an essential part of the meaning and experience of the music?

We need, surely, to re-examine the notion of disinterestedness as applied to works of art. A good place to begin would be the well-known remark of John Scotus Erigena about how a wise man might regard a beautiful vase: 'He simply refers its beauty to the glory of God alone. He is not seized with the temptation of avidity, no poison of greed infects the intention of his pure mind, and he is not sullied by any lust.'

So, at a level which will not raise any great difficulty we can say that in taking an aesthetic attitude to something we are not considering the honour or fame it brings to its maker or owner, we are turning our attention away from its financial value, and we are not regarding it as something to be consumed or possessed (although that does not mean that its content might not stem from or have a bearing on sensory appetite). We are content for the object to be what it is, we are valuing it for what it is, for its own sake, it would be said. Perhaps one might also think of the work itself as something which, in Ruskin's terms, accepts the world and humanity in 'all its light and shadow, without anxiety or lust or spite or remorse', or at least take it as an aesthetic criticism if a work—in the Leavisite phrase—'does dirt on life'.

But what we might think of as this uncontroversial baseline level of disinterestedness is quite considerably ratcheted up by Kant and his followers in aesthetics, so much so that we think it doubtful that Kant could accept the full implications of what Ruskin has just said.

For Kant disinterestedness is not just the suspension of appetite or greed in one's attitude to the work. The work itself has (ideally) to be disinterested in the sense that it has no interest other than the aesthetic, and that in so far as it does, and has moral, political, historical or religious content, in viewing it aesthetically, we abstract from this content. In the *Critique of Judgement*, section 2, Kant says that everyone (!) must admit that a judgement about beauty in which 'the least interest mingles is very partial and not a pure judgement of taste'; the pleasure yielded by an aesthetic experience is purely contemplative and brings about no interest in the object, in contrast to a moral attitude, which is essentially practical (section 12); and in section 17

Kant says that a thing's beauty rests on presentation and not on concepts or on any idea of the thing's purpose. To bring content or considerations of purpose or morality into our judgement would be to make an interested judgement; it would be mixed, rather than purely aesthetic. We should focus on the outward appearance of the object, and in doing so abstract ourselves from our cognitive, moral, religious and all other interests in viewing and judging it. All interest, he says, 'ruins a judgement of taste, and deprives it of its impartiality' (section 13), and he also speaks of the role of the free play of the imagination in aesthetic judgement.

Kant does, it is true, distinguish between free and what he calls 'merely' dependent beauty (section 16). Free beauty is when we admire something for its appearance alone, with no thought of its purpose, or what it should be ideally. A flower is Kant's example here (and according to him no one but a botanist has any idea of what sort of thing a flower should be, and in seeing a flower as beautiful we are not looking at it botanically). The lesser, dependent beauty is when our reaction to the object is mixed with some notion of how it ought to be. So Kant himself sees Maori tattoos, pleasing in themselves, as unpleasing because they are unsuited to the figure of a human being, particularly, he says, to a warrior, as presumably Kant believed that these patterns would detract from the intended effect of putting fear into the enemy. (He had obviously not seen the ha'ka.)

It is hard to see how moral, religious, political and other interests could fail to get a foothold here. For whether a decoration or a work degrades or disfigures a human being surely requires some idea of what a human being or human life more generally should be (and into this judgement, moral, cultural, political, metaphysical and religious notions are bound to intrude). Kant is clearly struggling with dependent beauty, so much so that he actually says that the purity of the aesthetic judgement is 'injured by the combination with beauty of the (moral) good.'

The upshot is that the Kantian doctrine of disinterestedness will sooner or later lead to and underpin pure formalism in aesthetic practice. Historically indeed we have seen just such an aesthetic in figures like Roger Fry and Clive Bell, who saw 'significant form' (rather than content) as the key criterion of aesthetic virtue. So what we are to concentrate on in a painting are the forms and relations of forms, and the relations and combinations of lines and colours, rather than any meaning or content, in order to appreciate the pure aesthetic quality of the work, as if in looking at Raphael's *Crucifixion*, for example, we can somehow filter out what is about. (It is true that Bell and Fry were influenced by G.E. Moore rather than by Kant directly, but there is more than a hint of a Kantian heritage in Moore's attempts to isolate separate skeins of experience, each with their uncontaminated essence and irreducibility.) And in this Kantian or neo-Kantian tradition of aesthetic theorising, we can also think of Clement Greenberg in his argument that all painting, properly conceived as just paint on flat surfaces, aspires to the condition of abstraction. It would also be fascinating to consider whether there might not be links here with the traditional Islamic fear of contaminating the aesthetic with the representational.

On the other hand, if we are beginning to question the full Kantian elaboration of disinterestedness, and while as we suggested earlier one can have a disinterested or aesthetic attitude to works replete with human interest, we would still want to distinguish the human interest in art proper from preaching, propagandising or pamphleteering. If that is part of the motivation of Kant and of those more generally who would espouse some doctrine of art for art's sake, it is easy to concur. At the very least, we should be able to say that in so far as a work is guilty of any of these things it is less valuable as a work of art.

Some remarks of Frank Kermode in contrasting D.H. Lawrence's novels with what Kermode calls his doctrinal writings (in which some of the same ideas are expressed) are helpful here:

> The novels do not have a design upon us; their design is upon the unqualified, uninspected dogmas of the treatises and letters, which must be made to submit to life. Why, asks Lawrence, is the novel the highest form of human experience? 'Because it is so incapable of the absolute ... in a novel there is always a tom-cat, a black tom-cat that pounces on the white dove of the Word.' The novel is *quick* and 'contains no didactic absolute ... everything is true in its own relationship, and no further ... a theosophist cannot be a novelist ... A theosophist, or a Christian or a Holy Roller, may be *contained* in a novel. But a novelist may not put up a fence.'

So Lawrence in 1925. The novel, the tale, could not become Fascist without becoming dead.[2]

In the light of this discussion, we could helpfully compare the woodcuts of the Apocalypse produced by Albrecht Dürer in 1499

---

[2]   Frank Kermode, *Lawrence* (London: Fontana Books, 1973), p. 30.

Four Horsemen by Albrecht Dürer

Four Horsemen by Lucas Cranach

with the slightly later set produced by Lucas Cranach (in 1523) — two superficially similar works dating from precisely the period about which Koerner was writing. Cranach's Apocalypse images certainly have designs upon us. They are very literal and very plain representations of the Biblical texts, more like cartoons, a succession of not entirely unified images, which need to be 'read' successively for the scene or content to come over to us. They are far more polemical and overtly anti-Papal than those of Dürer and also far more literal and faithful to the word of the text. They are also at times, frankly, an aesthetic mess, very hard to see as coherent wholes at all. Dürer's images, by contrast, are filled with imaginative inventions, including the use of what some see as self-portraits of the artist himself as the visionary (St John), and a daring aesthetic manipulation of the two levels of heaven and earth, culminating in an aesthetically satisfying vision of the two coming together with the artist's beloved Nuremberg as the heavenly Jerusalem. In Dürer's images aesthetic sense and unity always takes precedence over literal fidelity, which is no doubt partly why they are seem much more weighty than those of Cranach. And by means of Dürer's aesthetic interpretation new light is thrown on the Apocalypse itself, as is the case with many examples of genuinely artistic presentations of religious ideas. Would Byzantine spirituality be what it became without the icon, or medieval Christianity without plainchant? The point, surely, is that through music and painting and other aesthetic media, realities can be disclosed or revealed or created which the word can only hint at. Part of the significance of aesthetic modes of presentation is their power to do precisely this, to evoke spiritual and human realities with their own life and vibrancy, which words may indicate or point to, but not more than that. One of the unfortunate implications of the Kantian notion of the aesthetic is to deny to works of art this power, or to suggest that they have it only to the extent that they step outside the aesthetic mode, contaminating its purity with extraneous thoughts and feelings.

We know from historical sources that Cranach was operating under direction from Luther to stick to visual representations of the word and to go no further, but we are not talking here about the artist's own intentions, whatever they might have been, but rather about how the works might appear to an audience. The artist or writer might have all sorts of interests in producing his work, including making money or getting fame, right up to promoting a cause or a world view. But from the aesthetic point of view, the question is the extent to which the work itself can be perceived independently of any of this. No doubt Lawrence had a world view, which his novels were designed to explore and even to promote. The question we have to consider, though, is the extent to which 'life' in the novel enables the reader to perceive the result as more complex, more multi-faceted, maybe even more true than the message.

Something of this appears to us to be going on in Dürer's Apocalypse illustrations. It is my contention that he uses aesthetic means to convey to the perceiver a set of visions which are psychologically and religiously convincing, and that this is achieved through the experience of those images. That the experience itself is essential here is a piece of Kantian aesthetics I do accept, the idea being that what is conveyed in the experience is beyond what could be conveyed by a verbal description of the work, and even more beyond any verbalisation of the work's 'message'. To this extent, as already suggested, a religious tradition may develop as much as through its artistic expression as through its dogmatic formularies, and its art become a central part of its practice and constitutive of the attitudes of its adherents.

In the light of Dürer's images I would draw attention here particularly to the way in which Dürer integrates the realism of his earthly scenes and above all his Jerusalem with the miraculous heaven. It is noteworthy that not only is Dürer's Jerusalem his own Nuremberg, as already mentioned, but also that in his final image Dürer departs from a literal reading of *The Book of Revelation* to construct his own compelling sense of heaven and earth now brought together, in contrast to the obvious separation of the two realms in his earlier images. We could also fruitfully contrast Dürer's and Cranach's versions of the two beasts. In Dürer's version God is presiding over the whole scene, as a creative presence, intimating that as creator He is also creator/artist of the vision, with God's imaginative visions, unlike those of the human artist actually becoming reality where those of a human artist remain imagined, however fully realised; by contrast Cranach simply follows the literal text, presenting a bare depiction of the two beasts, with no sense of their status as created or imagined, and no sense of the contrast between the human imagination and that of the divine. Dürer is thus religiously and even philosophically compelling where Cranach is just literal, in a way exemplifying the Lutheran doctrine that the image has (or should have) no power beyond its bare literal meaning. There is also a striking difference in the way that our two artists depict St John, the visionary. Cranach seems not to care about him aesthetically or in any other way. He actually looks different in different images, whereas for Dürer he is always the same, fully and intensely drawn, even a self portrait it has been argued, but a key unifying figure in the whole set of images.

We might suppose that from Hegel's point of view, Dürer working at the end of the fifteenth century, with all his infusion of religious feeling into his images, belongs to the Late Middle Ages. Cranach, working a couple of decades later, has emptied his images of anything but the literal. Religion and inner spirituality has fled from them. And in a way this emptying of the image of content beyond the image itself could be seen as paving the way for the Kantian notion of aesthetic disinterestedness. For now the (truly) religious work is devoid of aesthetic interest or force, the aesthetic retreating to works which have no interest other than the aesthetic.

But whatever its historical influence, the Kantian notion of the aesthetic as a realm of disinterestedness and its anticipation in the Lutheran view that religious art should be plain art, devoid of the non-literal is thoroughly unsatisfactory as a general aesthetic doctrine. To consider only our examples we see with Dürer that images can quite properly convey what Kant would see as impure interests. But this further interest in the images is itself conveyed by aesthetic means and is also integral to the aesthetic experience we have in looking at the works.

Our example of the religious depth achieved by Dürer as opposed to Cranach in their respective Apocalypse illustrations stands here only for a much more general point. It is time to ditch the Kantian notion of disinterestedness as a mark of the aesthetic, and to acknowledge the potential the aesthetic has for casting light—or darkness—over the whole landscape of human life. It would be absurd to say that a deep moral sensibility is not an integral part of the aesthetic of *Anna Karenina*, that *Tristan* is contaminated by its evocation of sexual desire, that Turner's *Dido Building Carthage* and Berlioz's *Les Troyens* are not crucially dependent for their effect by what we (authors and audience) all (at one time!) knew happened to Carthage in part as a result of the events referred to in the works, or that there may not be something powerful—and powerfully decadent—in the themes Francis Bacon chooses to depict and in his way of handling them; nor is there any need to. Kant notwithstanding, the subject matter of the aesthetic is the landscape of humanity, the whole if it.

Chapter 5

The real or the Real?
Chardin or Rothko?

We will begin by considering some themes from Proust's wonderful essay on Chardin, *Chardin and Rembrandt*.[1] Proust speaks of the young man 'of modest means and artistic taste', his imagination filled with the splendour of museums, of cathedrals, of mountains, of the sea, sitting at table at the end of lunch, nauseated at the 'traditional mundanity' of the unaesthetic spectacle before him: the last knife left lying on the half turned-back table cloth, next to the remains of an underdone and tasteless cutlet. He cannot wait to get up and leave, and if he cannot take a train to Holland or Italy, he will at least go to the Louvre to have sight of the palaces of Veronese, the princes of van Dyck and the harbours of Claude. Doing this will, of course, make his return to his home and its familiar surroundings seem yet more drab and exasperating:

> If I knew this young man I would not deter him from going to the Louvre, but rather accompany him there ... I would make him stop ... in front of the Chardins. And once he had been dazzled by this opulent depiction of what he had called mediocrity, I should say to him: Are you happy? Yet what have you seen but dining or kitchen utensils, not the pretty ones, like Saxe chocolate-jars, but those you find most ugly, a shiny lid, pots of every shape and material (the salt-cellar, the strainer), the sights that repel you, dead fish lying on the table, and the sights that nauseate you, half-emptied glasses and too many full glasses.[2]

---

[1]   In Marcel Proust, *Against Sainte-Beuve and Other Essays*, trans. J. Sturrock (Harmondsworth: Penguin Books, 1988), pp. 122–31. Although beginning with Proust, this chapter as a whole is an attempt to develop some of the argument of Oliver Soskice in his article 'Painting and the Absence of Grace', Modern Painters, Vol. 4, No. 1, Spring 1991, pp. 63–5.

[2]   *Ibid.*, p. 123.

Proust then goes on to note that if one finds all this beautiful to look at, it is because Chardin found it beautiful to paint; and the underlying reason he and you find it all beautiful is because you have already unconsciously experienced the pleasure afforded by still life and modest lives, a pleasure Chardin had the power to summon to explicit recognition with his 'brilliant and imperative language'. In sum:

> from Chardin we had learnt that a pear is as alive as a woman, that common crockery is as beautiful as a precious stone. The painter had proclaimed the divine equality of all things before the mind that contemplates them, before the light that beautifies them.[3]

He thus brings us out from a false ideal of conventional beauty, to a wider reality, in which in accordance with what Proust says, we are enabled to find beauty everywhere. Perhaps Proust is wrong about this: perhaps, as we have suggested in 'Prospects for Beauty' (Chapter 3), there are areas in which there is no beauty to be found, in a dying child's bootless agony, for example. But the underlying drift of what Proust says, and the substance of Chardin's aesthetic is surely right: that there is a real beauty in the midst of everyday domesticity, a beauty that may well be overlooked by aesthetic young men and other visionaries, who have a false ideal of beauty, one constrained by grandiosity and sublimity. Proust does not say this either, but one aspect of the false ideal of beauty is doubtless the tendency—so prevalent in the contemporary world—to treat the mundane as disposable; to fail to cherish it, to let it grow old and so become touched with humanity through use and familiarity; to fail to design it with care for its conformability to our sensibility, but to crush all that with a brash and ultimately impersonal dehumanizing aesthetic of function.

Another aspect of Chardin, to which we will return, is the way in which in his still lives, in contrast to those of some of his brilliant Dutch predecessors, such as Kalf or Coorte, the objects emerge shyly, from a soft and often indeterminate background, against which they quiver in the light almost on the edge of visibility. Their being seen, and us seeing them is then represented by Chardin as what it is, a human achievement: the objects are summoned, as Proust puts it, 'out from the everlasting darkness in which they had been interred'. We may well be reminded by all this of Cézanne's words 'le paysage se reflète, s'humanise, se pense en moi'. These

---

[3]   *Ibid.*, p 129.

words, indeed, encapsulate the theme of this article, particularly if they are considered alongside Cézanne's own mature *oeuvre*, which consists not of dead versions of life, so to speak, but of canvasses in which the appearances of things are vividly reconstituted for us out of the equally visible pigments of the paint (which is one reason why photographic reproductions are particularly faithless to the reality in the case of Cézanne).

In his essay, Proust goes on to contrast the reality Chardin evokes for us with what he calls the transcendence of reality in Rembrandt; in some of Rembrandt's works, objects become no more than the vehicles by which something else, another light, another meaning, is reflected. Whatever we might say about Rembrandt himself, it is possible to discern in western painting an oscillation of emphasis and interest between the everyday and the transcendent. Early Italian painters such as Duccio and Fra Angelico made little attempt to be fully realistic, being more concerned to give expression to the religious truths underlying the myths they painted. It was not that in their painting there was a complete inability to represent the appearances of things; they do and they can, but that is not the focus of their interest. In Raphael we find, to sublime effect, a balance of the physical and the religious, a balance which begins to be lost, though to stunning effect, in the opulent sensuality of Titian and Veronese. It is not for nothing that Titian has been seen as ushering in the materialism of the modern age, though to see him simply in such terms is to discount the spiritual overtones and allegorical subject matter of paintings such as *The Flaying of Marsyas* and *The Death of Actaeon*. Given that painting is about the appearances of things, and that it is thus intimately related to our experience of seeing, it is even arguable that no painting can be regarded as materialistic in a reductionist sense; thus Monet, who is often taken to be the epitome of modernistic materialism in painting, certainly emphasizes sensation at the expense of anything deeper or more inward, but his work also testifies to the intrinsic interest and value of our perspective on the world, and would thus resist analysis of that perspective as 'mere' epiphenomenon.

If Monet was not interested in his art in anything specifically religious, there were other painters in the nineteenth century who were, and who, for a time, managed to combine a stylistic naturalism with an overtly religious content. We can think here of the Nazarenes in Germany and the Pre-Raphaelites in England. But this affected naïvety could not last. As Peter Fuller graphically described in

Theoria under the assault of Darwinism, the hope expressed in *The Light of the World* quickly turned to the desolation of Holman Hunt's *Scapegoat* and Dyce's *Pegwell Bay*.[4] In the former, a visit to the Holy Land failed to elicit anything more uplifting than a mangy animal and a waterless, wasted landscape. In the latter, women and children hunt for fossils on an empty beach beneath a sickly sky across which Donati's comet is passing. The symbolism would in both cases have had a direct impact on the intended audience, even if it needs conscious retrieval on our part. Moreover, if the natural world could no longer be seen as directly revelatory of the divine hand, what point was there in its literal depiction, particularly when the camera could do that painlessly? At least some of the Pre-Raphaelite Brotherhood retreated into highly-charged medieval fantasy.

Other religiously motivated artists worked in more oblique ways than the Pre-Raphaelites. Caspar David Friedrich's romantic landscapes turn out to be carefully crafted allegories of the Christian's journey through the world, but in them there is little enough sense either of the divine nature of the world—which is all too often a hostile environment redeemed only by the distant presence of a cross or of a vision of a cathedral, or of the concrete detail of the Christian myth.

Another approach is that of van Gogh: to transform the natural in a visionary manner: to see stars, olive trees, cypresses and the like, not as they appear in everyday life but as transfigured symbols of a deeper more vibrant life pulsating beneath the empirical surface, and visible to the man of faith. Van Gogh and Friedrich, whatever their differences in approach and in painterly quality, concur in their desire to preserve what they would see as the essence of the Christian message and in their refusal in the main either to represent that message literally or to see the natural world as it is to the normal eye as a straightforward manifestation of the divine. And in all these respects, they have been followed by many artists in the subsequent century.

With the decline of natural theology and the erosion of dogmatic Christianity, the problem for a religiously motivated artist is to devise a way of presenting the essence of religion without illegitimate recourse to either creed or nature. It is hardly surprising that some artists should have sought abstraction as a way forward, nor indeed that some critics and commentators have seen Barnett Newman and Mark Rothko as among the supreme religious painters of our time. Newman indeed told us that we should take him in this

---

[4]   Peter Fuller, *Theoria* (London: Chatto and Windus, 1988).

way, providing elaborate references to Kabbalistic themes in his titles and commentaries. I must confess to some difficulty in accepting Newman on his own terms. His huge rectangular expanses of flat colour punctuated by vertical stripes are not easily experienced as pointers to the numinous, although the canvasses can, like those of Rothko, engulf the perceiver by their sheer size, and one can be amazed for a time at Newman's sheer effrontery.

By comparison with Newman, Rothko's major canvasses are not so big (a mere two metres wide in many cases), but they all produce an experience of engulfing the perceiver, as much by their working from a ragged, indeterminate edge to quasi-rectangular expanses of deep colour, as by their size. They are, in a way, perfect expressions of the world as a stage on which everything is about to happen, or has already happened. In Rothko's work, there is no trace of the concrete, nothing appears; we are overwhelmed by hazy, empty sublimity. And before long, I find them deeply unsatisfying, longing to turn to the modesty and concreteness of a Chardin. Is engulfment, the wiping away of all determinations and horizons, what life—and art—is all about? If it is, then human effort and perception and perspective are, in the final analysis, mocked. There is, in fact, more than a grain of truth in Patrick Heron's barbed comment: 'that having painted 800 such canvasses, Rothko was led nowhere, but to the dealers and suicide!'[5]

This excursion into the history of painting is not simple self-indulgence. I have engaged in it in order to illustrate as vividly as I can the reason why I am unable to rest content with approaches to existence and experience which would undervalue human perception and human experience.

Either there is some cosmic point to human existence, or there is not. In either case, the value of human experience remains irreducible, despite temptations on both accounts to discount it.

Let us suppose, first, that human beings are simply products of a mindless, purposeless cosmos, thrown up by the random or mechanistic activities of more basic particles. Then it will be true that our perspective on the world (including our perceptions, our feelings and our meaning) is itself a by-product of more fundamental processes and reflective of no deeper reality or purpose. It may even be that knowledge of these fundamental processes and the laws which govern them would enable us to predict human perceptions

[5]   Patrick Heron, 'Can Mark Rothko's Work Survive?', in *Modern Painters*, vol. 2, no. 2, Summer 1989, pp. 36–9.

and actions. Relative to the more fundamental processes which underlie our perceptions, the modalities of our perceptions (colour, taste, smell, touch, sound) will be regarded as consisting of secondary qualities, qualities which arise only as a result of the interaction of colourless, tasteless, odourless, textureless and silent particles with our sense organs. But even if this were true, our perceptions, and artistic works devoted to the exploration and development of human perspectives would not lose any value they have for us. The value of a Monet landscape lies not in its genesis, but in the satisfactions and delights and insights it affords us, satisfactions and delights and insights which would not be corroded completely even were we to adopt the scientific view from nowhere, that which displaces the human subject from the centre of things, and sees human life and perception as part of more inclusive causal processes. Even accepting a story of this sort at an intellectual level, we still feel and experience things as we do, and it is in our lives and experiences as lived and experienced that value lies.

Indeed, even seeing our *Lebenswelt* as the product of primary material processes does not make what is revealed in our world false. It is open to us, even while accepting the scientific view as causally fundamental, to regard what is revealed in our experience as a legitimate disclosure of the world, one which is available only to us. Just because the world of so-called secondary qualities arises only in the interaction of particles with our sense organs, it does not mean that that world is unreal or in some derogatory sense subjective, any more than the pictures a television set emits are unreal or subjective just because a television receiver has to transform invisible radio waves into visible images.

The idea that there is in human perception a singular and irreducible revelation of the real world becomes even more plausible if we see human existence as cosmically intended in some way. For what, from the cosmic point of view, could be the point of human existence, other than that the cosmos should be experienced and understood in a human way? It is worth noting here that not even God, being a-temporal, a-spatial and immaterial, could know what it is like to be a human being; however much God might have foreknowledge of our thoughts, experiences and actions, this foreknowledge would necessarily be schematic, abstract and theoretical; however much God knows of the informational content of our experiences, He would not know our mode of experiencing and feeling that information.

It has for long seemed to me, as it did to Oliver Soskice in 'Painting and the Absence of Grace', that if we are here for a purpose, and if human life has something unique to contribute to the cosmos, it is this:

> Sind wir vielleicht *hier*, um zu sagen: Haus,
> Brücke, Brunnen, Tor, Krug, Obstbaum, Fenster
> hochstens: Säule, Turm ... aber zu *sagen,* verstehs,
> ob zu sagen *so,* wie selber die Dinge niemals
> innig meinten zu sein.

> [Are we perhaps here to say: House,
> Bridge, Well, Gate, Jug, Fruit Tree, Window
> —at most, Pillar, Tower? ... but to say—oh!
> to say in this way, as the things themselves
> never so intently meant to be.][6]

That is, we are here to experience and articulate something about things, something which things themselves can neither articulate nor experience, but which also (as Rilke goes on to say) is beyond the power of angels to know and experience.

We can, of course, see value in doing what Rilke says we are here to do, even if we are not put here to do anything, and that valuing need not be impugned by scientific explanations or views from nowhere. It is, perhaps, strange then that religion, which does see us as being on earth for a reason, all too often downgrades our Rilkean task, for doing what Rilke says we are here to do is the one thing we alone can do; and is the reason I place a higher value on the aesthetic experiencing of the world than many theological writers. I see the contemplation of what arises in human practice as the singular contribution we as humans can make to the cosmos. That is to say, through our practices and the associated sensory apparatus, we divide the world up and disclose it in various ways, but because we are self- conscious we can reflect on these perceptions and evaluate the significance of what is revealed in our practices and perceptions. Because of our status as sensory *and* intellectual, we alone are in a position to enjoy particular perceptions of the world, and to evaluate the fruits of those perceptions. A merely sensory consciousness could not reflect on what it perceives, while a purely intellectual being (an angel) would perceive or experience nothing.

Religion, though, is always tempted to take us all too quickly from the human to something we cannot envisage or articulate at all. In so

---

[6]   R. M. Rilke, *Ninth Duino Elegy,* lines 32–6.

doing, it all too easily downgrades and wipes away the human. Soskice refers in his article to Hölderlin's *Griechenland*, '... where the longing for eternity knows no bounds Divine things are overcome with sleep. There is no trust in God, no proportion ...'

I find more than a trace of this lack of proportion in John Hick's *An Interpretation of Religion*.[7] I am now going to turn to this book as it is, I believe, a brave and radical attempt to salvage something of religious value from the downfall of dogmatic religion; or, more precisely, from the dilemma which arises for any would-be religious believer from the existence of a plurality of religious faiths, all of which seem to have some good claim to be regarded as offering genuine insights into the divine.

Hick is also faced with the problem that straightforward dogmatic religion is, to many, hardly credible in the late twentieth century. For him, there is to be no return to a Pre-Raphaelitic naïvety. Moreover, he is well aware that Christianity is not the only credal contender. Right at the start of his book he speaks of the transcendent being pereived through different and distinctive cultural lenses.[8] Nevertheless, he is convinced that there is a Real behind the different religious traditions: that is to say, that the God of Abraham, Isaac and Jacob, the Holy Trinity, Allah, Vishnu, Brahman, the Dharmakaya/Nirvana/Sunyata, Zen and the Tao, all represent ways of affirming the same ultimate.

Presumably Zeus, Jupiter, Wotan, and the other limited, personal deities are not included in Hick's list because they are limited; they are themselves subject to fate and to contract and are not transcendent. Be that as it may, and leaving aside the point that Jahweh, Jesus and Allah are all conceived in personal — and hence in determinate and to that extent limited terms, I want now to consider the implications for us of conceiving what he calls the real, as Hick does, as a metaphysical or noumenal ground underlying all religious objects, whether personal (as often in the Western tradition) or impersonal (as characteristically in eastern traditions): that is, something divine and real behind the various humanly mediated revelations or intimations of divinity.

There is, indeed, as Hick points out, a drive in human thought to seek the utterly transcendent or the self-subsistent ground of our beliefs and valuations. We are not just conscious, we are also self-conscious. We have beliefs and values, and we are aware of

---

[7]   John Hick, *An Interpretation of Religion* (London: Macmillan, 1989).

[8]   *Ibid.*, p. 8.

having them. I am aware that any belief or judgement I make is mine, and that my perspective is just that – *my* perspective on a world which has an existence independent of me, and in which there are other agents also making judgements of value. I thus become aware that my belief or judgement is not the only possible belief or way of according value. I become aware of my route through the world as only one of many possible routes, and thereby open to question.

My self-consciousness may well be sparked into reflective activity by the realization that there are people other than me and cultures other than mine. But once activated, we begin to realize the limited nature of any actual sets of beliefs or values we have. We thus formulate for ourselves the conception of an absolute truth, an absolute good. But in formulating such notions, we realize that no merely human sets of beliefs or values can be guaranteed to be absolute: all will be more or less limited by the particular perspective we adopt.

Hick sees a great upsurge of self-conscious dissatisfaction with local and particular beliefs and customs around the fifth century BC, the time of Confucius, Lao Tzu, the Buddha, Mahavira, Zoroaster, the Hebrew prophets, and Socrates. As he puts it, following Karl Jaspers, at what is dubbed, the 'axial' age,

> Individuals were emerging into self-consciousness out of the closely-knit communal mentality of their society .... Religious value no longer resided in total identification with the group but began to take the form of personal openness to transcendence. And since the new religious messages of the axial age were addressed to individuals as such, rather than as cells in a social organism, these messages were in principle universal in their scope.[9]

This 'post-axial' quest for individuality and universality is in fact based in our very nature as self-conscious beings, as I have been arguing, and is not just a product of specific historical circumstances, however much some circumstances might encourage its development. The drive to individualism and the search for universal, unlimited truth and value are inherent in human nature, and cannot be totally suppressed. Nevertheless, we should realize that both these tendencies carried with them two, probably connected problems. First, they weaken local culture and secondly they encourage a

---

[9]   *Ibid.*, p. 30.

religion of unknowing, whose effect may well be to undermine the human.

In saying that individualistic and universalistic attitudes loosen culture, what I have in mind is the complaint raised by Aristophanes (in *The Frogs*) and by Nietzsche (in *The Birth of Tragedy*) against Socrates. In their view, the greatness of ancient Athens stemmed in part from the fact that its citizens were united in reverence for a myth or set of myths which bound them together (and which also, doubtless, enabled them to make culturally crucial distinctions between the best and the rest of society, between themselves as Athenians and other Hellenes, and between Hellenes and barbarians). But Socrates and, to an extent, Euripides, taught ordinary men to question the myths and to cease to respect their superiors or to regard Greeks as Greeks first and as men second.

In *The Decline of the West*, Spengler characterized the transition from what he called Culture to Civilization in the following terms, which certainly have a bearing on Hick's characterization of axiality:

> In place of a type-true people, born of and grown on the soil, there is a new sort of nomad, cohering unstably in fluid masses, the parasitical city-dweller, traditionless, utterly matter-of-fact, religion less, clever, unfruitful, deeply contemptuous of the countryman, and especially that highest form of countryman, the country gentleman.[10]

Spengler goes on to speak of the 'uncomprehending hostility' of the new city-dweller to 'all the traditions representative of the Culture (nobility, church, privileges, dynasties, conventions in art and limits of knowledge in science)', of his 'keen and cold intelligence that confounds the wisdom of the peasant' and of his apparently new-fashioned but actually quite primitive and instinctual naturalism in all matters of sex and society.

While there will in city-dwelling civilizations tend to be a decline of local and particular ways of doing things, in favour of the universal, the reproducible, the purely functional and the disposable, intellectually the decline of (Spenglerian) culture presages an attempt to discern a unity underlying apparently disparate forms of similar activity. This, of course, is what Hick attempts in the case of religion, and whose aesthetic analogue is the *oeuvre* of Rothko. I say this in the

---

[10] Oswald Spengler, *The Decline of the West*, trans. C. F. Atkinson (New York: Barnes and Noble, 1926), p. 32.

case of Rothko because I take it that what he is presenting is not just colour as an end in itself, but colour as a symbol of the ineffable.[11]

The attempt to fuse what, on the face of it, is unfusable (e.g. Islam, Christianity, Hinduism and Buddhism) together with the religious drive to find an underlying ultimate reality, conspire to produce a religion which is, practically speaking, without content. Drawing, indeed, on ancient religious texts and traditions, Hick speaks of God, Brahman, the Dharmakaya as unlimited, 'not to be equated without remainder with anything that can be humanly experienced and defined'; the Real in itself cannot be said to be 'one or many, person or thing, substance or process, good or evil, purposive or non-purposive';[12] 'we postulate the real *an sich* as the ultimate ground of the intentional objects of the different forms of religious thought-and-experience'.[13] Even if it is said that there is *something* (the Real) which underlies all the phenomenal divinities, the fact is that we can say nothing about this real. It is hard to see the difference between faith in a non-describable Real and agnosticism.

I hope that by now the point of my earlier reference to the work of Mark Rothko is clear. Instead of anything specific we are, in both cases, being offered a void, an emptiness, which is said to be pregnant with noumenal meaning and to underlie the merely phenomenal. Hick does urge us to respect and to maintain the disparate phenomenal manifestations of the Real (i.e. the actual world-religions). But given the superior viewpoint he is urging us to adopt, whereby each of these religions is seen as a radically incomplete version of something utterly ungraspable, of which we are told there are other equally valid (though I would add) mutually inconsistent manifestations, it is hard to see how one could in all good conscience continue to worship in, say, a Christian church or a Muslim mosque.

---

[11]   This might raise the question as to what I would say about a work, such as an Ellsworth Kelly, say, in which the aim might well be taken to be just the presentation of an experience of colour, as it is in itself and for itself, in which a painting 'stands', as a large and public sense-datum. Leaving aside the gigantism such works are typically prone to, I would have to say that this is a further area in which I would distance myself from a Proustian equality of all things; that there is more meaning, more humanity, in a wine glass or a firedog than in a patch of yellow, however large or small, and that the effort of a painter to render the one is potentially more worthwhile from a human point of view than the effort to represent the other. We value Vermeer's little patch of yellow but we do not value it just because it is what it is in itself. We value it because it is part of an extraordinarily gentle and precarious humanization of the world.

[12]   Hick, *An Interpretation of Religion*, pp. 236, 246.

[13]   *Ibid.*, p. 350.

Even if the exclusivist and particular claims of the actual world religions could somehow be mutually reconciled against the background of a noumenal we know not what, I am dubious about the moral and human effects of worshipping and directing our efforts to a Being as indeterminate for us as Hick's unknowable Real. If this Real can be said to be neither person nor thing, good or evil, purposive or non-purposive, loving or hating, as Hick avers, what ultimate reason is there for us to love, to be good, to respect others or to engage in purposive activity at all?[14] Hick does indeed struggle manfully with the Buddhist sunyata (emptiness, transcendence of all perspective); sunyata seems to be the natural end of life if the Real is as Hick conceives it.[15] At any rate, it is hard to value human activity or to see how our way of perceiving things could be a worthwhile revelation of a Reality which is essentially unknowable.

Hick doubtless would say that there is a reason for us to cultivate loving and truthful attitude, given that we are aiming to eradicate our ignorance and delusion with respect to the Real, and also that such attitudes are propagated by all the great world religions. But I have to say that from Hick's perspective of radical agnosticism, even loving and truthful attitudes on our part will get us no closer to the Real: we will still have nothing to say about it, and nothing to grasp, except possibly by some incommunicable, and hence dumb, religious experience. I can, indeed, see nothing in Hick's account to rule out a Real whose ultimate nature was not, say, closer to a Nietzschean will-to-power than to a Catholic Sacred Heart; nor indeed am I convinced that compassion for suffering humanity is always to the forefront of the world religions, as opposed to a stoical indifference towards individual life and suffering in face of cosmic dramas of global, rather than individual redemption or transformation. What is there in the notion of the unknowable, transcendent Real to rule but the possibility that our idea of a compassionate divinity is simply the ultimate fantasy of a deluded humanity whose final fate is to be broken on the wheel of existence? And I do not think it can be denied that some religious seekers after an ultimate divine reality have found not bliss but an emptiness, even a cruelty, too terrible to contemplate.[16]

---

[14] *Ibid.*, p. 350.

[15] See also *ibid.*, pp. 288–92.

[16] In the light of that dark night of the soul which is a recurring theme throughout the history of religious practice, I have to say that the efforts made by Hick in his

Against such a background the emptiness and, perhaps, the rhetoric of Rothko would be vindicated against the painstaking and human modesty of Chardin, and what Chardin presents to us as an all too-fragile achievement will be swallowed up in the abyss of the divine. At the same time, it is doubtless true that we come to see Chardin's achievement as the achievement it is just when we begin to understand that we are standing above an abyss, cosmically speaking, and that human domesticity and human perception rest on no secure foundation. In terms of my illustrative analogy, then, Rothko's Real might be seen to serve as the background from which Chardin's reality, and ours, emerges and is perceived.

---

book (pp. 304–6) to link religious practice to 'politico-economic liberation' (i.e. anti-capitalism) can seem sentimental and misguided religiously as well as economically. His endorsement of the 'basic intent' of Marx, Lenin, Trotsky and Mao, as a 'dispositional response of the modern sociologically conditioned consciousness to the real' (p. 306), serves to underline the extent to which religious thinkers, of all ages, get embroiled in the delusions of their time. Invoking a Real underlying the delusion will be of little consolation to those whose lives, domesticity and all, are ruined by projects of politico-economic liberation.

Chapter 6

'Two Cultures' Revisited

Vanity of Science: Knowledge of physical science will not console me for ignorance of morality in time of affliction, but knowledge of morality will always console me for ignorance of physical science.

(Pascal, Pensées No. 23)

Pascal's pensée is calculated to irritate leader-writers, politicians and curriculum theorists, among whom there is almost universal agreement that knowledge of physical science is a key component of any suitably modern education. This consensus is routinely signalled by a reference to 'the two cultures', a phrase that has by now become the inevitable cliché whenever anyone wants to deplore ignorance of physical science either among humanists or among the population at large, or, more rarely, whenever someone wants to point to philistinism among scientists.

A first reaction to the second of these matters might be to observe that philistinism is not confined to scientists; if the experience of no-doubt jaundiced academics can be trusted, it is alive and well among young people. Even more striking, one might, in looking at university literature departments and the fine art world, point to rampant philistinism within the professional heart of the humanities. In any case, while Matthew Arnold might have raised discussion of some topics related to our theme in terms of philistinism, philistinism was certainly not a category used by Pascal to interpret the world. Nor, I think, would it have commended itself to Dr Leavis in his now infamous, but today largely misunderstood wrangle with C. P. Snow over the 'two cultures'. How, though, can a controversy be both infamous, cliché-generating and largely misunderstood? Easily, one surmises, given that even at the time few seemed to understand clearly what was at stake, and given that this obfuscation of issues extended to the principals themselves, as well as to contemporaneous by-standers and commentators. Even today, at a distance of more than a quarter of a century, one can read Snow's original lecture and Leavis's impassioned battery of response and still fail to see the wood for the trees.[1]

There can be little doubt that at one level, Leavis was outrageous. Snow's lecture was certainly irritating, even at times silly, in ways we will come to. Nevertheless, what he was actually proposing was largely inoffensive, largely platitudinous in fact, which is probably why it has been so warmly embraced by leader-writers, politicians and curriculum theorists, as well as sixth-form masters preparing their pupils for Cambridge entrance exams (something which particularly got under Leavis's skin). What we have in *Nor Shall My Sword*, splendid invective though it is, is very much a case of the full weight of the Leavisian artillery being unleashed on a small and slender, but, as it has turned out, remarkably resilient blade of common grass. What Snow said in his original lecture was that while it was a pity that so few scientists read literature, it was also equally to be deplored that so few humanists knew any science. He urged that education should remedy the divide between what he called the 'two cultures', and begin to produce what would nowadays be called scientifically literate humanists and (I suppose) plain literate scientists. Actually, in his initial reply ('Two Cultures?'), Leavis concurs with Snow over the need for improvements in scientific education, and also in regretting the existence of 'two' cultures, dividing, so it seems, the educated sections of the country into two mutually uncomprehending classes. Although Leavis is particularly scathing about Snow's talk of *two* cultures, it is not as if Snow thought cultural duality a good thing: he actually saw himself as advocating its eradication. But, from Leavis's point of view, while Snow's professed concern here is justified, his concern—or at least the way in which he conceives his concern—is not enough, 'disastrously not enough'.

In fact, despite an ostensible even-handedness about science and the arts, and their role in education, Snow in his sub-text is far from being even-handed. He does not confine himself to pointing out the material advances made by science and technology over the past two centuries or so, or to advocating better or more specialist technical education; If he had, there could have been little cause for complaint, even from Leavis. But as Noel Annan put it, Snow was

[1]   C.P. Snow, 'The two cultures and the scientific revolution', Rede Lecture (1959). Leavis's response is collected in F.R. Leavis, *Nor Shall My Sword* (London: Chatto and Windus, 1972).

determined to 'strike a blow for science and put the narrow human-ists in their place'.[2] Whereas scientists and technologists are hard at work improving material conditions, representatives of what Snow calls 'traditional culture' are 'natural Luddites'. Whereas our natural human condition is one of horror and individual tragedy, we do have social hope, hope largely, it seems, in the matter of providing for the masses more jam tomorrow: 'common men can show extraor-dinary fortitude in chasing jam tomorrow. Jam today, and men aren't at their most exciting; jam tomorrow, and one often sees them at their noblest' — a nobility made possible only by the transforma-tions wrought by 'the' scientific culture. If we don't take these scien-tific and technological transformations in our stride, it makes us 'look silly' — a dig, doubtless, at the litterateurs who are unable to recite the second law of thermodynamics or who fail to recognize that Rutherford is what Snow styled the Shakespeare of science. But, in Snow's book, literary culture is not just silly and/or irrelevant. Whereas 'statistically' slightly more scientists are religious unbe-lievers compared with the rest of the intellectual world, 'nine out of ten of those who dominated literary sensibility (like Yeats or Pound) were not only politically silly but politically wicked'.

The tone of Snow's lecture, the crassness of his judgements and his button-holing man-of-the-world insensitivity all enraged Leavis. For Leavis, Snow is not just ignorant, he is portentously ignorant; that is, 'he is a portent in that, being in himself negligible, he has become for a vast public on both sides of the Atlantic a master-mind and a sage'. Leaving aside this and other invective (non-entity, intel-lectual nullity, banality, ineffable blankness, embarrassing vulgar-ity, as undistinguished as it is possible to be). What Leavis thinks is that Snow is simply a reflection of the received wisdom of his time ('he has been created as authoritative intellect by the cultural condi-tions manifested in his acceptance'). This impression time has done little to dispel. Yet, if there is anything in the debate beyond invec-tive (on both sides, it must be said, for Leavis's own entry into the arena had been provoked by Snow's initial over-statements and answered in intemperate terms by at least some of Snow's defend-ers), we must be clear what it is. Once again, an initial glance may produce bafflement, not least because of the many striking similari-ties between the two protagonists, both provincial grammar-school boys, both eventually anti-modernist on art, both elitists on educa-tion, both anti-religious, and both broadly on the left in open politics.

[2]   Noel Annan, *Our Age* (London: Fontana, 1991), p. 383.

However, despite everything so far said, there is a point of real significance which underlies the Two Cultures Debate, and which continues to be missed by most of those who consider the matter or refer to it. To bring this out. we could do far worse than point to one of Leavis's apparently more surprising remarks:

> I don't believe in any 'literary values', and you won't find me talking about them: the judgments the literary critic is concerned with are judgments about life. What the critical discipline is concerned with is relevance and precision in making and developing them.[3]

Leavis was, as has often been pointed out, a moralist and not an aesthete about literature (which is why his attack on Snow would be ill-represented by calling it an attack on philistinism). And, whatever we think about the efficacy of the average literary critic in developing judgements about life, an education in science will fail to address the relevant issues. The reason for this is in no way a criticism of science *per se*; indeed, it stems from science's very strength, what is sometimes, but perhaps unhelpfully, described as science's value-freedom.

It is important, though, to be clear about what might sensibly be meant by speaking of science as value-free. What is meant is not (or should not be) a denial of the fact that science is a matter of human interest, or that values of various sorts are involved in taking part in scientific work and in choosing the focus of that work. These include what might be seen as values external to the scientific enterprise itself, such as the particular desires which motivate individual scientists and the ends chosen by those directing and funding research, but we should not forget the internal values generated by scientific work of any description. These will include the need to solve a particular problem thrown up in the course of research, or the need to produce results replicable by fellow scientists, or the need to produce theories which survive empirical testing. What is right about thinking of science as value-free derives from the subject matter and the methods of science. The subject matter of science is the description, analysis and explanation of natural processes, as they are caused and brought about by other natural processes according to natural laws and regularities. The methods of science involve the observation and measurement of phenomena by any competent, suitably placed observers, whatever their beliefs, motives or cultural

---

[3]   Leavis, *Nor Shall My Sword*, p. 97.

backgrounds, and the rigorous testing of theories against such observations and measurements, again by any scientist or scientists, regardless of ideology or background. The widely canvassed notion of science as presenting an absolute view of the world, or, alternatively, as a view from nowhere, represents an ideal unattainable by human observers, limited as we are by our concepts and sensory apparatus. Nevertheless, there is something right about it in so far as in science the attempt is made to chart the course of nature (or of various facets of nature) as it goes on independently of human interest, however close to our interests the investigation of some facet of nature might be.

Thus, for example, things very important to us, including colour, sound and taste, are relegated by science to the status of secondary quality, causally and scientifically irrelevant to the fundamental processes of nature. The picture modern science presents of the world is of a humanly unrecognizable world, one in which not only secondary qualities are removed, but in which the familiar objects of everyday use and appearance become lattices of particles, fuzzy at the edges and occupied largely by empty space. We are familiar with this effect from Eddington's famous discussion of the two tables, but the start of a similar process of scientific kenosis of human meaning is well described by Proust:

> the town that I saw before me had ceased to be Venice. Its personality, its name, seemed to be lying fictions which I no longer had the courage to impress upon its stones. I saw the palaces reduced to their constituent parts, lifeless heaps of marble with nothing to chose between them, and the water as a combination of hydrogen and oxygen, external, blind, anterior and exterior to Venice, unconscious of Doges or of Turner.[4]

Proust is writing of the sense of depersonalization which came over him as part of his remorse for allowing a piece of selfish cruelty to his mother. But a dispassionate scientific account of Venice would know no more of its human meaning than did Proust in his neurasthenic state. In a scientific account, water does indeed become hydrogen and oxygen, palaces complexes of molecules, the very name 'Venice' a fiction, and Doges and Turner and their works but insignificant moments in the natural history of but one short-lived

---

[4]   Marcel Proust, *Remembrance of Things Past,* vol. 11, trans. C. K. Scott Moncrieff (London: Chatto and Windus, 1969), p. 320.

species, of no more interest or value than any other moment or moments.

To put all this another way, science aims at an observer-independent account of the world, transcending human meaning, culture and ideology. Its success derives from its success in approximating to this aim, for it is in so far as we go beyond looking at the natural world in terms of its first meanings for us that we are able to penetrate further its causally essential core, and so become rather more adept at manipulating and directing it than those who remain at the level of first impressions. The lesson of post-Galilean science is that there is no reason to suppose that the effects and processes we identify in our first transactions with nature will turn out to be those which are fundamental from a causal point of view.

What all this amounts to is that science has come to abstract from many of the properties which are of importance to us in our everyday lives. Even more, it teaches us to look at the world in a way which prescinds from its value for us. We look at it as it is in itself, according to its causal determination and structure, and not at how it affects us or how we might like it to be. Even where, as in medicine, say, or in some technological application, we are dealing with matters of direct value to us, and precisely because of their value to us, in science and in technology we take a detached view in order to establish just what the processes of nature are. In science, we decentre from the meaning and value the world has for us; it is in that sense that science is value-free, and it is precisely for that reason that science cannot constitute a culture, or even half a culture. In the explanations and descriptions given by science, the terms in which discussions of value are framed are rigorously excluded, as well as many of the predicates signalling the manner in which we feel attraction or repulsion to the world, and in terms of which our normal human concerns and interests are expressed and conceived.

If 'culture' refers to the context in which parts of the world are singled out as having meaning and value for us and the background of evaluative agreement against which particular judgements of value are made, then it becomes clear that there certainly can be human cultures which contain no science in our modern sense. There have been many cultures in which there has been no systematic attempt to get behind empirical appearance and to remove oneself, if only for a time, from considerations of value. It would be wrong to think that in such cultures it has been impossible to lead a fully human life, and it would certainly need argument to show that modern Western culture represents progress in domains outside the scientific and technological, or indeed to show that even within our culture scientific and technological as it is, a perfectly good life could not be lived in more or less blissful ignorance of the details of modern science, which, I take it, is Pascal's point. Moreover, even though in our history and culture science plays an important role, and we certainly need some people well up in science, science itself cannot make judgements of value (what Leavis used to call 'judgments about life'); further, many of the explanations and concepts of science occlude or simply by-pass the considerations which are relevant to life as lived.

It is of course, true that an exclusive concentration on scientific modes of thought can affect the way in which judgements of value are made. In particular, it can lead to an importation of quantitative considerations, and a tendency to see social and moral problems in terms of hygiene and environmental manipulation. Leavis's hostility to Snow was partly due to the fact that he discovered such tendencies in Snow. But to treat the Two Cultures Debate as being mainly about an old-fashioned moralism objecting to what Leavis called technologico-Benthamism (and for which he himself was in his turn dubbed Luddite) is to miss the fundamental point. The point is that culture is concerned with the living of life as a whole, and that science, quite properly, prescinds from the terms in which concerns relevant to that can be discussed or even raised. If, as Leavis implies, a non-literary education may fail to advance relevance and precision in this area, this is not so much because scientists have the wrong values as because science in itself does not address questions of value at all. (It is striking that Leavis, just as much as Snow, is unprepared to look to religion as a source of the required relevance and precision. We could in a way see the whole dispute as one in which each party turns to his own favoured discipline to supply the gap left by the passing of religion, another point at which the two are rather closer than either would have wanted to admit.)

What, though, is culture? Whence are what I am calling cultural judgements derived, and how are they to be justified? A striking feature of what I am calling culture is that, historically, cultures have been embedded in specific and local traditions. Unlike modern science, which just because it aims at universally acceptable, observer-independent theories, transcends particular religions, ideologies, and races, culture by contrast is particular, and has been recognized to be so since the time of Vico (1668–1744).

It is here that we encounter theories of *Verstehen*, that is the idea
that when we study a culture, part of what we should be asking is
what it feels like to be a member of that culture and what it is to share
in its traditions, history and commonality. The implied contrast here
is once more a contrast with natural science. In speaking about the
behaviour of atoms or genes, say, we are not asking what it is like to
be an atom or a gene, if only because it is not like anything to be an
atom or a gene; nor do we have to enquire into the tradition or
culture of particular groups of atoms or genes, for groups of atoms or
genes do not have traditions or cultures marking them off from other
atoms or genes. And for most philosophers of science a complete
account of atomic or genetic behaviour will have been given when
we are able objectively to predict the behaviour in question, given
initial conditions and the relevant laws. Understanding human
behaviour demands both more and less. It involves less because it
does not require more than very general predictability or general
laws. Indeed, and this is a key point of difference, locating an agent's
motives and self-understanding within a specific tradition or culture
tells us the terms in which he will conceive his actions, but not what
actions he will do.

Understanding human behaviour, on the other hand, requires
more than predictions of behaviour because understanding an
action will always involve reference to an agent's reasons, and,
implicitly, given the value-ladenness of the notion of reason, reference to values, those of both agent and observer. But, it will be said,
we can know nothing of an agent's reasons without some grasp of
his cultural background, and of what it might feel like to be an agent
in that sort of society. And so we return to the particularity of
culture, and of cultural understanding. In contrast, scientific understanding is general and impervious to the changes and contingen-
cies of human history (that is, the behaviour of atoms and even genes
follows laws which, if valid, are true for the whole of space and
time).

The idea that human conduct and the norms underlying it are intimately affected by history and by the development of culture runs
counter to the tenets of the European enlightenment. The enlightenment, strongly influenced, be it noted, by scientific modes of thinking and by a progressivist attitude to human history, took human
nature to be as invariant and unchanging as a carbon atom or a mole-
cule of water. It also believed that there was one rational standard —
that, roughly, of the eighteenth-century liberal-cum-sceptical intel-

lectual — to which all mankind could and should aspire. Informed by a rationalistic, scientific picture of the world, and by a similarly enlightened reading of human history, the prejudices and rivalries which caused hatred, fanaticism and factionalism could be eliminated. As Diderot put it, the ideal is a

> philosopher who, trampling underfoot prejudice, tradition, venerability, universal assent, authority — in a word, everything that overawes the crowd — dares to think for himself, to ascend to the clearest general principles, to examine them, to discuss them, to admit nothing save on the testimony of his own reason and experience.[5]

The assumption is that having done all this, genuinely independent thinkers will converge on a universal rationality. In matters of conduct, enlightenment thinking tended to stress the goals of self-preservation and pleasure-seeking which the new moral sciences were allegedly revealing as the mainsprings of human action. Once we were freed from the obfuscations and repressions of religion and the old order, and allowed innocently to seek pleasure and self-preservation, we would also be able to act with rational benevolence to our fellow-men. Rationality regarding our own nature and desires would reveal a harmony between our own ends and those of others. And, accustomed by science to the disengaged scrutiny of nature, we would similarly be induced to transcend egoism in our own behaviour.

In a sense some of these ideals were put to the test in the French Revolution: at least some of the revolutionaries conceived themselves as attempting to harmonize interests by means of universal rationality unfettered by old prejudice and authority, which, it was held, militated against such painless harmonization. The Russian Revolution, too, is a classic case of an attempt to reform men by remoulding society on rational principles. Both these instances, and others one can think of, certainly highlight the pitfalls of rationalism in politics. But a more telling, because more fundamental, objection to the enlightenment view of human nature is given by those who, like Vico, stressed the effect on human beings of their cultural and historical background. With characteristic force and hyperbole the basic point is put by de Maistre: 'In the course of my life, I have seen Frenchmen, Italians, Russians ... I know, too, thanks to Montesquieu,

---

[5]   In his article on Eclecticism in the *Encyclopaedia*. Quoted in Arthur M. Wilson, *Diderot* (Oxford: Oxford University Press, 1972), p. 237.

that one can be a Persian. But as for man, I declare that I have never met him in my life; if he exists, he is unknown to me.'[6]

Being rooted is not simply the condition of man's existence and identity, it is also the basis of a calm and fulfilled human life: 'All known nations have been happy or powerful to the degree they have faithfully obeyed (the) national mind, which is nothing other than the destruction of individual dogmas and the absolute and general rule of national dogmas, that is to say, useful prejudices.'[7]

Prejudice is a good because it binds communities and nations together and gives otherwise rudderless human beings a sense of purpose and direction. This is more than Burke's notion of prejudice as the deposit of long experience and wisdom, or than Hume's test of time, or even than Chesterton's plea that in our search for instant solutions to our problems we do not disenfranchise the dead, though de Maistre would certainly not have dissented from any of these sentiments. It is rather the idea that a community, or anything approaching a community, must be firmly embedded in a cocoon of all-embracing and unquestioned thought and feeling, a thought expressed around the same time by Herder:

> Prejudice is good in its time and place, because it makes people happy. It takes them back to their centre, attaches them firmly to their roots, lets them flourish in their own way, makes them more impassioned, and, as a result, happier in their inclinations and purposes. The most ignorant nation, the one with the most prejudices, is often superior in this respect. When people dream of emigrating to foreign lands to seek hope and salvation, they reveal the first symptoms of sickness and flatulence, of approaching death.[8]

Herder's motivation may seem entirely praiseworthy: a desire to defend the primitive and the rural and the communal against the hubris of the urban sophisticate. It is hard not to see his words as an anticipation of Nietzsche's ideas about the centrality of myth to a strong people, and of the impact of Socratic rationality as a type of sickly internal emigration loosening the bonds of allegiance to common values and myths which hold a community together. And it is hard not to see his whole stance through the prism of rather

---

[6]   J. de Maistre, *Oeuvres Complètes*, 14 vols. (Lyons: Vitte, 1884–87), vol. 1, p. 74.

[7]   *Ibid.*, p. 376.

[8]   J. G. Herder, 'Yet another philosophy of history concerning the development of mankind', quoted in *J. G. Herder on Social and Political Culture*, ed. F. M. Barnard (Cambridge: Cambridge University Press, 1969), pp. 186–7.

darker nineteenth- and particularly twentieth-century interpretations of culture and nation.

Our recent reflections on culture have begun to take us into deep,
if not murky, waters. We began by looking at the differences
between scientific theories and the terms in which discussions of
value are framed. In particular, in scientific theories, abstraction is
made from ethical and evaluative considerations, and often even
from the properties and predicates on which such evaluations focus.
If by 'culture' is meant the context in which what Leavis calls
judgements about life can be made, then science can be at most one
specific element of culture as a whole. Science will in various ways
inform discussions of value, by, for example, outlining what it is
possible to do, or by explaining some of the causal background to
specific human capacities or tendencies. But it cannot in itself
provide justifications for evaluations or decisions, even including
the decision to engage in science itself. The fact, if it is a fact, that the
reductive and quantitative approaches characteristic of modern
science have entered so much of our political and moral thinking
does not show that science itself is forcing our mind-sets in that way,
or that being a faithful scientist implies that one is bound to do this.

What it shows is that a particular culture has begun to move in a
Benthamite direction, and critics would say, has begun to look at
moral and political questions in terms and conditions which are
inappropriate. But scientific investigations, properly conceived,
neither encourage nor licence such a shift of mind or emphasis.
Leavis, in his criticisms of Snow fails clearly to distinguish the thesis
that science cannot be a culture from the thought that our culture (or
Snow's) encourages inappropriate incursions of quasi-scientific
modes of thinking (what might be called 'scientism'). Leavis clearly
hopes that a literary education will help to alert sensitive people to
the dangers of scientism, and in this he may well be right. Important
as this is, it remains subsidiary to the main argument, and also
vulnerable to Snow's *ad hominem* about the reactionary tendencies of
writers other than Ibsen (to the extent, anyway, that it is (a) true and
(b) if true, undesirable).

However, when we begin to look at the notion of culture, as it has
been developed and been analysed in practice, we notice that it is not
a matter of there being just one context in which values have developed. Culture is not centred on mankind as a whole, but rather on
specific groups. There appears to be something facile about the
assumption of a single human culture, and something dangerously

hubristic about the assumption that all cultures are converging on a single point, or converging on a single set of values. In Herder's case, indeed, it was dismay at the hubris involved in enlightenment rationalism which led him to stress the plurality of culture and the incommensurability of value—and one doesn't have to be objectionably Spenglerian to question whether the superiority of twentieth-century liberal democratic culture over, say, fifth century BC Athens or thirteenth-century France is simply self-evident.

However sympathetic some of the sources of his thought may be, there are obvious disadvantages in Herder's position. If he himself refused to rank cultures, or even to compare them, his view that human cultures are incommensurable gives him no redress against the position of one who, like Fichte, simply declares the German people the *Favoritvolk*, the favoured nation. A Herderian position would in any case, seem to argue for a form of apartheid, multicultural if not supremacist; that is to say, if each human being's identity rests on his or her assimilation to his or her national culture, should the aim of social policy not be to preserve groups (and hence individuals) in their purity, rather than encourage or even allow cultural assimilation?

Against the holism of Vico, Herder and their followers, the enlightenment stressed the individual. While enlightenment thinkers like Diderot and Condorcet certainly underestimated the rootedness of individuals in particular traditions and cultures, nothing so far said shows that they were wrong to stress the autonomy of the individual. The remarks I have quoted from de Maistre and Herder suggest that happiness comes from sinking one's individuality in the nation. Far from suggesting that this is inevitable, they are quite conscious of the possibility, the danger as they would see it, of doing the opposite. So, even while recognizing the importance and significance of cultural roots, it remains an open question as to just what one should take to follow from this. The situation here, indeed, is analogous to that regarding science: just because science is an important aspect of culture, it does not follow that ethical or political issues should be discussed as if they were scientific questions; just because my culture is a significant aspect of my identity, it does not follow that I should envisage my activities in exclusively nationalistic terms, or seek to subordinate my personality in that of the nation.

In his book *La Défaite de la Pensée*, Alain Finkielkraut has drawn an interesting contrast between Herder's attitude to national culture — and by extension those of Fichte, Nietzsche, Spengler and many of our contemporary multi-culturalists — and that of Goethe.[9] In his essay on German architecture of 1772 written shortly after he had met Herder and had been impressed by him, Goethe had praised the Gothic at the expense of the classical, which was, we may suppose, the *international* style of the eighteenth century. In the form of an address to Magister Ervinus (Erwin von Steinbach), the architect of Strasbourg Cathedral, Goethe comments how the Italian would describe the Minster as in niggling taste, with the Frenchmen childishly babbling 'Puerilities' while 'triumphantly snapping open his snuffbox, à la Greque'. Moreover,

> the first time I went to the Minster my head was full of the common notions of good taste. From hearsay I respected the harmony of mass, the purity of forms, and I was the sworn enemy of the confused caprices of Gothic ornament ... no less foolish than the people who call the whole of the foreign world barbaric, for me everything was Gothic that did not fit in my system ... [10]

And yet, on actually seeing it, 'how surprised I was when I was confronted by it', and, as a result of the magical and above all natural impression given by all its ornament and detail, he quickly came 'to thank God that he can proclaim that this is German architecture, our architecture. For the Italian has none he can call his own, still less the Frenchman.'

The German Gothic is a characteristic art. As such it is the only true art 'unadorned by, indeed unaware of, all foreign elements, (and) whether it be born of savagery or of a cultivated sensibility, it is a living whole.'

Hence among different nations you will see countless different degrees of characteristic art, and in the case of Strasbourg, what we have is an example of the 'deepest feeling for truth and beauty of proportion, brought about by the strong, rugged German soul on the narrow, gloomy, priest-ridden stage of the *medii aevi*.'

Even as late as 1823, Goethe endorsed the favourable impression the Minster had made on him in 1772, but by then his attitude to national culture had been somewhat transformed.

Finkielkraut in his book focuses on a conversation Goethe had with Eckermann on 21 January 1827. Goethe had been reading a

---

[9]   Trans. D. O'Keeffe as *The Undoing of Thought* (London: Claridge Press, 1988).

[10] 'On German Architecture' (1772), in *Goethe on Art*, ed. John Gage (London: Scolar Press, 1980), pp. 103–12.

Chinese novel, expecting to be struck by its strangeness and difference, but he had been struck instead by its closeness in theme and treatment to his own *Hermann and Dorothea* of 1797, and also to the English novels of Richardson. Of course men were rooted in particular places, and up to a point creatures of their traditions, histories and geographies, but these divisions and fragmentations could be transcended, particularly through art:

> I am more convinced that poetry is the universal possession of mankind, revealing itself everywhere and at all times in hundreds and hundreds of men. One makes it a little better than another, and swims on the surface a little longer than another — that is all ... we Germans are very likely (not) to look beyond the narrow circle that surrounds us. I therefore like to look about me in foreign nations. The term 'national literature' does not really mean much today. We are moving towards an era of universal literature, and everyone should do his best to hasten its development ... While we value what is foreign, we must not bind ourselves to some particular thing, and regard it as a model.[11]

And he says that if we want a model we must look to the ancient Greeks, where the beauty of mankind is universally and constantly represented. The rest we must look at historically, taking for ourselves what is good, as far as it goes. On 14 March 1832, shortly before his death, Goethe appeals even more forcefully to universal standards:

> as a man, as a citizen, the poet is bound to love his native land ... but the native land of his poetic powers and poetic action is the Good, the Noble, the Beautiful, which have no particular province or country, and which the poet seizes on and forms wherever he finds it.

The poet, for Goethe, is like an eagle, hovering and gazing over whole countries, it being of no consequence to him whether the hare he pounces on is running in Prussia or Saxony. What then could be meant by love of one's country, other than setting aside the narrow views of his countrymen and so ennobling their feelings and thoughts?

The Herderian position on culture will deny this, and insist that each individual becomes even more rooted in his or her own particu-

---

[11] See J. P. Eckermann, *Conversations with Goethe* (London: Everyman's Library, 1970).

lar culture, though whether this is intended as an epistemological or a moral-cum-political claim, or a mixture of the two, is not always entirely clear. As an epistemological claim, it is, of course, refuted by the experience of Goethe with the Chinese novel, by the experience of anyone today who reads Homer with some understanding, and at a significant but lower level, by the universal popularity of originally American pop music. It is this last phenomenon, indeed, that might lead many to see something attractive in Herder's position from a moral or aesthetic point of view. Doesn't universalism lead to a destruction of much that is worthwhile, and to an abrogation of value-judgements, leading in the end to a universal mediocrity? Here, I think, one has to beware of a sentimental form of primitivism. Vulgarity and worse do not occur only in Disneyland, but *may* be evident in village culture. And, as the example of Goethe himself shows, transcultural borrowing and assimilation can be conducted on the highest level.

In fact, on analysis, it turns out, perhaps paradoxically, that a Goethean position is far more conducive to the making of value judgements and to the preservation of the worthwhile than Herder's. For it was Herder who denied the possibility of making value judgements across cultures and who thus in effect deprived the admirer of a peasant culture of any firm ground on which to criticize the incursions of satellite television or Coca Cola. In a Herderian dispensation, he will appear simply to be defending the picturesque against the popular, having been deprived of any notion of any objective value on which to argue his case.

Goethe, by contrast does appeal to a universal sense of value, which is manifested in but transcends particular cultures. He is neither committed to the defence of everything in a culture he admires overall, nor need his defence of ancient cultures against modernization be simply a lament for the passing of the old: he can point to universal values its passing will offend. To return to Leavis, his complaints against the effects of industrialization need not be sheerly Luddite, mere obstinacy in the face of universal progress. Paradoxically, then, it is Herder, with all his affection for the particularity of primitive cultures who reduces their defender to the position of the Luddites castigated by the likes of Snow. Goethe, with his references to the Good, the Noble and the Beautiful, and with his extolling of the man who stands *above* nations, opens up the logical space needed to rank and assess cultures and their elements. There is, then, no contradiction between an appeal to universal values and a defence of particular aspects of particular cultures. Quite the contrary: what would be contradictory would be to attempt such a defence while denying any transcultural standards of assessment.

If such denial is what is meant by pluralism, then Leavis's strictures on pluralism are well taken:

> 'Pluralism' denotes a sitting-easy to questions of responsibility, intellectual standard, and even superficial consistency, the aplomb, or suppleness being conditioned by a côterie-confident sense of one's own unquestioned sufficiency — or superiority.[12]

Leavis's target here is Noel Annan; whether his sally is justified in that case, it could certainly be said that the sort of non-judgemental pluralism he criticizes here received an early exposition in Herder, and after various incarnations on the political right and on the political left, is with us today as those forms of multi-culturalism which would refuse to allow one to judge the worth of other cultures or their customs. In most, if not all of its incarnations, there has also been the sense from proponents of pluralism that they consider themselves somehow superior, intellectually and morally, to those benighted folk *within* particular cultures, who insist on the unique correctness of their views.

But one does not have to subscribe to the enlightenment view of human progress or deny the fact of our own situatedness in particular traditions or cultures to think of values as universal. Indeed, a proper account of judgment would be that it is both individual in expression and formulation, and, in intention, universal: while judgements may indeed depend on backgrounds of communal agreement, they cannot in the first instance be communal. Any judgement is made by an individual who then takes some responsibility for it. As Leavis himself puts it, speaking of judgement about poems, 'a judgment is personal or it is nothing; you cannot take over someone else's'.

And in describing the process by which critical judgements are then discussed, amended and ratified, he goes on to speak of the collaborative-creative process in which the poem comes to be established as something 'out there', of common access in what is in some sense a public world.[13]

Leavis goes some way here to capturing both the individual and the universal poles of judgements of all sorts — that they are made by

---

[12] Leavis, *Nor Shall My Sword,* p. 32

[13] *Ibid.,* p. 62.

individuals, while seeking general or universal agreement. He then goes on to make the important point that a culture can exist only in so far as it provokes renewed responses from the individuals in it, 'who collaboratively renew and perpetuate what they participate in—a cultural community or consciousness'. In other words, a culture, if alive, is always changing in response to the judgements and reactions of those who live in it.

What all this amounts to is that while individuals stem from their cultures, as rooted in them, if you like, they are never completely determined by them. They are individuals, and in making their judgements, they appeal implicitly at least, to standards of correctness which stand above the particular, and by which the particular is judged, whether the particular is the individual person or his or her society. And there are some types of judgement no human being can avoid having to make. The point about the 'two' cultures is that necessarily we all make judgements about what Leavis calls 'life'; in this sense—to return to Pascal's initially quoted pensée—we all have knowledge about morality, knowledge which is vital to us all in a way in which knowledge about science is not. While there is a clear sense, as we have seen, in which scientific judgements are cross-cultural, it is not the case that even in a scientifically dominated culture, each individual will have to engage with science. On the other hand, we do all have to make judgements of value; and while our value judgements are initially in the presuppositions common to our culture, in making them we take a personal responsibility for them, which gives us the chance at least of loosening the bonds of cultures as given, and of moving into a more universal environment.

Chapter 7

Art and Censorship

A few years ago we spent a wonderful morning in the van Gogh gallery in Amsterdam. Of course we knew all the paintings, we had seen them all in reproduction, and the building was more like a bank vault than a setting for art. But what art! At first sight how small and uniform the paintings were in reality: yet every blade of grass, every flower in a field, every olive tree, every vibration in the sky, every patch of colour, every brush stroke, testified to life and to a life vibrating beneath the surface form. In a true sense, van Gogh was an artist inspired, an artist breaking convention, artistic and social, but nevertheless an artist transforming life with a vision of the enhancement of life; in his vision he invites each one of us to look again at the natural forms around us, to feel the spirit or the gods dwelling in them. It is a vision of enchantment and of humanity in a disenchanted world. Art—painting—can, then, be a source of spiritual nourishment as Kant and Schiller and Ruskin in their different ways thought it should be.

Later on, we crossed over to the Museum of Modern Art, where at the time pride of place was given to work by the Italian artist Francesco Clemente. Here too was an artist apparently concerned with life in a general sense, but his was an art which in Nietzsche's terms was quintessentially decadent:

> an art of tyrannizing. A coarse and strongly defined logic of delineation; motifs simplified to the point of formulas ... within the delineations a wild multiplicity, an overwhelming mass, before which the senses become confused; brutality in colour, materials, desires.[1]

Clemente's art was an art of garish screams, of skulls, of raving eyes and snarling teeth. And so was borne vividly and unforgettably on me that while art can transform our material existence, not by

---

[1] F. Nietzsche, *The Will to Power*, ed. Walter Kaufman (New York: Vintage Books, 1968), section 827.

denying it or by etherealising it, as, perhaps Burne-Jones might be accused of having done, but by leading us as, van Gogh did, to experience the material world as the best picture of the spirit, it can also, in the Leavisite phrase, do dirt on life.

Of course, I had in a sense known that already from my encounters with the work of Francis Bacon, technically a far more accomplished artist than Clemente and one who may be credited with an intensely personal style and vision. For that very reason Bacon is far more insidious than Clemente's abrasive rhetoric, in his relentless reductions of the human form to writhing meat and his strippings of the achievements of civilized life to the grasping of naked desire, in unfurnished rooms lit by unshaded light bulbs. I have to question the taste of the man who chooses to ply guests with drinks beneath a Bacon portrait.

Later I learnt, too, of Mary Kelly's display of used nappy liners in her so-called *Post-Partum Document*, of artists exhibiting their own turds, of Gilbert and George's videotapes of young men getting drunk on Gordon's Gin, and of their works with titles like *Buggery Faith*, *Friendship Pissing* and *Tongue Fuck Cocks* and images to match, of Robert Mapplethorpe's photograph of one man urinating into another's mouth, and of another in which his own buttocks are exposed with a bullwhip protruding from between his legs, of Andres Serrano's *Piss Christ*, a photograph of a crucifix submerged upside down in the artist's urine.

Art can do dirt on life, or attempt to; many of the things I have just described sound like the rather pathetic efforts of callow fifth-formers to shock their parents and teachers. But then fifth-formers do not yet get Arts Council Grants and Turner Prizes for their infantilities. Nevertheless there can be art which is fuelled by hatred, by childlike destructiveness, even by evil. What should be our attitude to artistic works which do or attempt to do dirt on life? (My examples here are all from the visual arts, but analogous cases can easily be found in the worlds of literature, film and dance.)

The philosopher Arthur Danto has this to say about feminist art (and I daresay defenders of Mapplethorpe and the rest would say similar things about certain types of self-advertisingly homoerotic or political or anti-racist art):

> So often feminist art, when performative, is funky, aggressive, contestive, flagrant, shocking, daring, extreme, and meant to be responded to as dangerous: it uses frontal nudity, blood, menstrual fluid, and the like almost magically ... it is not intended to

be beautiful, symmetrical, composed, tasteful, let alone pretty or
perfect or elegant. It is everything that a painting by Matisse, for
example, is not. So it is in its favour that it should be ugly, disordered, offensive, not to mention tacky, flawed and raucous.[2]

And he adds: 'its conception of success has a kind of merit'. Leaving aside the questionableness of referring to Matisse's work as
pretty and elegant, it follows from all this that it is all right to scribble
'shit' or 'fuck' or 'kill all men' over some blood or crudely executed
daub so long as you have the right feminist or anti-racist intention.
You might even get exhibited in a New York gallery or win the
Turner Prize or a grant from the Arts Council for England or the
National Endowment for the Arts. Is having the right para-political
intention and being accepted by a gallery or art-funder what counts
as success in Danto's model artistic universe? I ask this question in
all seriousness, because from Danto's description and from what I
have seen of the work of Mary Kelly and the rest, it is very hard to see
what other criterion of success is being used. We have need to
remind ourselves here that it is crucial to any developed tradition of
artistic expression that the audience or viewer should be able in
looking at a work of art both to identify the artist's intention in
producing the work, to come to an assessment of his or her success in
executing that intention, and also (as the contrasting examples of
Bacon and van Gogh show us) to come to terms on a human level
with the results of that execution.

But perhaps, as Danto himself suggests, the aim of feminist and
postmodernist art generally is to be perceived as aesthetically *bad*, to
sneer at the genius, to make fun of the masterpiece, to giggle at
aesthetic values altogether; 'the injunction is to begin a non-
exploitative history in which art is something put to immediate
human ends, rather than destined for the brilliant collection.'[3] This
sounds like self-indulgent hand-waving, to me, but I believe it represents a dangerously confused state of mind as well.

In the first place, was not van Gogh responding to immediate
human needs, just as much as the manufacturers of Mary Kelly's
baby's nappies? (And to suggest that van Gogh, of all people —
whom Danto had discussed at some length in the paragraph prior to
the one just quoted from — was intentionally aiming at what Danto
refers to as the brilliant collection, the dramatized auction room, the

---

[2]   Arthur Danto, 'Bad aesthetic times in the USA', in *Modern Painters*, vol. 2, no. 2,
      Summer 1989, pp. 55–9, at pp. 55–6.

[3]   *Ibid.*, p 57.

sanctuary of the museum or the tomb of the expensive art book, is in the case of that artist as gross and damaging a perversion of the truth as one can imagine). But then secondly, if, as I suspect, the phrase 'being put to immediate human ends' is a euphemism for preparing for political revolution, it is hard to see how sneering, giggling and making fun of the good is a good way to prepare. Not only that, but after Hitler, Mussolini and Trotsky we should surely by now need no further reminding of the social and human cost of political revolutions brought about by would-be artists on the basis of manifestoes largely filled with artistic bombast and the type of sloganising and simplification politicized art is prone to. Good artists have never been particularly apt at politics, and nothing I have seen in the work of these self-proclaimed bad artists gives reason to suppose that they have an ability in political and social analysis which outstrips their evident artistic inadequacies.

If we cannot take an artistic doing dirt on life as a serious political gesture, what should be our attitude to it? I am trying, if nothing else, to show that perhaps because of the widespread acceptance of the modernist cliché of the artist as a rebel, as a culture-critic, there is a great amount of art being produced and publicly promoted these days which is bound to infringe and is often intended to infringe public standards of taste and decency. I am not talking of erotic art which can lead to real celebrations of human love and human sexuality, but of art which conspires with the puritanical to present sex and sexuality as essentially depraved and to present sexuality in perverted forms.

In 1990 Senator Jesse Helms, partly as a response to the public funding of the Serrano and Mapplethorpe exhibitions in which the works I mentioned earlier appeared, proposed an amendment to the appropriations bill for the National Endowment for the Arts in the United States Senate which would have cut off all public funding for artists who

> promote, disseminate or produce obscene or indecent materials … including but not limited to depictions of sado-masochism, homoeroticism, the exploitation of children, or individuals engaged in sex acts, and which taken as a whole do not have serious literary, artistic, political or scientific value.

I should emphasize that Helms in his Amendment was not intending to censor art, but only to restrict public funding according to standards of public decency. His attitude was that if Mapplethorpe wanted to show his photographs and Kelly wanted to exhibit used nappies and others were inclined to respond to the invitation, they should not be prevented from doing so, but that they should not be helped to do so either from public funds. I cannot resist making the point here that many artists in the feminist/post-modernist camp echo Josef Beuys in saying that everyone is an artist. By their own lights this may well be true: anyone can drag an old VW into a museum or order a cast of a heap of earth or put a pile of bricks or a few pebbles on the floor or fill gallery walls with the type of graffiti which too often disfigures public transport or parade around a gallery wearing funny masks and hats. But if in this new, emancipated sense of 'artist' anyone or everyone is an artist, why should some be paid for it? Or is it just that some are rather better than most of us at latching on to those very institutions of the capitalist state apparatus which many avant-garde artists would in more public mood profess to despise?

The Helms Amendment was eventually watered down by force of liberal opinion to an anodyne document about peer group assessment being enough to ensure that standards of decency are met in the disbursement of state and federal funds for the arts, although Helms and his supporters did not give up their campaign in the Senate or elsewhere. I have to say, though, that the Helms Amendment was unworkable anyway, glossing over essential distinctions such as that mentioned earlier between the erotic and the pornographic, and also between types of offence works of art might cause. Nevertheless, I think that people who really care about art and about what is happening in art should be grateful to the Senator for taking art more seriously than most of those in the art establishment do. He realized instinctively that it can be a powerful force for good and also for harm, that there is a morality involved in art, and that the say-so of the artistic establishment is not enough to guarantee that works exhibited are not disgusting, incompetent and nihilistic in intent.

Like Senator Helms, I think that censorship of the arts is likely to be counter-productive, even if motivated by the best of intentions, and will not work. In all probability the censor will sooner or later go for the wrong target, he will bring ridicule on his own head and the artist censored will become a hero and bask in the resulting publicity which might otherwise have eluded him. I do, though, believe that the public funding of the arts raises questions about public taste and decency which ought to be addressed more directly than they often are and that people involved in the arts should be far more honest and open about what they are about if they choose to dwell on what is negative and disgusting in human life. While an artist might choose to depict scenes of, let us say, atrocity or sexual perversity as therapy for himself, a question is raised as to the attitude the rest of us should take to such work. Critics I see especially as having a significant role here, but one which they frequently neglect for fear of seeming moralistic. But what is a critic if not at bottom a moralist?

The relation of art to truth and goodness must be a fundamental concern of any serious criticism of it. I will, though, end on a consoling note for anyone who has followed me thus far; in the late 1980s, even with Arts Council backing, massive critical acclaim, sponsorship from Beck's Beer and the publicity of their Turner Prize, Gilbert and George attracted only 39,000 people to their Hayward Gallery exhibition compared to 364,430 for the Renoir exhibition at the same place. The public still take art seriously enough to make talk of outright censorship unnecessary, though they will correctly continue to question arts funding policy.

Chapter 8

To Swim with Strong Strokes in the Lake of Antique Poetry

In 1856, Hector Berlioz was hard at work on his masterpiece, *The Tro-jans (Les Troyens)*, a work which had been incubating in his mind for decades. Its seeds had been sown in his childhood days in the small town of La Côte Saint-André near Grenoble. In 1814 at the age of ten his father had taken him out of school, 'having decided to look after my education himself', as Berlioz recorded.[1] His father was a doctor and taught him scientific things, but more important he taught him poetry and Latin. They used to read *The Aeneid* together in Latin. After some initial resistance on Hector's part, bit by bit Virgil's char-acters became impressed in the young man's psyche, never to be dislodged from it. And so it was that he wrote to his sister Adèle in 1856:

> Working at my opera intoxicates me. I swim with strong strokes in this lake of antique poetry. What gratitude we owe these great spirits, these mighty hearts, who give us such noble emotions as they speak to us across the centuries. It seems to me that I've known Virgil and Shakespeare [his other great passion], that I can see them.[2]

Perhaps some today would quail at the notion of great spirits, at the thought of mighty hearts and above all at the very concept of a noble emotion. These are certainly untimely thoughts, which can

---

[1]   Hector Berlioz, *The Memoirs of Berlioz*, ed. and trans. David Cairns (London: Panther Books, 1970), p. 38.

[2]   Hector Berlioz, letter to his sister Adèle Suat, 22 June 1856 (quoted in David Cairns, *Berlioz, Servitude and Greatness, 1832–1869* (London: Penguin Books, 2000), p. 606.

make us uncomfortable. Certainly I can give no other explanation than unease with Berlioz's professed intention for what I saw on the stage of The English National Opera a few years ago, what purported to be Part Two of *The Trojans* (the part dealing with the story of Dido and Aeneas). Aeneas, according to Virgil, like 'the lord Apollo in the spring', with his hair bound 'in fronded laurel, braided in gold', walking 'with sunlit grace upon him', this son of Venus, portrayed as a shaven headed punk; Dido, Sidonian Dido, Queen of Carthage, and a figure of truly regal stature, leader and more to her people, clothed in gold and scarlet, according to Virgil, on the Coliseum stage in a business suit as if she had just come from some board-room meeting, setting targets and adumbrating outcomes; the cave, in which Dido and Aeneas consummate their love, according to Virgil the ritual opened by Primal Earth herself and Nuptial Juno, and attended by torches of lightning and nymphs crying out wild hymns from the mountain top, simply a trap door in a bare stage down which the lovers inelegantly clamber; the Trojans themselves (who are, of course, going to be the Romans) boorish mercenaries, carrying shells and other impedimenta of modern warfare (no doubt in case in entering the theatre we had temporarily forgotten about Iraq); no great palace, no hall filled with mementoes of Troy, which provoked Aeneas's great invocation 'sunt lachrymae rerum', itself the inspiration for one of Liszt's finest pieces, but instead a set of such calculated ugliness as to expunge from our minds any thought of the Carthage of antiquity or of Turner's great painting.

That presumably was its point, and the point of all such directorial aberrations, an attempt to domesticate the greatness of the past in a spirit of egalitarianism. In the name of relevance and accessibility the meaning and potential of the works of the past have to be brought to our level and to our mentality, either because we are incapable of transcending the parochialism and the levelling spirit of our time or because the thought that we might be encouraged to do so would be too subversive, certainly on a publicly funded stage.

But it is not just a question of taxpayer subsidy. Mention of *The Trojans* conjures up thoughts of Troy, and of *The Iliad*, and inevitably of the film *Troy*. People who see the film, but who know nothing of Homer, will, if they remember what they see, come to believe the following things.

Patroclus is Achilles's younger cousin (not his older companion and probably his lover). Aeneas was a mere boy at the fall of Troy (and not a seasoned fighter on the plain of Troy). The Trojan War lasted about four weeks (and not ten years). Menelaus was killed by Hector after his single-handed duel with Paris (and so never returned to Sparta with Helen, there to welcome Telemachus in the Odyssey, and help him in his quest for Odysseus). Briseis was a member of the Trojan royal family. There is no warrant for this in Homer or in Greek mythology more generally, but in the film it allows the introduction of an entirely spurious sub-plot and some highly questionable characterisation of Achilles as the sort of man likely to respond favourably to a feisty barrack room female who dares to stand up to him.

Continuing the same theme, Hector himself is very much a man of our age spouting anti-war speeches and helping Andromache with child-care (!). In Homer Hector loved fighting and was as cruel to his victims as Achilles; the fact that he also understood the cost of war, at least what he foresaw would be the cost to his own family and people, no doubt adds an additional poignancy to his character and situation. But Homer achieves his condemnation of war — to the extent he does condemn it — not by words, but by graphic descriptions of the horrors of war and how those horrors turn men into things and women into booty (they still do); spears lancing beneath the brows, down to the eye's roots, skulls cracked to splinter, brains splattered inside helmets, shrieking heads tumbling in the dust, spears skewering men through the groin and guts, liver split, skewered hearts jerking in their last throes, until blood stains the dust and the plain and night blinds men's eyes … but men who, in each case, are differentiated and characterised in a few brief epithets, epithets often recalling their homes and flocks and fields. For whatever reason, in respect of war's horror, the film *said* where Homer *shows*, and so lost much of the power of the original.

In the film, Agamemnon is no more than a scheming, power mad politician. He was mad with over-weening pride in his conflict with Achilles, true, but he was also a brave and terrifying fighter, 'lord of fighters', according to Homer, withdrawing from the desperate battle around the Greek ramparts, and in which he personally kills several Trojans, only because wounded; for the Greeks he was a symbol of nobility, even if flawed, so much so that in Plato's *Republic* he is reincarnated as an eagle. In the film, Agamemnon was killed at Troy (and so never returned to Mycenae and his fate at the hands of Clytemnestra and Aegisthus). There is in the film no hint of the Judgement of Paris, which started the whole thing, but in the film Paris and Helen walk off together after the fall of Troy (instead of

Paris being killed at Troy and Helen going, willingly enough, back to Sparta with Menelaus). And in the film Paris is saved in his earlier duel with Menelaus by Hector, rather than being whisked away from the field of battle by Aphrodite and into bed with an initially reluctant Helen, and so we lose not only one of the most erotic passages in ancient literature, but also one of the key episodes in *The Iliad's* cumulative treatment of the theme of war and peace.

This last takes us to a much bigger issue than apparently gratuitous tampering with a text, the gods. Apart from an embarrassingly improbable Thetis there are no gods in the film *Troy*, because, I suppose, in the twenty-first century we (we, the film going public, that is) don't believe in them. But how can we have any sense of the mentality of the ancient Greeks, of that tantalising mixture of familiarity to us and at the same time of utter strangeness and distance from us (as the great poet George Seferis always used to emphasise), unless we at least acknowledge that they did feel and see things differently from us? How can we make any sense of their myths, of their philosophy, of their history, of their art without this? In so far as much of our mentality and of our art descends from theirs, by going to the roots which may still be living and powerful, beneath the surface, but which through centuries of Christianity and scientific enlightenment we have systematically occluded to ourselves, we might actually learn something about ourselves. But more than that, in entering into the classical Greek mind, and about their conception of the world and the gods to the extent we can, we might just learn something, period, something which Christianity and enlightenment has occluded at least on the surface.

In the words of Seferis, it is this:

> In Homer everything meshes, the whole world is a woof of organic 'umbilical cords'; the earthly, the heavenly world, animals, plants, elements, the hearts of men, good, evil, death, life — that ripen, vanish and them flower again. The mechanism of the gods performs nothing supernatural, nothing *ex machina*; it retains coherence, nothing else.[3]

It is just this coherence and plenitude which is lost when an ancient work is translated insensitively into a modern idiom. Instead of a vision, even a *Weltanschauung*, from which we might learn something old and something important we simply refract ourselves and

---

[3]   George Seferis, *A Poet's Journal: Days of 1945-51* (Harvard: Belnap Press, 1974), p. 49.

our own prejudices back from the myths of the past: Agamemnon becomes a contemporary politician, such as George Bush (or what some of us think of as George Bush), Odysseus just the ubiquitous fixer and spin-doctor, Briseis a gutsy liberated female, Hector a new man role model, etc., etc.

We profess to be shocked at Garrick's alterations to *Romeo and Juliet* and to *King Lear*, at Victorian bowdlerisations of Shakespeare, and congratulate ourselves on being beyond all that sort of stuff; but I can see very little difference between these aberrations and what Richard Jones did to *The Trojans* or Hollywood did to *The Iliad*, and what countless other opera directors, theatrical producers and film makers routinely do to the works of the past. Far from swimming in the lake of antique poetry, or even leading the audience to its shore, they appear to see their role as to shallow out the lake altogether so as any paddling we might do in it conforms to the dictates of contemporary mental health and safety.

In response to what I have so far said, it might be replied that the history of literature is, in part, a history of the re-working of old themes in the light of new mentalities. Indeed, Homeric themes and their continual re-working run like a golden thread through much of our culture: the tragedies of Aeschylus and Sophocles, *The Aeneid*, Shakespeare's *Troilus and Cressida* (no gods there!), Racine's tragedies, Goethe's *Faust*, Berlioz's *Trojans* itself, Joyce's *Ulysses,* and so on. In this context we should surely draw a distinction between a distorted production of an antique work and an attempt to revivify an old myth for a modern audience. *Troy* is thus vindicated where ENOs *Trojans* stands condemned.

I accept part of this reply. There is indeed something far worse about a self-conscious and deliberate distortion of the spirit of an existing work than a harmless variation on an old theme. But there is still a question as to the light or otherwise the new variation throws on the old theme, and also as to the extent to which the new variation adds to or subtracts from the original. We might suppose that nothing could actually add to *The Iliad* or even to *The Odyssey*. Compared to Homer, Virgil's attempt to synthesise both epics and to vindicate Troy and Rome at the same time has been judged by Simone Weil (no less) to be cold, pompous and in bad taste. [4] Still, in dissenting from this — and in part because of Berlioz's intuitive artistic understanding of it, and even more, no doubt, because of Dante's assimilation of

---

[4]   Simone Weil, *Intimations of Christianity Among the Ancient Greeks* (London: Routledge, 1987), p. 52.

its author into his own great poem—one can point out that *The Aeneid* has furnished our collective mind with its own enduring images and poetry, and continues to do so.

It is doubtful that the film *Troy* will do that, as I have already implied in my analysis of it, but my real criticism of it is that by its very verisimilitude of setting and costume it will mislead people into thinking that they have been given Homer. It proclaims itself as having being 'inspired' by Homer. At best it is a colossal lost opportunity and at worst it is as misleading as setting Wagner's *Ring* in a nineteenth-century factory or with the gods as 1930s gangsters. It is a domestication of something which should resist domestication, a testament to our own parochiality of mind (or at least of the parochiality of the director), and sabotages its potential. (Perhaps, to show that what I am complaining about does not infect only popular culture, I should say that the way Plato is usually taught in British universities is just as parochial as Petersen's film, for those doing the teaching nine times out of ten simply ignore the mythology and mysticism which permeates all Plato's thought, as if these things were too naïve and embarrassing even to notice.)

Revisionist directors and producers will say—as do many contemporary teachers of literature—that the reason we have to revise the obvious intentions of earlier authors and composers is because we have to make difficult and alien texts relevant to the needs and interests of potential audiences. They will also claim that in their re-settings they are clearing away the gratuitous accretions and misplaced reverence which have become attached to these texts over the centuries and making them relevant to our own time, in much in the same way as cleaners treat old paintings, restoring them to a pristine and original freshness.

Actually this is not an analogy which necessarily helps their case. The history of the restoration of old paintings and buildings has been as much a history of how succeeding ages have imposed their own aesthetic on works of the past, and in so doing have contributed to the destruction of what they claim to be restoring. We can think in this context of Viollet le Duc's ruthless stripping out of Gothic buildings in the nineteenth century of everything he found superfluous to them, and in so doing stripping the sense of a great building as a changing, living thing; and also of the tendency of today's picture 'restorers' to replace the subtleties and delicate modulations of a Venetian painter like Titian with the harsh lines and garish colours of acrylic, advertising and postcards (a phenomenon which was made abundantly clear the Titian exhibition in London in 2003 when the National Gallery's *Bacchus and Ariadne* was placed next to the Prado's much less savagely handled *Andrians*).

But, one wonders, why do we want relevance anyway? It is, of course, as close to dogma as anything in current educational practice that all material has to be made relevant to the needs, interests and backgrounds of pupils, as I have just remarked. This dogma is all of a piece with the whiggish presumption that our society and our mentality is the prism through which the past and other eras should and must be viewed. But it is just that, dogma and presumption.

In fact, for able pupils at least, relevance is likely to dampen interest and enthusiasm. This is in part because of the fruitful complexity and density of works like *The Aeneid* or *Paradise Lost*, to say nothing of the critical literature about the great works of the past. In this critical literature we see the contribution of some of the most reflective minds of the past to the understanding and literature of the past, which itself becomes part of the weight of the meaning of those works. All this helps to explain why able pupils, at least, often actually prefer studying Milton or Shakespeare or Donne to Ian McEwan or Margaret Atwood or *Captain Corelli's Mandolin*. The incidentals of plot aside, the latter authors and books tell them what they know (or think they know) already, and there is little of any great interest to say about them, or certainly little of any great interest that has been said about them.

By contrast is not difficult to inspire interest in the languages and images of *Paradise Lost*, say, and once interest has been inspired the great lake of antique poetry is before one. To attempt to pretend that *Paradise Lost* has immediate or obvious connections with the life (or simulacrum of life) which is portrayed in *EastEnders* or *Coronation Street*, or that such material might provide a way in to it is condescending to all involved. It is, as Matthew Arnold put it, not the way of culture; according to Arnold, culture 'does not try to teach down to the level of inferior classes', nor does it 'try to win them with ready-made judgements and watchwords'. [5] It is, of course, partly because Milton is not 'ready-made', trotting out the clichés of the day like a television soap that he can still speak to us today, as his great learned, poetic and religious sensibility wrestles — and maybe all too obviously and uncomfortably and unsuccessfully wrestles — with the most profound of themes.

---

[5]   Matthew Arnold, *Culture and Anarchy* (1869), quoted in the Chelsea House, New York edn, 1969, p. 31.

At a deep level, no doubt Milton does speak to the condition of those portrayed in *EastEnders*, as indeed he speaks to the rest of us; but that in *EastEnders* itself, its characters would recognise their predicament as having anything to do with 'man's first disobedience' or indeed from human disobedience at all is inconceivable. It is inconceivable precisely because there is in contemporary prejudice, as reflected in the popular culture of our time (and no doubt itself deeply permeated by the romanticism of Rousseau), no logical space for the thought that our lives might be tainted by disobedience of the sort Milton and, in their different ways, St Augustine and Dante and Baudelaire and Dostoyevsky and Tolstoy and T.S. Eliot were all obsessed by.

Personally, and contra Rousseau and his myriad followers both high and low, I believe that mankind is naturally disobedient. Original sin, even as we try to ignore it, is part of our condition, even if not necessarily in the way Milton describes; also redemption of the sort hinted at by Eliot may be an ever-present possibility, though again not necessarily in the way Eliot adumbrates. But even for those unable to see the world in this way there is no denying that the notions of disobedience, original sin and redemption are deeply influential in Western consciousness. As Nietzsche recognised more clearly than most, and even as our most progressive thinkers strive to avoid the implications of the point, our whole morality and sensibility — our predicament, if you like — continues to be informed by concepts and feelings which really make sense only in a Christian context, including the otherwise philosophically baffling notions of human rights, equality and colonial guilt, which play so large a role in our politics (of all parties) and in popular culture. In the sense that it takes us back to the mythology which spawned these concepts and feelings *Paradise Lost* throws light on our predicament, but only if we take it on its own terms, if we swim in its lake and begin to understand how it might be to live and move and have one's being in such a mentality.

In their own way, so do *The Divine Comedy*, and also *The Oresteia* and *The Iliad* ... for, to continue the theme of disobedience, the notion of disobedience to God or the gods, and the continuing effects of that disobedience is ever present in Greek epic and tragedy. To take but one example, the destruction of Troy itself is a colossal offence to man and to the gods, as was the brutal deed which launched the Greeks on their way, and which proved ten years later to be Agamemnon's nemesis; none of Greek thought and literature can be understood without understanding that their greatest mythological triumph was also a great offence, and recognised by them to be an offence, polluting all involved — and their descendants. Simone Weil put the point about hidden continuity between the Greeks and us by talking of intimations of Christianity among the ancient Greeks.[6] We might just as well put the same point by speaking of echoes of ancient Greece in Christianity.

So, what I am saying, to put the matter programmatically, is that to benefit from antique poetry we have to let it speak as it is. We have to submit ourselves to the works, bend ourselves to them. We do not ask ourselves what impression they make on us, or how we feel about them, before we have studied them in and for themselves. Even less should we get pupils into the habit of asking themselves how they would feel if they were Hector, say, or Dido, or getting them to transpose Hector and Dido into a twenty-first century context; this would be of a piece with thinking that history can be done by getting pupils with a pristine and untroubled twenty-first century mentality saying what an agony aunt might have said to Lady Macbeth (an actual example from a recent public exam in England), or how they themselves might have felt had they been a slave in ancient Athens or in the trenches of the Somme or in the Crusades. For whatever our pupils might think they would have felt in these situations or as these personae, without an education which distances them from the prejudices of their own time, it would not be how the historical agents or literary characters of earlier times felt.

It may be worth underlining here that as far as surface culture goes, the average white comprehensive pupil from the London suburbs is hardly closer to the worlds of Homer or of Virgil than is a Bangladeshi girl from Tower Hamlets or the child of Somalian refugees — there is actually a kind of benign equality of distance here! But wherever we start from, what matters is that we ask the poets and their characters what is they have to tell us, striving as far as we can to hear what, across the centuries, they have to say to us. Then, and only then, is our response to the point, and our response must be to them and to what they say, not to some modernised version of them. Then and only then will the response be part of a genuine conversation through the ages, and not a self-enclosed dialogue whose only voices are those of our own time. We do not, like modern directors, attempt to domesticate works which through the test of time have

[6]   See the essays in Simone Weil, *Intimations of Christianity among the Ancient Greeks*, Routledge and Kegan Paul, 1957.

showed their power to transcend place and time. We do not, like those Matthew Arnold criticised, condescend to those we think are socially or ethnically or culturally unprepared for the best or for what is distant from them. We give them the best and what is distant, as a common entitlement and as the basis of a common culture literacy, and then we let nature—and upbringing and the free decisions of individuals—take their course.

There is, though, a question of ability, on which I have already touched. Is the lake of antique poetry for people of all abilities? Some have certainly thought so, including Simone Weil who wrote, simply but uncompromisingly, about Sophocles's *Antigone* for French factory workers. In Saul Bellow's *The Dean's December* we are told of a teacher, who, notwithstanding the instructions from the educational authorities, found only the savage poetry of Macbeth could touch the souls of children from the Chicago ghetto: 'only poetry had the strength to rival the attractions of narcotics, the magnetism of TV, the excitements of sex, or the ecstasies of destruction.'[7]

One would like to think so. But there are dangers here, too, in the agenda of inclusiveness. Should we simply assume that art is for all, when we do not know who are included in the all, and when, in conversations of this type 'all' is likely to signify people *en masse*, people as reflected in the mirror of the mass media, people without any of the education in antique poetry and the rest they would need in order to come to any sort of appreciation of it? That the mass of the people now are hardly more educated now in cultural matters than they were in Matthew Arnold's day, and now, if the number of cultural self-help groups which existed among the Victorian working classes is anything to go by, far less sensible of any hunger in this respect, is itself a striking comment on our education system and our culture.

But, to return to the masses, here is Berlioz again, this time for a sardonic comment on a certain sort of inclusiveness:

> How right they are, the great critics, when they say, Art is for all. If Raphael painted his divine madonnas, it was because he understood the exalted passions of the masses for the pure, the beautiful, the ideal. If Michelangelo wrested his immortal Moses from the bowels of the marble and raised up with his hands a glorious temple, it was of course to satisfy their yearning for profound emotions. It was to feed the sacred flame which burns in the hearts of the people that Tasso and Dante sang. Let all works not admired by the mob be anathema! For if it scorns them, it is because they are

---

[7] Saul Bellow, *The Dean's December* (London: Secker and Warburg, 1982), p. 187.

worthless. If it holds them in contempt, it is because they are con-
temptible. And if it formally rejects them with catcalls, let the
author too be rejected! He has shown a want of proper respect for
the public, he has outraged its intelligence and wounded its deepest
sensibilities. Away with him to the mines![8]

There is a hard path to be trodden here. The best must be offered,
unadulterated. But in the confidence that we are offering the best,
we must not be deflected when, as will inevitably happen, 'the
public' in its collectivist voice, or in the persons of those purporting
to speak on its behalf, rejects the best as élitist or as too difficult or as
just irrelevant.

Here is another image, relevant to our theme, midway between
those mines to which the exiled artist has been consigned and that of
a Benthamite public irredeemable by culture and education,
pig-headedly preferring pushpin to poetry:

> Suppose human society to be a pyramid whose base is every-
> one's due, and whose apex is the highest attainable human excel-
> lence. Somewhere between base and apex we must each find our
> place; but never must the standards of excellence be lost or
> corrupted, for to realise the highest excellence is perhaps the task
> of our race in the economy of the universe. Those who give
> expression, whether in knowledge or in moral or aesthetic
> beauty, to the highest things, are giving to the world patterns of a
> perfection to which all must strive, which is latent in all. Through
> the creations of the few we all live, somewhat, in Genji's court, in
> Plato's Academy, in Mme Verdurin's salon.[9]

I have to say that I have my doubts about living in the Verdurin
salon itself, as opposed to inhabiting the comedy and irony of
Proust's matchless description of it, but Raine's underlying intuition
is surely right. We have to aspire to the highest things, to the extent
that we can. For teachers, particularly of literature, the most important task and the one for which ultimately they will most be thanked
is to open eyes and feelings to those highest things.

It will be obvious from what I have said that I believe there is value
in the world and in some works of art, objectively speaking; and that
even if it needs a human sensibility to perceive the value in (say) *The
Iliad* and *The Iliad* is a human creation, nevertheless that it is valuable
is not just a projection of their own feelings on the part of those who

[8]   Berlioz, *Memoirs*, p. 204.

[9]   Kathleen Raine, *Autobiographies* (London: Skoob Books, 1991), p. 123.

perceive it. What they perceive, its meaning and its value (to the extent it is valuable) is there, whether particular individuals perceive it or not. To the extent that people do not perceive it, they are diminished. Good art, says Iris Murdoch,

> thought of as symbolic force rather than statement provides a stirring image of a pure transcendent value, a steadily visible enduring higher good, and perhaps provides for many people, in an unreligious age without prayer and sacraments, their clearest experience of something grasped as separate and precious and beneficial and held quietly, and unpossessively in the attention.[10]

Think, I would suggest, of *War and Peace*, of Titian's *Flaying of Marsyas*, of Bach's *Chaconne*. This is at least part of the reason for swimming in the lake of antique poetry, and part of the reason for us submitting ourselves to it. And in the confrontation with the other thing and its value, for a time the grip on us of what Murdoch calls the 'soft fat ego' is loosened. This is the most fundamental reason why in approaching great art the route is not through our own ego, not through our own prejudices, not as refracted through our own unchallenged feelings and self awareness. Of course, as Iris Murdoch also emphasised, there is also plenty of art which is not great, and which simply feeds the soft fat ego with wish fulfilment and flatters its view of the world, so, instructed by our experience of the best, we must learn to discriminate, and pass this sense of discrimination on.

But, bad and mediocre art aside, in the contemplation of good art we let the thing and its value speak for itself. We value it in and for itself. To adapt a striking image of the poet Hölderlin, in our contemplation of it, a great work of art is like a rock against which the wave of our sentimentality is scattered. In its presence we cease to be the centre of our world, and the structure of our feelings and sensibility is re-formed. In a sense that a work of art precisely does not stem from or reflect from the surfaces of our existing needs, interests, cultural background etc is in its favour. It may be something which can work on us, rather than the other way round.

Part of what I want to say is hinted at in the passage already referred to in Essay 3 from Rilke's *First Duino Elegy*.

> Beauty's nothing
> but beginning of Terror we're just still able to bear,

---

[10] Iris Murdoch, *The Fire and the Sun* (Oxford: Oxford University Press, 1977), pp. 76–7.

and why we adore it so is because it serenely
disdains to destroy us.

So, the thing is there, apart from us, impermeable and still, impervious to us, yet so attractive to us, and attractive in part because it has no need of us. And yet, and yet. Rilke goes on:

> Many a star
> was waiting for you to perceive it. Many a wave
> would rise in the past towards you; or else, perhaps,
> as you went by an open window, a violin
> would be utterly giving itself. All this was commission.
> But were you equal to it? [11]

Our imaginative response to beauty is part of the divine economy of the world. But our response must be one of giving, rather than of taking, of letting be, rather than of grasping, of letting go of ourselves rather than of wrapping the thing up in the rags of our needs, interests, cultural backgrounds, etc. As Rilke says in 'Archaic Torso of Apollo' (of 1908) of the 'intact stone' torso, which is all that is left of the kouros, it gives light like a star, prompting the command 'You must change your living.'

I know that the metaphysical view underlying what I am saying here is unfashionable. The fashionable view is that when we apply aesthetic and moral predicates to things, be they works of art or natural objects, what we are really doing is expressing our feelings, feelings which we then project on the things. Further, the human world, the world in which things are endowed with human meaning is something which we add to the world and add without ultimate warrant in the nature of things. The fashionable view — fashionable particularly in university departments of humanities — is the view which was attacked, quite effectively in my view, by C.S. Lewis in the first chapter of *The Abolition of Man*, in which Lewis analyses the views of the writers of a school literature textbook. [12]

The writers of this book, whom Lewis calls Gaius and Titius, say that when Coleridge talks about the travellers at a waterfall, one of whom calls it 'sublime' and the other 'pretty', and agrees with the one and disagrees with the other, Coleridge is himself confused. For when the man calls the waterfall sublime, he is not saying anything about the waterfall, but only about his own feelings. That he is

[11] Rainer Maria Rilke, *Duino Elegies*, trans. J.B. Leishman and Stephen Spender (London: Chatto and Windus, 1975).

[12] C.S. Lewis, *The Abolition of Man* (Oxford: Oxford University Press, 1943).

saying something objective and about which Coleridge can disagree is a confusion ever present in our language: 'We appear to be saying something very important about something: and actually we are only saying something about our own feelings.'

As Lewis point out, the view of Gaius and Titius flies in the face of the age old conviction that even to inanimate nature certain responses are more appropriate than others, and that this conviction underlies all the great philosophies and religions of the past. I would add that, far from being a confusion, the age old conviction is actually the only one which makes any sense of our language and behaviour, and of the world itself (and not just the human world) which is infused with value. Nevertheless, Lewis spoke in vain, at least as far as many modern critics are concerned, who seem to think that in discussing beauty and other aesthetic properties, all you can talk about are people's responses, which might, of course, at a deep level provide some rationale for the obsession with audience response which we found in government policies on the arts and education.

Thus Robert Macfarlane in *Mountains of the Mind* says that,

> when we look at a landscape, we do not see what is there, but largely what we think is there. We attribute qualities to a landscape which it does not intrinsically possess — savageness, for example, or bleakness — and we value it accordingly. We read landscapes ... The way people behave towards mountains has little or nothing to do with the actual objects of rock and ice themselves. Mountains are only contingencies of geology ... [13]

And apart from their geology, all the rest of what we think about them has been 'imagined' into existence by human beings down the centuries.

In support of this view Macfarlane quotes Byron's Childe Harold staring down into the waters of Lac Leman: 'To me/High mountains are a feeling'. Using Byron in this way is very misleading. What the Childe actually says is,

> I live not in myself, but I become
> Portion of that around me, and to me,
> High mountains are a feeling, but the hum
> Of human cities a torture; I can see
> Nothing to loathe in nature, save to be
> A link reluctant in a fleshly chain,
> Class'd among creatures, when the soul can flee,

[13] Robert Macfarlane, *Mountains of the Mind* (London: Granta Books, 2004), pp. 18–19.

And with the sky, the peak, the heaving plain
Of ocean, or the stars, mingle, and not in vain.

And a couple of stanzas further on, he asks

Are not the mountains, waves, and skies, a part
Of me and of my soul, as I of them?

What Byron is saying is that, far from his feeling about the mountains being a projection he reads into them, he and they are part of a unifying quasi-pantheistic process in which he achieves his higher vocation in fleeing to them and mingling his feelings with theirs and with what their nature summons forth from him. The sky, the mountains, and the ocean's heaving plains are chemistry, geology, biology, but they are more than that; and that more we can respond to. In so responding, we complete one turn of the Rilkean (or is it Hegelian?) circle in which we are formed by these things at the same time as progressively rendering their spirit and meaning articulate and conscious.

Against a perspective of objective value in the world, at least in part summoned up in human perception of and activity in that world, but really there nevertheless, I would conclude by saying this.

The lake of antique poetry, like the archaic torso, is one way in which we get in touch with and articulate the value in the world. It is also, of course, an important component of that value itself, in that in its expression of that value, it is itself part of what we value. But the lake is not part of our everyday utilitarian concerns, and, to mix metaphors horribly, what it expresses and is transcends the quotidien of our time and of its. In immersing ourselves in it we can come to understand and value aspects of the world and aspects of human life which we would not appreciate were we to remain on the level of the everyday, cocooned in our own egos and in their own fleeting concerns and the transient opinions which hold sway in society at any time.

One of the things which we will come to realise in taking the great works of the past on their own terms is that in most of what was written before 1800 (and in a fair amount since) there is an assumption that there is an order of value not of human making, and that our vocation as human beings is in part to respond to that order. Of course, now that God is dead, or is presumed to be dead, much literature and art is premised on the assumption that whatever value there is in the world and in our lives is put there by us. We invent right and wrong, to use the title of an influential philosophy text, and much else besides in the realm of value, as Gaius and Titius and Macfarlane would have it.

So one fruitful outcome of taking the great literature and art of the past on its own terms would be that it allows us to feel, from the inside as it were, what it might be like to live and experience the world as itself replete with value. Foreign as such a sense is to us, or to many of us, even if God is dead there is something to be said for knowing what it would have been like to live in a world filled with the presence of God or gods, if only because we still live in the hollowed-out shell of such a world.

For some there will be something of a paradox here. The works which presuppose a settled value and order not of human making are all themselves works of human making. They are as much human creations as, in the modern view, values are. Further, in our art and literature we reverence human creativity above all else, perhaps especially because we believe ourselves to inhabit a universe with no ultimate meaning or purpose. What we seem to be saying is that, in reading the literature of the past, we are reading human creations, theatrical, contrived and idiosyncratic creations—yet we are gaining through these works insights into a world not theatrical, contrived or idiosyncratic, and certainly not one of human creation. Moreover these works of art might for many of us today be the most powerful way of gaining such insights, more powerful for us than many a directly religious text or service.

My intuition is that much of the literature and art of the past can and does have such an effect, and that in reading it and living through the experiences we are offered by it, suggestion of paradox evaporates—but only so far as we submit ourselves to it, and are prepared to take it on its own terms, terms at once close to us, but equally and often strangely foreign.

Chapter 9

Art and Technology

An Old Tension

This is not the first time the title 'Art and Technology' has been used, but to distinguish what I have to say from Walter Gropius's Bauhaus exhibition of 1923, I am subtitling my paper 'an old tension', where the architect spoke of 'a new unity'. In a way Gropius has been proved right; the structures of the future avoiding all romantic embellishment and whimsy, the cathedrals of socialism, the corporate planning of comprehensive Utopian designs have all gone up and some come down. We have a mass media culture also largely made possible by technology. Corporatist architecture, whether statist 'social housing' or freemarket inspired, films, videos, modern recording and musical techniques are all due to technological advances made mostly in the last century. Only in a very puritanical sense could what has happened be thought of as inevitably bringing with it enslavement. All kinds of possibilities are now open to artists and architects, which would have been imaginable a few decades ago. No one is forced to use these possibilities in any specific way.

If I have a complaint about what has happened in the arts this century, it is not that technology is constraining imagination, or making slaves of us. It is rather that it isn't constraining it enough, that technology is removing those very constraints which made art a matter of craft, rather than an unfettered display of expression and imagination.

It was common at one time to praise the avant-garde architects of the first half of the century for (in Pevsner's words) 'courageously' breaking with the past, and accepting 'the machine age in all its implications: newmaterials, newprocesses, new forms, new problems'. [1] We are now in a better position than Pevsner was in 1943 to judge whether this courage was advisable or not: whether it was

[1] Nicholas Pevsner, *An Outline of European Architecture*, 5th edn (Harmondsworth: Penguin Books, 1957), p. 281.

something forced on the artist or architect of integrity by new materials, etc., or whether it was, rather, a question of the possibilities offered by new materials leading to the deformation of an old craft. Certainly this century we have had an aesthetic of functionality which intentionally broke with the past and in so doing produced buildings which were by any normal human standard uncomfortable and inconvenient, precisely because they swept away much ornamentation and detail whose role, we now know, was not merely decorative.

It is part of modernist propaganda that the aesthetic of the Bauhaus and Le Corbusier was forced on us by new materials and techniques. That this is false is shown by the fact that there are architects today who are using those very materials and techniques to produce a new classicism, just as Giles Gilbert Scott earlier this century had used reinforced concrete to largely unmodernist effect. In particular, Scott refused to expose concrete, regarding it as visually crude.[2] Modernists would doubtless accuse Scott of being untrue to his materials, but with decades of what David Watkin has called the 'graceless weathering' of concrete, that doctrine is itself looking a little tawdry today.[3] It is, in any case, an *aesthetic* doctrine, not one forced on us by materials or by technology. We are perfectly free to reject its sillier and uglier implications on aesthetic grounds, as indeed Ruskin, its original proponent, would have done. Ruskin was not seeking to do away with all ornamentation, but only with what he regarded as the dishonesty of certain types of ornamentation, all of which goes to show once one gets away from the simplicities of modernistic sloganizing, even the meaning of the doctrine of truth to materials is far from clear.

The artist, according to Ruskin,

> is pre-eminently a person who sees with his eyes, hears with his ears, and labours with his body, as God constructed them; and who, in using instruments, limits himself to those which convey or communicate his human power, while he rejects all that increase it. Titian would refuse to quicken his touch by electricity; and Michael Angelo to substitute a steam-hammer for his mallet. Such men not only do not desire, they imperatively and

---

[2]   See David Watkin, *A History of Western Architecture* (London: Barrie and Jenkins, 1986), p. 557.

[3]   *Ibid.*, p. 558.

scornfully refuse, either the force, or the information, which are beyond the scope of the flesh and the senses of humanity.[4]

Unlike Ruskin, I am not confident about what Titian or Michelangelo might or might not have done, had they lived the age of electricity or of the steam-hammer, or of acrylic paint, or of computer-assisted design, or of epoxy resin. But what I do know is that with all our technological advances, there is no one painting today who can convey colour, shade, flesh or cloth as Titian and dozens of his contemporaries could. It is also significant in this context that our supposedly advanced 'scientific' restoring techniques have in the case of Titian often simply had the effect of removing the glazes and varnishes on which his flesh tones, shading, perspectives and half-tints depended. Compare, for example, the ruin of *Venus, Cupid and an Organist* in the Prado, or the garish *St Margaret* from the Heinz Kisters collection with the uncleaned *Annunciation* from Naples.[5] And it is hard to think of any sculptor of note today even interested in carving forms of classical beauty from blocks of marble, let alone worth mentioning alongside Michelangelo.

If Titian and Michelangelo belonged to a technologically primitive age, it is as if their technological limitations simply spurred on their mastery of technique, whereas our technological advancement has led to a loss of technique. Technique is certainly central to art, for reasons we will come to. Indeed, one of the unfortunate effects of the entry of technology into the world of art has been the downgrading of technique and the upgrading of the idea. The thought is: why bother with painting when I can get what I want much more easily and quickly with a camera? Why should I run the fearsome risks inherent in carving, in which a few bad strokes can ruin the integrity of my stone, when I can do what Michelangelo did not have available, that is model in clay and infallibly point-up my block of stone

[4] John Ruskin, *Deucalion* (1875–83), vol. 1, chapter 2, section 4. In writing this paper. I found myself increasingly drawn to Ruskin, and to what he has to say on the subjects of art and technology. This paper is not a paper on Ruskin, nor do I accept everything Ruskin said on everything. (How could I when Ruskin is *notoriously* inconsistent?) But even though Ruskin is not normally regarded as a philosopher, what I write could be nevertheless regarded as a philosophical homage to one of our greatest writers on art. Ruskin's works are most easily available in the collected edition of his writings, edited by E.T. Cook and Alexander Wedderburn, London: George Allen, 1903–12, 39 volumes.

[5] All this was revealed in the great exhibition of Titian and his contemporaries in the Grand Palais in Paris in 1993. See the catalogue of that exhibition, *Le Siècle de Titien* (Paris, 1993), especially illustrations 176, 250, 251.

(or even get an assistant to point-up for me)? Why should architects learn to draw the human figure-knowledge, which for centuries formed the basis of a feeling for architectural proportion and sensibility, when computer-assisted design can apparently make their lives so much more exciting?

Computer-generated graphics and designs now take us far beyond the static camera or the nineteenth-century sculptor's pointing machine, allowing the instant realization of complex and many-layered conceptions, human input into the result being infinitesimal compared to what is required in painting even the most formulaic canvas. From what appears to be the opposite end of the artistic spectrum, Richard Long, who is paid large sums to walk from one place to another and take photographs as he goes, says that he likes 'the simplicity of walking, the simplicity of stones ... common means given the simple twist of art ... *sensibility without technique*'.[6] This sort of conceptual art may seem a far cry from the high-tech of the studios of contemporary architects and video producers, but in both cases we have lost the ancient and noble idea of art as *technè* or craft, in which all that was done was done by human hand and controlled by human intelligence.

Plato, in common with his fellow Athenians of the fifth century BC, put painters in the same category as shipwrights, builders and 'other craftsmen'; that is people who mould their materials, with craft or artistry (or *technè*, fitting each bit to harmonize with the others 'until they have combined the whole into something well ordered and regulated'.[7] Skill (*technè*) is needed for art, but over and above that, some imaginative power to order and co-ordinate the parts in a manner appropriate to the intended effect. Part of Plato's point in discussing painting is to contrast activities, which make use of a recognizable *technè*, with poetry, which according to Plato does not, relying instead on an uncertain and morally unreliable inspiration (and is indeed the sensibility without technique admired by Long). Nevertheless, Plato's prejudice against poets aside, the linking of art with crafts such as building is a healthy antidote against that form of idealism regarding art which technology encourages. We need to remind ourselves of the way in which art grows out of our embodiment and affects us via our senses.

---

[6]   Richard Long, *Words after the Fact*, text in his 1980 catalogue for the d'Offay Gallery, London.

[7]   Plato, *Gorgias*, 503e.

Where we come to the work of a true artist, we get a full-bloodied humanism:

> The day's work of a man like Mantegna or Paul Veronese consists of an unfaltering, uninterrupted series of movements of the hand more precise than those of the finest fencer: the pencil leaving one point and arriving at another, not only with unerring precision at the extremity of the line, but with an unerring and yet varied course — sometimes over spaces a foot or more in extent — yet a course so determined everywhere, that either of these men could, and Veronese often does, draw a finished profile, or any other portion of the face, with one line, not afterwards changed. Try, first, to realise to yourselves the muscular precision of the action, and the intellectual strain of it: for the movement of a fencer is perfect in practiced monotony; but the movement of the hand of a great painter is at every instant governed by a direct and new intention.[8]

It is because *everything* is a craft-based work of art governed by a direct and new intention, that a painting is potentially of far more critical and aesthetic interest than a photograph, say. In a photograph, the photographer governs and intends only the general shape and outline depicted, and the outcome is not the result of a constant and continuous reflective interaction with the material over a long period.

In creating a work of art the artist occupies a dual role. He is both maker and audience, or, rather as maker, he constantly puts himself in the position of his audience, judging for himself just how what he makes will appear to the audience. In the light of this knowledge, he will modify what he does (and sometimes, as in the case of Bruckner, he will modify what he does in the light of actual audience response). If the creator of a work of art puts himself in the position of his imagined audience, the audience attends to a work of art not as to a natural phenomenon (such as a cloud, a crystal, or an untamed landscape), but as to something driven by human intelligence and expressive of human emotion. In so doing, the audience is confident that it is not indulging in the exercise of pathetic fallacy, that is, it is not imputing to unplanned and unintended phenomena characteristics which are properly attributed only to planned and intended things. A work of art is produced by a human being in order to express some vision and set of intentions its creator has in making it. As such, a work of art is of interest for what it reveals about the human world, the world in which intentions, institutions and tradi-

---

[8]   John Ruskin, *Lectures on Art* (1870), lecture 3, section 71.

tions introduce meaning into an otherwise meaningfully empty universe. As located in the human world, works of art are liable to the same types of evaluation as other human works and deeds: 'there is no moral vice, no moral virtue which does not have its precise prototype in the art of painting', says Ruskin, and the same can be said of the human attributes other than the moral.[9] (It does not, incidentally follow from this that the *artist* who gives expression to, say, modesty or chastity is himself chaste or modest: that there is always (?) an element of theatricality about art does not mean that a Raphael or a Wagner might not understand human feelings very far from their own behaviour and evoke them in their work.)

What, though, would we say were we to do a Turing test on a work of art, and discover that something we had imagined to be the work of human artist and assessed as such, had in fact been generated by a computer? This question takes us to the core of the issue which concerns us, for it raises in a dramatic way the connection between the work of art as a product, and its history or mode of production. What I am going to argue for is for a form of externalism regarding works of art: that their visible form or intelligible content is not all they are, that part of what makes them what they are is in fact that they have been produced in a particular way, as a result of human intentional activity, one aim of which is to produce a realization in the audience that the artist has intended that the audience have an experience of a particular sort.

This does not mean that there cannot be failures in an artistic attempt to express a particular vision, nor that the result may not be ambiguous in various ways, and so fall below or above the sense the artist has as to what he is doing. But that we can judge a work to have failed against what we take to be the artist's intention is a justifiable and often illuminating commonplace of art criticism, but one which is to the point only where a human action is concerned. Similarly, that a work of art is ambiguous in various ways may tell us something about hidden aspects of ideas or feelings, hidden even to the original proponent of them, but which emerge precisely in executing the intention to articulate the surface feelings artistically.

In exploring the relation between works of art and their producers, we need initially to distinguish between production and reproduction. There are certainly works of art which can be mechanically replicated, even after their creators have lost interest in them, or even died. Sculptural bronzes, engravings and prints can all be

---

produced in the absence of the original artist, according to the matrix he has produced. (I leave aside the practice at least some sculptors and print-makers have of embellishing and refining the final results.) What, though, we have in these cases is mechanical reproduction or replication, rather than mechanical production. The artist is held to be responsible for the product, because he is taken to know how the final results will turn out, and to have designed his plate or model accordingly. We may speak here of mechanical replication rather than mechanical production, because in a sculptural bronze or an engraving the detail of every finished line and contour is or should be under the control of the artist: contrast that with a photograph in which much of the detail inevitably has little to do with the photographer's intention, or even, in typical cases, his knowledge. (This, of course, contributes to the sense of *actualité* conveyed by many photographs. but it is *actualité* at the expense of art).

Reproduction of a less elevated sort can also be envisaged in the visual arts and in architecture, where an original work is simply copied. One could certainly imagine fairly expert copying of wholes or parts of originals by means of machines, without human intermediaries. Such replication might even survive the Turing test; that is observers might be unable to tell that a particular drawing or building was the computer-generated copy rather than the original. If computers were able to generate copies of existing works of art indistinguishable from the originals, it might well be possible for them to produce formulaic works which drew on repertoires derived from existing works, but which were not copies of any complete works. What, if anything, would follow for our concept of a work of art from this possibility?

What would follow would be this. Computer-generated works of the type indicated might be indistinguishable from human productions, but the meanings which were attributed to them would be due to their sharing in the forms of typical human productions. They would be parasitically meaningful, deriving their meanings from the techniques and conventions which human artists had developed in their works.

However, the possibility that a computer might produce an original work indistinguishable, at least in respect of its appearance, from something produced by a human being, does not show that we are wrong to see works of art as, in their primary sense, productions of human intention and intelligence, and to accord them the value we do accord them at least in part because of that. In particular, works of art, like other productions of the human world, derive their significance from their ability to express and incarnate the way things seem to members of human communities. They are also intended to evoke aesthetic, moral, intellectual or emotional reactions from audiences. As things do not *seem* at all to computers or other machines, and as computers and other machines do not react with feeling and sensitivity, or even with unfeeling or insensitivity, computer-produced art is viable only to the extent that computers are programmed to exploit explicit human knowledge and to anticipate feelings which arise only within human experience.

Computer-generated art will in any case be unable to profit from that close and continuous monitoring of results in the light of human response which we spoke of earlier in connection with the glazing, shading and varnishing of the Venetian masters. It is hard to imagine that this knowledge could be algorithmically formalized and computed at all; works of art are, as Kant taught, essentially singular and individual. Their effects are not generalizable into other contexts, but are dependent on the ungeneralizable judgement of both creator and perceiver.

We are now in a position to suggest two ways in which art cannot be mechanical:

(1) The 'externalist' thesis, i.e. it matters whence artistic works derive.

Art is based on human life, its emotions, attitudes, feelings and institutions. While a purely machine-produced art, such as the fractal images produced by computers, may exemplify certain formally satisfying features, it necessarily lacks those references, explicit and implicit, to human life and sensibility, which make art more than a purely formal exercise. Art in the full sense is based in human experience. It does therefore matter where a work is grounded, and works not grounded directly in real human experience gain the honorific title of art only by being modelled on works which are. From such 'modelled' works we will not expect the same level or type of insight into the human condition as those that are created by human beings who have had the experiences relevant to their meaning, though we may learn something about the intentions and mentality of people in the art world who chose to exhibit them as though they were no different in interest from humanly produced works. It might also be a comment on a form of art, such as geometrical abstraction, which is *easily* mimicked by computers operating with little or no human guidance.

(2) *The singularity thesis.*

Art of distinction is necessarily individual and unique. It impresses partly because in it we see the free exercise of skill and judgement so as to produce new effects and original works. The skill and judgement is that of the artist who moulds what he does, exercising his skill in the light of his judgement. It is a cliché, but nonetheless true, that there is barely a movement in any of Mozart's mature repertoire of symphonies, concerti and string quartets which is not full of artistically fascinating surprises, truly a matter of, in Kant's terms, genius, the innate mental disposition through which, as Kant says, nature gives the rule to art.[10] So a Mozartian computer could never write a Mozart work: like any pastiche, it would lack just those qualities of guided but intuitive surprise, subtle melodic inventiveness, poignancy and control which characterize echt-Mozart.

The singularity thesis impinges on technology both as regards the need to experience a particular object and as regards ungeneralizable aspects of that object. In the first place as Kant insists, aesthetic judgements are judgements about single and particular objects. To make such a judgement, you have to experience the object in question. I can judge that, say, *Bacchus and Ariadne* is a beautiful painting only if I am perceiving *it* or have perceived *it*. An account of the painting without the experience will not be sufficient. Even if I were able, dubiously, to list all its properties there would be no guarantee that in some other context, even one just slightly different from that produced by Titian, those very same properties might not produce a quite different and even an unbeautiful result. I have chosen my example with care. There are in fact those who will hold that it is actually impossible to make a proper judgement about *Bacchus and Ariadne* in the twenty-first century, because since 1962 when it was 'restored', Titian's painting no longer existed. The result is that 'in the view of many informed critics its systematic and unimaginative cleaning has resulted in a tragic disruption of the fragile total unity of the painting'.[11] Readers may find this view confirmed if they go to the National Gallery in London today, and are struck both by the garish colours and the hard contours of the restoration. The influence of technology is double here: not only is it technology which has destroyed the soft lines and half-tints of the original, but the harsh

---

[10]   Immanuel Kant, *Critique of Judgement* (1790), section 46.

[11]   Sarah Walden, *The Ravished Image* (London, Weidenfeld and Nicolson: 1985), p. 139. In what I have said about cleaning I have relied closely on Mrs Walden's excellent analysis.

flattening aesthetic at work in the restoration is very much of that of the coloured photograph, the magazine and advertising.

What I say about restoration may seem to justify authentic performances of pre-nineteenth-century music, and to condemn any use of modern instruments in, say, Bach or Mozart. Actually, what I am saying has the opposite conclusion. It would clearly be wrong to play Bach as if he were a Liszt or a Brahms conjuring up waves of undifferentiated sound, or to fill in the sonorities of keyboard to Mozart's works without inserting the unwritten grace notes Mozart intended. But it does not follow that they cannot or should not be played on modern pianos. It is certainly arguable that Bach and Mozart were not exclusively aiming at the dead and staccato sounds characteristically associated with ancient keyboard instruments, and that the sonority and legato effects they clearly wanted can, by a Gould or a Perahia, be better conveyed on a modern piano, without sacrificing clarity or lightness, than by a slavish search for authenticity. Our current search for musical authenticity could well be the contemporary equivalent of the National Gallery's cleaning policies of the 1960s. The point is that in questions of art, what is required is judgement and insight respecting the individual case, and that blanket decisions covering whole classes of case (the technological approach) are likely to be wrong

If aesthetic judgements are characteristically singular and ungeneralizable, the artist in producing a work will also be guided by his 'genius', in Kant's terms, by a sense or talent for which no definite rule can be given.[12] What the artist must have is insight into how something will work, just which experiences it will produce in the individual case. According to Ruskin, in the case of Veronese's *Presentation of the Queen of Sheba* (Galleria Sabauda, Turin), what might otherwise and in the other hands be a mess of 'trivial and even ludicrous detail' in no way detracts from the nobleness of the whole.[13] One could, of course, lay down a rule, 'Detail is permitted (encouraged) to the extent that it doesn't detract, etc., etc.', but can there be a rule defining the appropriate extent? As Kant again, has argued, a genius (a Veronese) can produce models, which can serve as a standard or rule of judgement for others, but doing this will not indicate 'scientifically' how to enable others to produce similar products, if only because in matters of artistic judgement and

---

[12] See Kant, *Critique of Judgement*, section 46.

[13] John Ruskin, *Modern Painters* (1860), vol. 5, part 9, section 2 (London: Cook and Wedderburn, 1903-12).

creation, the artist himself does not know how his judgement works. What is at issue is the free play of the imagination, in which hitherto unassociated elements are brought together, so as to open out the prospect of an 'illimitable field' of association and representation. What is at issue is not a question of a closed logical deduction nor of the systematic steps a scientist might take in pursuing and testing a hypothesis.

A large part of what interests us in a work of art is an encounter, not with a machine or an algorithm but with another human mind, at once expressing itself freely, but also in control of what it is doing. I am not saying that there might not be aesthetic interest in computer productions, in fractals and the like. There is aesthetic interest in crystals, after all, and in landscape and cloud formations, an interest which does not diminish for the man unable to see such things as God's handiwork.

But there is a different, and from the human point of view, a superior interest in recognizing an aesthetic phenomenon as produced by a human being.

> Its true delightfulness depends on our discovering in it the record of thought and interest, and trials, and heart break-ings — of recoveries and joyfulness of success; all this can be traced by a practised eye: but, granting it even obscure, it is presumed or understood; and in that is the worth of the thing, just as much as the worth of anything else we call precious.[14]

An artist works with the intention that an audience should, in its experience of the work, come to have just that experience. In forming the work in the light of the experience it is intended to evoke, the artist will refine both intention and experience as he works. In doing this, he will, Richard Wollheim has argued, be drawing on 'thoughts, beliefs, memories, and in particular emotions and feel-ings, that [he] had, and that, specifically caused him to create as he did'.[15] He will also, doubtless, be guided by notions of what he thinks appropriate, aesthetically, morally, commercially, spiritually and in a host of other ways. A work of art, then, as it is being produced draws on much of the fabric of its creator's life, outer and inner, private and public, and, at the same time, contributes to the development of that fabric.

---

[14] John Ruskin, *Seven Lamps of Architecture* (1849), chapter 2, 'The Lamp of Truth', section 19.

[15] R. Wollheim, *Painting as an Art* (London: Thames and Hudson, 1987), p. 86.

If an artist is successful in his work, we can learn much about his inner life from contemplating his work, even without knowing much about his outer life. To put this another way, a work of art, if successful, draws on the artist's inner imaginative life and articulates aspects of it, and we learn something of that inner life from the works which stem from it, even without knowing much of the outer life in question. And, if Ruskin and Proust are to be believed, and the true life of an artist is that inner imaginative source on which he draws in his work, there can actually be disadvantages in knowing too much of the outer life, however much the outer life may have provided the bits and pieces which the inner self transforms. What is being said here is not that a work of art is or should be just a mirror of the feelings or biography of the artist. A good work of art involves a discipline, a *technè*, which will involve the artist in dissociating himself from his actual and current feelings. His work should, as T. S. Eliot insisted, be 'not a turning loose of emotion, but an escape from emotion ... not the expressions of personality, but an escape from personality'.[16] But, as Eliot adds, this impersonality is not something ungrounded in personal experience and passion; 'only those who have personality and emotions know what it means to escape from these things'.

It is a consequence of this view that while art should not be read as pure autobiography, and while artists need not (and should not) aim at displaying the detail of their own personality, art which cannot in any sense be regarded as successfully expressive of its creator's inner life and vision will, to that extent, be of less interest than that which can. Shakespeare and Homer are often regarded as the most impersonal of artists in that their work seems, by being so rich and deep and all-encompassing, to transcend their empirical existences and personalities. One could say, on the contrary, that part of what we admire about them is the manifestation of an inner life and vision which was so comprehensive and full of insight.

I believe that it would be nonsense to think of a computer having an inner life in this sense, or of its inner life being composed through its reactions to an outer world, including the human world, but even if a computer did have an inner life, it would not be a human or even an animal life. (Biology and animal life are crucial here.) So a whole dimension of appreciation, so central to our interest in humanly produced works of art, would be absent in the case of computer-

---

[16] T.S. Eliot, 'Tradition and the individual talent', in *The Sacred Wood* (London: Methuen, 1960), pp. 47–59, at p. 58.

produced works, which we ought therefore to view as more akin to crystals than to drawings or paintings. As Frank Palmer puts it, one of the things we value in works of art is 'our negotiation with a human mind other than our own'.[17] And in this negotiation we simultaneously extend our experience and at times find corroboration for our own feelings and viewpoints. At other times, we doubtless find challenges to our own feelings and viewpoints, but the challenge is a challenge precisely because it is a human being—a fellow-traveller on the journey through life—who sees and feels differently from us. Have we missed something? Are we hiding something from ourselves? Or are we dealing with a moral or aesthetic idiot?

In the passage about Mantegna and Veronese from which I have already quoted, Ruskin says of the great artist's power and control,

> determine for yourself whether a manhood like that is consistent with any viciousness of soul, with any mean anxiety, with any gnawing lust, any wretchedness of spite or remorse, any consciousness of rebellion against law of God or man, or any actual, though unconscious violation of even the least law to which obedience is essential for the glory of life and the pleasing of its Giver.[18]

Ruskin's attitude is surely preferable to the prevailing attitude of our time, to degrade any hero by any means possible, but it is unsustainable as it stands. Not only are many great artists on a human level mean, spiteful and even worse; some have made it their aim to present human life as mean, spiteful or worse.

Nevertheless, as often when he is most obviously wrong on the surface, there is something Ruskin is hinting at, something true and important, something which should lead us to take a Bacon or a Céline or a Picasso seriously, even while rejecting the morality of what they have to say and averting our eyes decorously from the sordid details of their biography. Art is closely linked to fantasy. Most people's fantasies are second-hand and often imprecise, rhetorical and incomplete to boot. Many works of art simply mimic other works of art, other people's fantasies in other words, without resting on any basis of skill or observation. The danger of this happening is particularly acute in the mechanistic arts, such as film and

---

[17] F. Palmer, *Literature and Moral Understanding* (Oxford: Oxford University Press, 1992), p. 159.

[18] Ruskin, *Lectures on Art*, lecture 3, section 71.

photography, where owing to the nature of the medium involved a verismilitudinous gloss is inevitably given to any material, even to the most shallow. Where in a novel, dialogue and characterization of the level to be found in the average film or television drama would immediately reveal its unreality, on screen the mechanism involved ensures a semblance of an unbroken and unquestionable truth. By contrast, an imperfectly executed or observed drawing or painting is easily seen through, both for its lack of skill and its absence of originality.

In Ruskin's terms, though, Picasso and Bacon would rank as powerful artists: men with new and direct intentions, and the skill and exertion to convey them in visual form. Analogously, in the field of literature, few writers of the past century come anywhere near Céline in their ability to re-create a whole world and its meaning, a harsh and vexatious world to be sure, but to do so with neither remorse nor sentimentality.

The visions conveyed by Picasso, Bacon and Céline are neither unworked nor second-hand, and if, in the end, we find them transgressive or ignoble, this is not because they are unrooted in intelligent encounters with human reality. Rather they emphasize aspects of human reality we might prefer to overlook or feel need to be counterposed with other perspectives. Unlike pure fantasy, they are true to the extent that they demand a considered response from those who find them uncomfortable, and not just the instinctive rejection of pornography or of a Nazi tract.

Works of art, then, are human creations, made with skill and craft to evoke and express human meanings. They are also and characteristically singular objects, unique in themselves and reflective of one person's intelligence, sensitivity and skill.

Even if a work of art is reproducible, it cannot be machine-generated, for that will be to undermine the role of the artist and the role of work of art as something intended as such by another human being. Equally, its appearance should not be too slick, belying its origins in the struggle of an imperfect, but free human being with his imperfect material: too much ostensible perfection may simply reflect an attempt to deny human freedom, spontaneity and creativity. Art which aims at complete suppression of human freedom and a complete hiding of the artist's personality is, to that extent, an inhumane and imperfect art, even, or perhaps especially where the motivation for such suppression is religious or otherworldly. Beautiful as such art may sometimes be, it may at the same time witness to an attempt by the society from which it derives to suppress and deny human autonomy, and to treat artists as means rather than as ends. To the extent that this is evident in the art, we, with our respect for human autonomy, are bound to find the art less than complete.

Such, indeed, was Ruskin's view:

> Go forth again to gaze upon the old cathedral front where you have smiled so often at the fantastic ignorance of the old sculptors: examine once more those ugly goblins and formless monsters, and stern statues, anatomiless and rigid; but do not mock at them, for they are signs of the life and liberty of every workman who struck the stone; a freedom of thought, and rank in scale of being such as no laws, no charters, no charities can secure; but which it must be the first aim of Europe at this day to regain for her children.[19]

Great art, in Ruskin's view, is never perfect, or finished like machine work. We, as human beings, are fallen and multiply imperfect; it is the aim of mass production, of the division of labour and of technological aids to production to occlude this fact. The perfections afforded by technology are degrading in comparison to the old crafts precisely because they *are* perfect: 'it is only for God to create without toil; that which man can create without toil is worthless', it allows no room for any creative or expressive lapse.

Part of what is at issue here is an aesthetic question. Michelangelo's David or the Rondanini Pietà? Michelangelo as a whole or Canova? Raphael or Leonardo? The Hermes of Praxiteles or the Anavyssos Kouros? Ruskin's own preference for the Gothic over the Classical and particularly over the neo-Classical is well known, though his arguments for the preference are far from convincing. Apart from anything else, he underestimates the freedom for invention and ingenuity which the classical orders permit, while at the same time over-estimating the extent to which the twelfth- and thirteenth-century cathedral builders were innocent of specialism, division of labour and technological advances.

At the same time, Ruskin's idealized and inaccurate characterization of the Gothic does bear on the question of technology in two ways, one of direct relevance to the artistic, and one of wider import. One besetting artistic sin is dominance by too easy a technique to avoid the business of hard creativity, creativity against a

---

[19]   John Ruskin, *The Stones of Venice* (1853), vol. 2, chapter 6, section 15.

background of rules and resistant material which, by curbing fantasy liberates true thought and true originality. The salon sculpture and academic painting of the last century was produced by men who had mastered much of the technique of, say, Canova or David, but who used their technical prowess to conceal the fact that they had nothing really to say, and were simply repeating old clichés. As Reynolds put it in his *Twelfth Discourse to the Royal Academy*, 'a provision of endless apparatus, a bustle of infinite enquiry and research ... may be employed to evade and shuffle off real labour—the real labour of thinking', (words which have application, I think, in areas nearer home).[20] To be sure, the Friths, the Makarts and the Geromes and the Gibsons bustled and laboured, and filled rooms full of sculpture and walls full of canvass, but one feels a slackness in the work and an emptiness in the conception—faults, if anything, made worse by their technical facility. One feels an avoidance of a true engagement with the medium, with its difficulties and hence with its possibilities.

The danger of meretriciousness, of the avoidance of creative engagement with the medium are clearly the greater the more the artist is working through technology, with a medium which does much of the work for him. Looking at the visual and musical material we are surrounded with for so much of our lives at the start of the twenty-first century, it is hard not to feel the force of Goethe's dictum that technology in alliance with bad taste is the enemy of art most to be feared, and hard, too, not to conclude that the very ease technology affords to fantasy and imagination may not be past of the cause of our artistic decline.

The wider import of these reflections on art and technology is simply to ask whether there might not be something important missing from a life or a culture in which technical proficiency dominates over other considerations. We have a culture or, perhaps better, a civilization of great technical proficiency, one in which the steam-hammers of the last century are now museum pieces not without their own beauty. Our society is not based on some hellish Nibelheim, but is one in which dreams of power and glory have, for the most part, been replaced by a universal aspiration for comfort and entertainment. We do not have the division of labour, as envisaged by Ruskin, whose result is men divided and broken so as to be capable of one thing only, so much as the abolition of *labour* and its replacement by a huge middle class of administrators and facilita-

---

[20]   Joshua Reynolds, *Twelfth Discourse to the Royal Academy* (1789).

tors. Indeed, I see the most accurate portrait of *our* age as painted not
by Ruskin, but by de Tocqueville:

> Above this race of man stands an immense and tulerary power,
> which takes it upon itself alone to secure their gratifications and
> to watch over their fate. That power is absolute, minute, regular,
> provident and mild. It would be like the authority of a parent if,
> like that authority, its object was to prepare men for manhood;
> but it seeks on the contrary, to keep them in perpetual childhood:
> it is well content that people should rejoice provided that they
> think of nothing but rejoicing ...[21]

There is much that could be said about de Tocqueville's vision,
and much of that is not directly relevant to our topic. I would,
indeed, distance myself from the hint of big brother, of conspiracy,
of a *single* tutelary power, in what is supposed to be a description of
democracy. But if, as I believe, we are in a situation in which for
many if not most people, basic needs are satisfied without much
effort of labour, this is because of the advance of technology. At the
same time, though, technology infantilizes, encouraging people to
be satisfied with the material delights it makes so easy, and to reduce
our sense of freedom and democracy to that of chasing among the
delights and 'life-styles' they make possible. As old crafts and skills,
and the apprenticeships they required, become redundant, there is
an increasing desire for a certain type of perfection, but of a bland,
mass-produced, unindividualistic type, unconducive to the labour,
risk and insight on which true art depends.

The question this leaves us with is whether the ease in living and
in entertainment made possible by contemporary technology is con-
tributing with us to an absence of the skill and taste on which good
architecture and good art depends.

---

[21]   A. de Tocqueville, *Democracy in America,* vol. 2 (1840), part 4, chapter 6.

Chapter 10

Science and Religion

Introduction

In this paper, I want to explore certain convergences and divergences between science and religion in a way which may strike some as somewhat unusual and maybe even perverse. If this is the case, then all I can say in mitigation is that what I have to say here reflects certain thoughts and experiences I have had. If what I say strikes a chord in anyone else, so much the better: if not, then I hope that it will at least stimulate people to explore the reasons for their disagreement with me.[1]

A second preliminary remark I want to make concerns my conception of religion and of science. To take science first, as this is less controversial, what I am discussing is contemporary science, realistically understood. In other words, I am taking the theories of science on their own terms, as attempts to understand and describe the world as it really is independently of us. Whether and to what extent scientific theorizing can deliver what it promises is, of course, controversial. However I hope it can be agreed, at least for the sake of argument, that the prospect of fulfilment of such a promise is and always has been part of the reason people have had for engaging in scientific activity. That we perceive ourselves to be in a world which is independent of us and not fully transparent to our first thoughts and impressions, and that we want to find out more about this world is a large part of the motivation for scientific enquiry. Even if science is also and importantly of great instrumental value to us, its instrumental value depends on its actually delivering truths about the world, truths which of necessity are independent of our desires and perceptions.

---

[1] This paper was originally given as part of a symposium of science and religion at the annual conference of the British Society for the Philosophy of Science in Cambridge in 1990. Versions were presented subsequently at Peterhouse Cambridge and the University of Bradford.

If science is seen as revelatory of a world which has an objective and independent existence apart from us, objectivity, at least in intent, is true of religion as I understand it and want to consider it here. For my purposes the notion of a revelation of a world independent of and transcending human perceptions and desires is crucial to religion. It may be that not all religions rest strongly on the notion of a revealed truth and that the notion of revelation is one particularly attuned to the great monotheisms of semitic origin (Judaism, Christianity, Islam), although I suspect that some notion of a humanly transcendent wisdom revealed in sacred stories and texts is to be found in most religions. Nevertheless, it is the comparison between revealed religion and mature theoretical science which particularly interests me, and which will concern me in this paper.

Religion and revelation

It was in the great period of confrontation between Western science and religion, in the nineteenth century, that strenuous efforts were made by theologians and defenders of religion to prove the naturalness of religion and its conformability to human reason and value. Following the work of Hegel and of David Friedrich Strauss, a flood of books appeared, all purporting to demythologize Christianity, to explain away the miracles of the gospel, to present Jesus as a fundamentally human and historical figure, and to represent the teachings of Christianity as a combination of Hegelian rationalism and secular morality. There were, of course, dissenting voices within Christianity, Kierkegaard naturally and Cardinal Newman, who in *A Grammar of Assent* memorably insisted that a man who failed to perceive the inscrutable mysteriousness of the revealed doctrine of the Trinity did not understand what it was he was being presented with. However, it was not until the *dies ater,* the black day in August 1914 when Karl Barth found nearly all the theological teachers he respected endorsing the war on the German side, that the tide began to turn against nineteenth-century rationalistic, and modernist theology, and the associated attempt to present Jesus as a secular historical figure dispensing some comforting and comfortable version of progressivist humanism.[2] In his *Church Dogmatics,* Barth was to contrast what he referred to as religion — 'the most dangerous enemy a man has on this side of the grave' — with the wholly other and utterly

---

[2]   My picture of Barth, and the quotations from his work, are drawn from Peter
      Fuller's discussion of Barth, in his *Theoria* (London: Chatto and Windus, 1988),
      chapter 17.

transcendent nature of God. For Barth religion was a fundamentally human construction; it is 'unbelief ... the one great concern of godless man'.[3] In religion 'man bolts and bars himself against revelation by producing a substitute, by taking away in advance the very thing which has to be given by God'.[4] According to Barth, 'in Jesus the communication of God begins with a rebuff, with the exposure of a vast chasm, with the clear revelation of a great stumbling block'.[5]

For Barth, God was *totaliter aliter*, wholly other, for the revelation of whom man must prepare himself by not attempting to presume on God's nature by creating religious substitutes for revelation. In theological terms, apart from naturalistic theologizing, Barth's great enemy is Pelagianism, that is, the denial of original sin and the suggestion that man can somehow perfect himself without admitting the need for divine grace. In contrast, the attitude of the truly religious person is one of humility and patience before the otherness of God: in philosophical terms this may lead to a form of extreme realism about God's nature, an admission that all our thinking about God prior to a divine revelation might be erroneous, a product of human fantasy. Barth is right from a religious point of view, at least to the extent that a religion which does not acknowledge the otherness of God, and the consequent need for revelation and grace initiated by God, is likely to subside all too easily into anthropomorphic fantasy and wish fulfilment. Where the otherness of God is not recognized, it will be all too easy for one's conception of God to be no more than a projection of human desires and feelings, a point surely underlined by the history of nineteenth-century rationalistic theology and biblical study in which God and Jesus are very clearly embodiments of the progressive secular wisdom of the age. (For this, of course, Strauss and other theologians were ruthlessly excoriated by Nietzsche.)

I realise that speaking in this way will pose considerable problems for those who do not believe in God or in Christian revelation. If, however, the religious impulse is anything at all it must embrace something of Barth's perception. In other words, it must rest in a strong sense of the limits of human knowledge, of the objectivity and transcendence of the divine, and of the consequent distance between the divine and the human.

[3] Karl Barth, *Church Dogmatics*, vol. 1, part 2, trans. G. Thompson (Edinburgh: T. and T. Clark, 1936), p. 300.

[4] *Ibid.*, p. 302.

[5] Karl Barth, *The Epistle to the Romans* (New York, 1960), pp. 98–9.

If the divine is to be object of worship it must lack all taint of contingency: it must be something which, in Aquinas's terms, is 'subsistent existence itself, in no way determined'.[6] A being which is not subsistent would be contingent and either dependent on something else or subject to chance. In neither case would it have that completeness and self-sufficiency which would make it right to worship it. It would be a struggler in the realm of existence, as we are ourselves, more powerful perhaps, but an Olympian Kronos or Zeus rather than that eternal being which in Dante's conception turns all else and to which all else tends, and which is turned by nothing in its turn.

Equally to think of God's essence as being in any way determined as be (again in Aquinas's terms) anything other than to exist is to suggest that God's essence is somehow capturable by human thought. One might, for example, want to think of God as having power, but this would be misleading because in our conception power is the ability to overcome obstacles, but for God there are no obstacles to overcome. To speak of God, therefore, as having power is at best an analogy, misleading if taken literally and the same would be true of anything else we might want to say about God, that he (!) loves, is changeless, etc., etc. All attempts to define God's nature are implicitly to confine God, to make the divine subject to specific and implicitly limited characteristics and hence to open the way to further questioning about the whys and wherefores of God's nature, whereas the direction of the religious impulse is—as we learn from Aquinas once more and from his contemporary followers such as Lonergan—to take us to an act of understanding which leaves no further questions to be asked.

If the religious impulse stresses the absolute otherness and self-sufficiency of the divine, it will also emphasise the limitations and imperfections of the human. The doctrine of original sin is an apt expression of the sense of the chasm between the human and the divine, and an apt way of curbing human presumptuousness, and also of drawing attention to the negative and selfish elements in human character. Although such things can hardly be quantified it is not, I think, coincidental that the worst societies people have had to suffer under in the last century were inspired by dreams of the Nietzschean superman and a materialist utopia: that is, by a principled and self-conscious denial of human imperfectibility and

---

[6]   St Thomas Aquinas, *Summa Theologiae* (left incomplete by Aquinas in 1273), Ia.II.4.

ignorance. Religion, in emphasizing human frailty and the distance between all human efforts and the truly good and beautiful, should clearly have a benign tendency to curb the pretensions to knowledge and wisdom which lead to political totalitarianism. In this respect, Islam may be seen as religiously inferior to Christianity precisely because it lacks any tradition of a distinction between the two cities, the earthly and the divine. To those quick to speak of Christianity as a theocratic religion, it is worth pointing out that despite well-publicized lapses, more often than not, Christianity has survived and presented itself as a force distinct from, and often actually opposed to the earthly city and merely temporal rulers. For the Christian God's kingdom may be initiated and intimated in this world, but it is not and can never be of this world, kingdoms of this world being inherently attended by the ineliminable imperfections of the human beings who run them, even and perhaps especially when those human beings are claiming a divine sanction for their rulership.

Science and religion: convergence

As I have been emphasizing the way in which religion, properly understood, will tend to reveal truths which could not be learned by purely human means, and will stress the otherness and objectivity of the divine, let me now, in turning to science, stress the strangeness and otherness of the world-view modern science presents us with:

> Once atoms had no colour; now they have no shape, place or volume ... There is a reason why metaphysics sounds so passé, so *vieux jeu* today; for intellectually challenging perplexities and paradoxes it has been far surpassed by theoretical science. Do the concepts of the Trinity, the soul, haecceity, universals, prime matter and potentiality baffle you? They pale beside the unimaginable otherness of closed space-times, event-horizons, EPR correlations and bootstrap models.[7]

Thus van Fraassen, but now consider John Polkinghorne on the subject of the intelligibility of quantum mechanics:

> perhaps we are in the midst of ... (a long) drawn out process of education about the nature of quantum mechanical reality. If we are indeed in such a digestive, living-with-it period, it would explain something which is otherwise puzzling. A great many

---

[7] Bas van Fraassen, 'Empiricism in the philosophy of science', in *Images of Science*, ed. P.M. Churchland and C. A. Hooker (Chicago: University of Chicago Press, 1985), pp. 245–308, at p. 258.

theoretical physicists would be prepared to express some unease about the conceptual foundations of quantum mechanics ... but only a tiny fraction of them ever direct serious attention to such questions. Perhaps the majority of them are right to submit themselves to a period of subliminal absorption.[8]

The realist about science, here speaking about the quantum world, is not unconscious of the difficulty of understanding the world his physics reveals, any more than Newman was unconscious of the difficulty of understanding the doctrine of the Trinity which his Church reveals. Indeed, in some ways the cases are rather similar: taken individually the various propositions of both the Trinity and quantum mechanics are quite intelligible. The problems arise when you try to put them all together. Maybe the solution is — as Tolstoy once suggested in the case of religion, and as Polkinghorne is suggesting in the case of science — to live with the contradictions, to submit oneself to a period of subliminal absorption in the hope or expectation that eventually a fuller, less paradoxical understanding might be achieved; we have to say, however, that if a theory really is contradictory, as opposed to simply strange and apparently contradictory, merely living with the contradictions may produce a mental adjustment to them, but it will not actually do anything to diminish the problem.

The realist about the physical world, just as the realist about the divine, might well make the following observation at this point. The human mind, although attuned to reality at certain points, is nevertheless a fallible instrument when it ventures outside its intellectual ecosystem. Is it, then, surprising that it cannot formulate a non-contradictory or unproblematic account either of the divine or of the quantum world? In both cases. the theological and the scientific, an explanation is forthcoming from within the relevant field of enquiry as to why the human mind cannot form an adequate account of the objects in question. In the scientific case, it would be the evolutionary story of the human mind and perceptual faculties being adapted to the perception and understanding of medium-sized physical objects in stable conditions, and not thereby necessarily well-attuned to the very large or the very small. (While some would emphasize the undoubtedly remarkable correlation of mathematical and physical understanding in modern physics — something *very* puzzling in the seventeenth century — I would stress the paradoxes

[8]   John Polkinghorne, *The Quantum World* (Harmondsworth: Penguin Books, 1986), p. 82.

and problems of quantum theory, as evidence of less-than-complete adaptability of mind to matter at this level.) The religious, too, will not improperly emphasise the distance between the human and the divine, a distance whose effects of incomprehension on our part are exacerbated by our fall from grace.

My conclusion at this point, is that in treating their respective subject matters realistically, both science and religion lead us into areas in which the human mind is prone to stumble into paradox and contradiction, and in ways that are strikingly similar.

Natural theology

What does it mean to have a religious attitude to the world? It is, surely, to take the world and our life and consciousness as being the expression of the mind of a Creating Spirit. It is to see the world as a veil behind which a divine purpose is hidden, and intermittently revealed. It is to see meaning and will underlying the immense, unrelenting and otherwise ultimately meaningless processes of change, growth and decay which make up the physical world. (I agree, by the way, with the traditional theological distinction between deism and Christianity: a truly religious attitude, such as is evinced in orthodox Christianity, would see God or the divine as intimately but silently involved in all material activity, although this may lead to theological difficulties in making the divine subject to the sort of open future classical quantum theory, to say nothing of doctrines of human free will, envisage.)

If there is a divine face behind the material world, can we learn anything of that face and its purpose from study of the natural world, from what might broadly be called natural theology? The first and most obviously relevant feature of the natural world is its orderliness: the way in which, despite its apparent diversity, complexity and size, its operations manifest a high degree of regularity and mathematically capturable order. Against Richard Swinburne and others who have argued in this way, I do not believe we are entitled to conclude from this that there is or is likely to be a divine designer.[9] The reason for this is that given by C. S. Peirce, namely, that the universe is by definition a unique phenomenon. We have no reason *a priori* to suppose that a highly ordered one is in more need of a divine creator than a highly chaotic one. And even if, as intelligent design theorists argue, we believe that there are problems with a highly ordered universe emerging through spontaneous evolution

---

[9] Richard Swinburne, *The Existence of God* (Oxford: The Clarendon Press, 1979).

from less ordered states, we do not have any experience of supernatural agents creating worlds out of nothing so as to know whether, in the case of this universe, such a form of creation is probable or not. But we can certainly conclude from the order in the universe that *if*, on other grounds, we are prepared to see the universe as the creation of a divine mind, then that mind must be in comparison with ours, one of great subtlety and intelligence, remembering, of course, that all such comparisons are strictly relative to our perceptions and natures, and cannot give us any direct knowledge of the divine nature.

Apart from the existence of manifold types of order within the universe, the presence of conscious and self-conscious life in the universe may also be seen as having some significance for religious thought. Some may question here whether the anthropic principle has much relevance, at least in a direct form. From science alone it may be hard to deduce anything of metaphysical significance about any chain linking what went on at the moment of the Big Bang to the emergence of conscious life on this earth however many billion years later. It may well be true that a tiny difference in the conditions obtaining at the Big Bang would have rendered the emergence of conscious life impossible. But it does not follow from that that the scientific evidence supports our seeing the whole universe from the Big Bang onwards as being directed by some extra-universal intelligence to the production of life and consciousness. Whatever exists now, clearly and tautologically has to have been foreshadowed in whatever prior conditions were necessary for its development, and from this tautological truth one might be able to infer a lot from what exists now about what there was and would have to have been ages before (such as covalent bonding at a very early stage in the history of the universe). But one certainly cannot infer from any of this that those prior conditions were put there deliberately to get the later result.

On the other hand, it would seem to follow that if the conditions which have led to life and consciousness on this planet were present at the very beginning of the universe, we should not regard their presence here and now as unlikely and highly unusual — which is what might seem to be the case if we look purely at inorganic physics and what might follow from that. From the point of view of physics and the purely physical sciences, life and consciousness do indeed look extremely mysterious. They might seem to be events of such improbability as to be the product of extraordinary concatenations of chance. The conditions necessary to produce life and consciousness do require a very high number of apparently independent factors to be present simultaneously, none of which appear to have any function or adaptiveness in isolation from their role in what is produced by the whole lot acting in unison. It is precisely this which so impresses the proponents of intelligent design creationism: that only an intelligent designer could have ensured that they were all there, together, at the right time, and until triggered all together, uselessly. Like the component bits of a mousetrap lying around unconnected on the floor, which are no use at all except as brought into the design of the mousetrap maker, the elements necessary for life would appear to have no purpose independently of the life designer. This apparently inexplicable 'irreducible complexity' as they call it, leads theorists such as Michael Behe and William Dembski to postulate an intelligent designer as the cause.

But, if the conditions necessary for life were all present at the beginning of the universe, might we not conclude on the contrary that life and consciousness, far from being unlikely, are actually extremely likely (and hence as likely to occur at a number of times and places over so large and lengthy a universe as ours)? Further, if this is so, we should think of the universe, right at the beginning, as far from being dead, lifeless and to be analysed reductively in terms of inorganic science, but rather as having an in-built drive towards the production of life and consciousness. Such, anyway, is the view of Christian de Duve, in his argument against Jacques Monod, to the effect that from the very beginning the universe was pregnant with life, and the biosphere with man.[10] It is precisely the denial of this probability which unite the intelligent design theorists with many of their atheistical opponents. Both sides stress the apparently unforeseeable appearance of life, one set appealing at this point to the iterated operation of random or chance events, the other to intelligent design, both sides in a sense offering no explanation at all for what we see. But maybe what we see (life, consciousness, etc) is not so mysterious from a cosmic point of view, or is mysterious only if we take too narrow a focus, overlooking the sense in which the conditions driving the universe towards the production of life and consciousness were always there, from the very beginning, doing just that. However plausible de Duve's analysis might be, though, we

---

[10]   Christian de Duve, *Vital Dust: Life as a Cosmic Imperative* (New York: Basic Books, 1995), especially p. 288; Jacques Monod, *Chance and Necessity* (New York: Knopf, 1971).

would not be any nearer deducing the existence of a designer (this time of life and consciousness) than we were in the case of physical order. In both cases we might just have a brute fact: universe as ordered, universe as pregnant with life and consciousness, and no direct route to a Creator beyond.

But even if the presence of conscious life in itself gives us no direct argumentative path to the Creator's nature or intentions, it may, like the presence of order, give us some clues as to the inherent nature of the universe — as essentially life giving and consciousness producing — and of its Creator, if there is one. In particular it may inspire us to focus on a notion of the Creator as one having a mind, as being *the* mind behind the physical world, and as having an interest in the evolution within the world of life and consciousness, and as revealed in part by that world.

It is from our experience of ourselves and our fellows that we see certain physical movements as expressive of intention and of mind. From a religious point of view, an analogy will be drawn between our embodied consciousness manifesting its intentions in bodily movements, and the divine consciousness permeating the physical world with its meanings and intentions. (We should, though, acknowledge that the problems involved in applying the concept of consciousness to God remain immense. For consciousness in us is typically successive and directed towards objects, while, for the orthodox, God is both timeless and requires no object outside himself. It is, perhaps, not coincidental that the notion of the Trinity has often been invoked to deal with these problems, though not, it has to be said, in a way that makes them any less intractable.)

It will be clear even from these brief remarks that I do not see natural theology as providing any direct proof of the existence of God. The world revealed to us by natural science is, at best, silent on the probability of a divine Creator, even if suggestive of elements of the nature of the Creator if there is one.

Science and religion: divergences

Does science undermine religious faith? Obviously it has done so and often still does, particularly when dogmatic religion over-reaches itself and makes empirically false claims. But such activity on the part of religious believers should be condemned as an aspect of the perennial temptation which man has to create his own religion in his own image. The question we need to consider is whether science means that a religious attitude to the world and a patient search for divine revelation is in itself misguided. Playing down the probative force of natural theology means that scientific investigation can *per se* have nothing to say either for or against a fundamental religious attitude or insight. What we have in science and in religion are at bottom two separate and non-conflicting modes of discourse. Science is the attempt to classify, describe and explain natural phenomena in mathematico-reductive terms: that is, it sees the great diversity of natural phenomena in terms of the quantifiably describable operations of smaller numbers of objects or processes, which are seen as causally responsible for the phenomena. In so doing, it abstracts from what it sees as causally irrelevant properties of the phenomena, secondary qualities and much else besides. From the point of view of human experience, the scientific picture omits much that is significant and important; this is no criticism of science as such, but only of the attitude of mind which would see scientific discourse as the only valid approach to the world.

It is this scientistic frame of mind rather than science as such which poses a threat to religion, but such an attitude has a certain shallowness. For one thing, it would repudiate as meaningless questions about the totality of the process within which the objects and processes science treats of operate. One can legitimately fail to follow the religious path in seeing the totality in terms of the intention and sustaining love of a divine will, and, for the sorts of reasons adduced in the section on natural theology, discount the probative power of religious explanations of that totality: but it would surely be misguided to insist that religion is not a genuine attempt to address a genuine question, a question which science cannot within its own terms even raise. In this sense, we can agree with John Polkinghorne that theology's 'regal status lies in its commitment to seek the deepest possible level of understanding', even if we do not follow him in thinking that theology (or any actual revelation) actually achieves what it seeks.[11]

From where might one come to see the universe in personal terms. and open oneself to the possibility of some revelation of the will and intelligence behind the universe? Not, it seems, from science, which for its own purposes strives to eliminate from its world-view everything that pertains to the personal nor, owing to the inherent weakness of the attempt, from the natural theological attempt to explain the existence of the world in terms of a divine creator. But the failure of natural theology and the ambiguity of the world

---

[11] John Polkinghorne, *Science and Creation* (London: SPCK Press, 1988), p. 1.

religiously-speaking, does not mean that the religious can rest on some Barthian notion of a revelation or grace which rests on no human pre-disposition to respond to revelation. At the very least, Barth's position makes it impossible to see why we might be able to respond to a purported revelation at all, or even to see some supposed good news as potentially divinely inspired. In face of the need to find some naturalistic basis for religion, combined with the religiously enigmatic nature of the physical world, the religious impulse to see the world in more than physical terms might most plausibly be seen as stemming from within. It might thus be seen as stemming, in the first place, from certain key aspects of ourselves as conscious and self-conscious beings (which is why seeing the universe as pregnant with life and consciousness may in the end come to have a religious significance in that it is precisely our self-conscious nature which brings to the world, through us and through our reflection on it, some realisation of its ultimate significance).

We can draw attention here particularly to that sense of the meaningfulness of our lives which derives from our feeling ourselves bounden by certain duties, duties towards truth, towards goodness, towards beauty, towards our fellow men, towards our ancestors and our children, duties we neither chose nor can abrogate without irreparable damage to ourselves as human beings and to the fabric of human culture and society. The religious impulse might be seen also as a response to the experience of a natural object or a work of art as beautiful: in which we see a thing not just as 'a fragment of nature' (in Wittgenstein's phrase), but as something which mediates between our own longing for perfection and some other world in which that perfection is actually realised. A sense of the unconditional nature of these duties and feelings is undoubtedly sustained by a mature religious faith and, for many religious people at least, is made an object of legitimate concern only on the assumption that the universe itself is guided by a personal force which our sense of duty and of beauty in some dim way reflect and which speaks to us and responds to us through those feelings and insights.

Certainly any purely secular account of mortality and aesthetics such as that offered by sociobiology will struggle to make sense of the absoluteness of moral obligation and of the apparently timeless and transcendent sense of rightness one sometimes has in the experience of something beautiful. The non-religious might respond by denying the full force of alleged feeling or sense in either case or by attributing the feelings to socio-biological or psychological causes.

The latter move fails to do justice to the intuition many have that thinking of the moral or aesthetic urge in terms of prior causal conditioning does nothing to diminish in them the sense that they remain here and now bound by the absolute demands of morality and aesthetics. If prior causal conditioning extraneous to the actual rightness or wrongness of the demands were all there was to it, once we realised that most, if not all, of our moral and aesthetic attitudes were initially given to us by instinct or upbringing, we would cease to think of ourselves as unconditionally obliged by them. The former move — that of denying the existence of the feelings in any full or unconditional sense — remains a possibility: but it is at least arguable that such a denial fails to take into account very significant aspects of human experience.

Even without being religious it is possible to find a religious attitude towards one's duties and also towards our need for grace in face of our evident proneness to moral weakness and self-deception ethically and aesthetically preferable to the various secular alternatives: such as the political utopianism of a Marx or the revaluational stridency of a Nietzsche or, to come closer to home, to the existentialist melodramatics of a Russell (in 'A free man's worship') or to the self-proclaimed immoralism of a Keynes (in 'My early beliefs').[12] To treat values and obligations as a matter of choice or as founded in choice and so to be abrogated at will, as Keynes implied, and to see human beings as constrained by nothing higher than their choices and able through those choices to create utopian societies, has not had happy consequences for civilization or for culture, as I hinted earlier. It may also do violence to the psychic health of the individual.

Whatever stand one takes on the acceptability of a religious understanding of the world and of human life, though, it is clear that at a deep level, science cannot be seen to conflict with religion, if each activity is properly conceived. The one looks at the world in an impersonal way, prescinding from fundamental questions of the meaning of the whole, while the other takes the whole as given and attempts to see it in terms of personal meaningfulness. Indeed, far from being in a state of mutual conflict, if anything I have just said is correct, science and religion could even be seen to be part of a mutually sustaining harmony. A religious attitude to the world can

---

[12] Bertrand Russell, 'A free man's worship' (1903), reprinted in his *Mysticism and Logic* (London: Allen and Unwin, 1917); J.M. Keynes, 'My early beliefs' (1938), in his *Two Memoirs* (London: Rupert Hart-Davis, 1949).

motivate the desire to understand God's creation better and more truthfully, and also to respect its integrity. Equally the sense of the objectivity and otherness of the world evinced in science can put us on our guard against those religions and ideologies *which* in effect, and as Barth warned us, idolize human subjectivity.

Coda: Anknüpfungspunkte

In this chapter, I have stressed the way that both science and religion treat aspects of reality far beyond normal human experience, the grasp of which may be beyond human intellectual powers. In order to stress the otherness of the subject matter, I have taken as examples of doctrines of science and religion, quantum theory and the Trinity respectively. I have taken a realist attitude to both these doctrines, as that is the only way to take them seriously. I have also focussed on writers, like Karl Barth and John Polkinghorne who, while being realists about their subject matter, are open and explicit about the difficulties the subject matter presents to our understanding, in theological terms about the way it may prove a stumbling block to belief: a scandal to the Jews and to the Greeks, foolishness.

There is, naturally, a danger in this approach. To insist on the divide between divine revelation and our natural experience, and on the way no human language can be adequate to the reality of the divine is to invite the Humean riposte that belief in a God of whom we can know or predicate nothing without falling into error is little different from atheism and liable to lead to scepticism concerning any purported revelation expressed in human and historically definite terms. The hapless Emil Brunner received a thunderous 'Nein!' from Barth for his *Nature and Grace* of 1934 for daring to suggest that there were some points of contact (or *Anknüpfungspunkte*) between human experience and the divine. Therefore it is hardly to be wondered at that others of Barth's followers were to take the Humean road, and proclaim the death of God. Theology's great quest remains that of finding a way of speaking and thinking about the divine, while maintaining its otherness, of maintaining the reality and believability of the divine without reducing it to an evident projection of human desires and fantasies. In seeking to locate the soil of religion in human inwardness, as we have done here, is doubtless to invite the Barthian riposte that such an approach to religion is merely humanistic projection. In reply one could say that the situation is that we, as humans, have certain inklings of transcendence which *are* difficult to naturalise, but which nevertheless are real and important. So the religious quest is not to be ruled out, even if any purported fulfilment of the quest raises as many problems as it solves.

But without labouring the point, is the situation in physics so different? Physics and the other mature sciences need points of contact too, between our highly limited and highly specific experience and the wider worlds the sciences reveal to us. This is a problem which is particularly acute in the case of quantum theory, where the theory itself is beset by paradox and contradiction, but it is one which is raised by any theoretical account of the world which goes beyond whatever we take the experiential data to be. How do we know that it is the account we have which is true rather than any one of the multitude of other possible accounts, all equally consistent with our experience? The problem will continue to arise even if we follow Hacking and Giere in taking technology legitimately to extend our experience beyond what can be observed by our naked senses.[13] Cyclotrons doubtless give us experience of protons and neutrons: they do not, however, reveal to us what protons are made of or how nuclear forces work. For reasons of which philosophers of science need no reminding, science is always going to strive for ultimate explanations and discoveries, which are beyond human powers to verify or falsify. On the other hand. to push too hard in the direction of empiricism will reduce all our science to some sterile version of instrumentalism.

Both science and religion, then, present us with the problem of the Anknüpfungspunkt. In both cases credibility and intelligibility require points of contact between our human world and the worlds of which they speak. There is a sense, too, which we have briefly touched on, in which there is within our human world a need to push out into both those other worlds. In so doing we necessarily begin to lose touch with our own world and, however unwillingly, to open ourselves to scepticism and unbelief on the part of our fellows.

---

[13] Ian Hacking, *Representing and Intervening* (Cambridge: Cambridge University Press, 1983); Ronald N. Giere, *Explaining Science: A Cognitive Approach* (Chicago: University of Chicago Press, 1988).

Chapter 11

Democracy and Openness

During the recent Iraq war there was a great deal of discussion of the desirability of bringing democracy to Iraq, and indeed to other countries which were suffering under ruthless and oppressive dictatorships. There was also the thought that if Iraq had a flourishing democratic system, its benefits would become evident within the Middle East, and other peoples in the area would be encouraged to press for more democracy in their own countries. Critics who expressed doubts about any of this were accused of treating the people of the Middle East in a patronising way, implying that they were not able to do what we in the West have managed for some time.

I certainly do not want to appear patronising, nor indeed do I want to reject the idea that democracy conceived in a particular way to be defined in the course of this chapter may ultimately be the best form of government for everyone, everywhere, particularly as there are countries such as Portugal and Hungary which have clearly benefited greatly from democracy over the past few decades and are in many ways models of a transition from dictatorship to democracy. And I think that it evinces a form of pessimistic determinism to say, as many do on both left and right, that there may be countries too poor or backward to become democracies. But I do want to raise a number of questions in order to make slightly more precise just what might be meant by democracy, by the sort of democracy it might be advisable to spread around the world and the conditions which might be propitious for introducing democracy in a benign form.

Consider the following cases

1. In an Islamic country, there is a bitterly fought and often violent election. The election is won by the radical or fundamentalist party, who have made it clear that they will institute Sharia law and various other practices regarded by others inside and outside the country as repressive. The army steps in and annuls the election, setting up a military dictatorship with its own different type of repres-

sion. One effect of this is that the country becomes a major exporter of asylum seekers, some of whom join Islamic terrorist groups outside the country around the world.

2. An African country is divided on tribal lines. People in that country vote almost entirely on tribal lines. One tribe is significantly larger than the others. There are democratic elections, but they are always won by one party, so democratic tribalism paves the way for a one party state.

3. A central European country is suffering from a continuing economic and social crisis following a disastrous war. Elections happen frequently, but tend to produce weak governments, which simply exacerbates the crisis. A new party arises, led by a strong leader, who identifies groups to blame for the continuing crisis. He promises to rid the country of instability and to curb the influence of the offending groups. The voters give him this power, and he then uses his majority in the democratically elected parliament to he set himself up as dictator.

4. Another Western country has for a number of years (with just one break) been run by a party of the social-democratic left, which has won a series of elections. This party is in fact financed by the trade unions and led by a combination of doctrinaire socialists and rabble rousing populists. The state runs pretty well everything including what the party's official doctrine refers to as 'the commanding heights of the economy' (i.e., decrepit, inefficient and over-manned steel, coal, aircraft, rail and motor industries, to say nothing of telecommunications and other public utilities), and controls (or attempts to control) the whole economy. Nevertheless, despite or perhaps because of all this, there are damaging strikes every year in both public and private sectors, which usually end in 'meaningful' settlements after 'constructive' negotiations (i.e., pay rises for the strikers of between ten and twenty per cent or more). Inflation is rampant, twenty per cent or so per year; taxes are as high as ninety-eight per cent on the highest incomes; there is capital flight; in some cities the dead are unburied and rubbish is uncollected for weeks; the government has to go the IMF to get baled out and is forced to institute draconian economic measures. It loses the next election, after its leader and the country's Prime Minister has returned from a mid-winter holiday in the Caribbean allegedly uttering the immortal phrase 'Crisis? What crisis?'

A few preliminary comments on our cases

The first case is based on the current situation in Algeria, following the success of the Islamic Salvation Front (FIS) in the first round of elections in 1991, and the army's cancelling of the second round in 1992, in which the FIS was heading for a clear majority. One lesson which might be drawn from it is that the effects of violent political events in one country may not be confined to that country. In this sense, then, we all have an interest in what happens in Algeria; we all have to consider whether democracy is or is not desirable in such a country, and whether we would support the intervention of the army in an election in circumstances like those which obtained in Algeria. (It is worth noting that completely open, free and fair elections in Egypt and elsewhere in the Islamic world, including possibly Saudi Arabia, would probably see victories by fundamentalists; but it is also worth noting that the allegedly 'secular' government currently ruling in Algeria is actually a brutal and ruthless dictatorship, and that in its attitude to women is currently trying hard to appear as hard-line as its fundamentalist critics.)

The second case might be Zimbabwe (or many other African states). But let us suppose it is Zimbabwe over the past twenty-five years or so, where the ruling party owed its success, initially at least, to its roots in the majority tribe. Actually in 2002 even some of the President's own supporters were beginning to turn against him, and he was in some danger of losing the election that year. Whether he would actually have lost it or not in a genuinely free election, we will never know, because the population was assisted in its democratic deliberations and in its vote-casting by groups of the President's supporters, armed thugs known as 'war veterans', whom the police, far from controlling, actually helped. But this was only the final stage on Zimbabwe's route from democracy to a one-party state with no respect for human rights, which was only underlined by the events following the 2008 election. We need to ask whether this passage was inevitable in the circumstances, and also perhaps about the meaning of fair elections.

The third case is a somewhat simplified sketch of Germany in 1933. The National Socialists under Hitler together with the parties which supported the Nazis did win an election that year, the last election in Germany until after the war. A democratically elected leader did then annul democratic procedures (by means of the Enabling Act, which gave the Chancellor power to make laws without consulting Parliament), leading to what philosophers have dubbed 'the paradox of democracy': that is, a democratic system democratically voting away its own right to operate democratically. In this context we might also note what has happened more recently in Europe; when the European Union attempted in effect to negate the democratically decided inclusion of Jörg Haider's Freedom Party into the Austrian government, and also when, in the French Presidential election of 2002, the whole apparatus of government and the media abandoned all pretence at impartiality and directed itself, unfairly many thought, to defeating Le Pen. So should democratic institutions act undemocratically in attempting to defeat those they see as enemies of democracy and likely if they got power to undermine democracy?

The final example is a sketch of Britain in 1979 and of the atmosphere leading up to 1979; unlike the other stories, it does have a reasonably satisfactory ending. The new leader was Mrs Thatcher who, among other things, took on the trade unions and curbed their undemocratic power. She got inflation down, privatised much of the economy, including the public utilities, and she reduced taxes generally (while actually generating more revenue for the government). But perhaps we could also consider the less happy case of Chile under Allende where a democratically elected government appeared to its critics to be expropriating private property on a large scale and was plunging the country into severe social instability, which was ended, after a fashion, not by an elected monetarist regime, but by an army coup. But when does a democratic redistribution of wealth become expropriation, and when does giving workers their legitimate trade union rights become syndicalist abuse of a labour monopoly (in which collectivised labour can hold a country to ransom, by means of closed shops combined with aggressive and often violent strikes in key industries)?

Aristotle and Plato

So from our examples, we have a budget of questions, too many and too complex to answer or even discuss in any detail. But clearly they all show ways in which democracy is not just being used to further undemocratic ends — which it clearly is in the cases considered — but more precisely, democratic structures are being used to decrease openness and freedom in the society as a whole. Underlying all the questions and cases is the meaning of a distinction made first by Aristotle in his *Politics* (1279a16). In Aristotle's own words it is clear that those constitutions which aim at the common good are right, as being in accord with absolute justice; while those which aim only at the good of the rulers are wrong. They are all deviations from the right constitutions. They are like the rule of the master over the slave, whereas the state is an association of free men.

While it is easy for us in the twenty-first century to see in dictatorships and oligarchies the type of deviation from the good constitution of which Aristotle speaks, it is less natural to see democracies in those terms; less natural, perhaps, but as our examples suggest, not necessarily incorrect. For Aristotle there are two ways in which rule by the majority can turn out, the first which he calls polity and the second he calls democracy. Polity is political control exercised by the mass of the populace in the common interest, whereas democracy is when the mass uses its power to further the sectional interests of the many, or as Aristotle says, of the men without means. Democracy is when the poor and numerous hold office, and use their office for the benefit of the poor and numerous, often using this office to despoil the better off (what might be *called* redistribution, but which may actually be little better than the legalised theft and the expression of the primitive resentment of the less well off against those who may well have worked hard to achieve their positional and economic superiority).

Democracy, as opposed to polity, may then lead to that characteristic vice of the many, a spirit of small-mindedness and of its working up by demagogues. Here, of course, Aristotle walks in the footsteps of his teacher, Plato. In Plato's *Republic* we find an almost wholly negative characterisation of democracy. Democracy arises in the first place when the majority in an oligarchic society begin to realise that the minority of wealthy people who are ruling are in fact no better than the majority, and because of their corruption by wealth, weak too. So in a movement which anticipates the awakening of the slave class in Hegel, the poor use their numerical might to take over from their masters. A form of egalitarian diversity and liberty ensues, which is close to anarchy in that there is no real authority and no hierarchy of value. There is no real constancy, either individual or collective; the same people appear one day as sybarites, the next day as ascetics; one day they praise military virtue, the next business values, the next study, and so on; and the same goes for the fashions in society as a whole. Those rule who manage to convince the majority that they are the 'people's friends'.

Among the people themselves, in the name of liberty, lower passions begin to dominate, and there is also a cult of youth:

> the parent falls into the habit of behaving like the child, and the child like the parent; the father is afraid of his sons, and they show no fear or respect for their parents in order to assert their freedom ... the schoolmaster timidly flatters his pupils, and the pupils make light of their masters as well as of their attendants. Generally speaking, the young copy their elders, argue with them, and will not do as they are told; while the old, anxious not to be thought disagreeable tyrants, imitate the young and condescend to enter into their jokes and amusements.
>
> *Republic*, 563a-b.

Eventually, in the ensuing lawlessness, democratic despots become dominant, paving the way for straightforward tyranny.

We do not need to accept everything Plato says to see that, phenomenologically speaking, he acutely captures some of democracy's inherent dangers and possible outcomes, a point to which we will return. But he is too negative, in part I conjecture because he holds a false view of political truth. It will be recalled that for Plato the ideal republic was one which would be ruled by philosopher kings, intellectuals who had devoted their lives to the study of dialectic, cut off from the rest of humanity and from ordinary human concerns. They would acquire a form of wisdom superior to the rest of humanity, and, armed with this wisdom, they would be able to rule and administer society with perfect justice. From this perspective any attempt to involve the majority of ordinary people without philosophical training in matters of government would necessarily corrupt the pure truth of the philosophers, and it would also mean that society would be dominated by factions and self-interest (much like what Plato saw in the Athenian Assembly and its Council, where those he believed signally unfitted to govern held sway, and, whose court of 501 jurors had, of course, condemned Socrates to death).

But Plato's model of ethical knowledge is fatally flawed. Morality and justice are not *a priori* concepts, discoverable by dialectic or pure reason alone. Without denying their objectivity, it is important to appreciate that what we know about these things emerges from human experience and from what we discover about human flourishing through the experience of life. They are, to that degree, empirical matters, constrained to a considerable degree by what we learn about the experiential interplay between human possibility and human limitations.

But even if this were not so, Plato's model of politics, too, is fatally flawed. For his rulers to be able to rule successfully, they would have to have knowledge of the whole of society, in order to see what policies were needed and how those policies turned out. It is just this knowledge which they are denying themselves by failing to involve the whole population in their decision making. For, however well intentioned and learned legislators might be, all actions and policies have unforeseeable and unintended consequences. To take a simple example, it might be felt that in a situation of housing shortage, private landlords are taking unfair advantage of their tenants by pushing rents up too high and threatening those who do not or cannot pay with homelessness. So the government acts to control rents and tenure to protect the security of tenants, which would in all probability be both just and popular democratically. But unfortunately the landlords respond by ceasing to let their property to secured tenants, whose situation is actually worsened as the supply of property to rent dries up.

No doubt it would be said that all this is now well known. Any future rent acts would be drafted to close off this eventuality, and that is no doubt true. But what is now well known was not well known when, in response to public pressure, British governments did first introduce rent acts in the 1960s, with the effects I have just described. No doubt future rent acts will have other, as yet unpredictable, consequences. The general point being made here is that the successful ruling of any society will require a constant flow of information to the rulers from the ruled, both in order to decide policy, but, even more important, to learn the effects of policies. It is just this flow of information which Plato's rulers are denied by their situation, and it will also be denied to any self-enclosed group of rulers who are insulated from the general public by groups of flatterers, place men and intermediaries who tell them only what they want to hear (which will be the inevitable effect of any dictatorship). Effective rule requires openness in the body politic, an openness which democracy is well suited to supply.

This was well understood by Aristotle in his defence of polity. In general, according to him, when there are many people, each is likely to have some share of virtue and practical wisdom, which is why he wants matters of value generally to be decided by the consensus of the many and the wise; the wise, to be sure, but also the many because of their experience, individual and collective. And although individually each of the many may be inferior in understanding to the experts, collectively they are likely to be as good or better.

Negatively, too, if we exclude the mass of people from politics we are likely to be incubating a 'huge hostile element in the state' (*Politics*, 1281b31). True enough, but the positive argument is stronger and more interesting. It is precisely the point we have been making, that those who best understand the effects of policies are those directly affected by them:

> there are tasks of which the actual doer will be neither the best nor the only judge ... An obvious example is house building: the builder can certainly form an opinion on a house, but the user, the household manager will be an even better judge ... and it is the diner not the cook that pronounces upon the merits of a dinner.

> *Politics*, 1282a17-23.

In our days of arrogant architects raised to peerages and celebrity chefs, Aristotle's common sense is salutary. And anathema as it might be to politicians and bureaucrats, in evaluating practical matters and particularly in public politics, the user or consumer should be in pole position and not the producer or planner.

Then again, while Aristotle is unillusioned about the possibilities of democratic corruption and the buying of votes, he also points out that the more power is diffused, the less the possibility of corruption; many are less easily corrupted than one or a few (and, as we have learned, corruption can take many forms and also can occur even among the most incorruptible once they have got power). But, more than that point, obvious enough to us if not to Plato, Aristotle also points out that if the people in the middle of society take a hand in politics, the results are likely to be better than if either the arrogance of the rich or the envy of the very poor are in the ascendant. 'Where the middle element' as he puts it, 'is large, there least of all arise factions and divisions among the citizens' (1296a8), and this desirable condition is more likely to obtain in large democratic states than in any other type of constitution, given the natural tendency of oligarchies, aristocracies and monarchies to concentrate wealth and honours on the few — and hence to prepare the way for factional strife.

But this middle element, if mature, numerous and powerful, will also be able to counter-balance the tendency in democracy to egalitarianism of a radical sort, which is inherent in the democratic assumption that at a certain level every man — and opinion — is equal or deserving of equal attention. What we are calling openness does indeed demand an assumption of this sort, because, for reasons already touched on, we do want every voice to have some sort of say and we do not want people to be dismissed and treated as nonpersons; the difficulty is to maintain this fundamental premise without lapsing into the potentially rancorous egalitarianism which would treat all opinions as equally worthwhile or valid, however well thought out and studied, and dismiss any differences of wealth and position, however obtained, as in themselves objectionable. And it is at this point that a strong and stable middle group in a society may be able to steer policy and practice in directions which are both democratic and measured in value and judgement. Of course, as Aristotle hints in his negative remarks about the bad form of democracy, a successful middle group and a successful polity will be far easier to establish in a society in which everybody has a degree of economic stake in that society and economic security to boot. The historic connection between liberal democracy and the ownership of property is not coincidental.

In sum, then, Aristotle, while no uncritical admirer of democracy, actually gives us some very substantial reasons for thinking that the beneficent form of democracy—polity as he puts it, a democracy dominated by a secure and stable middle group—is likely to produce better decisions, better feedback, less corruption and more political wisdom overall than rule by one man or a few or by some faction simply pursuing its own interests unchecked or by rulers unprepared to listen to all those they rule. This point in Aristotle is so strong that, given the high likelihood of corruption and stupidity in both monarchy and oligarchy, one wonders why he did not come straight out and declare polity the best form of government simpliciter. But it would, of course, have to be a polity in which general consensus through the middle group restrained the brute exercise of power by a bare majority acting purely in its own narrow and immediate interests.

De Tocqueville

Not even the most superficial consideration of democracy can avoid a brief reference to de Tocqueville's unparalleled analysis of democratic mores and the democratic temperament in Democracy in America.[1] De Tocqueville was, of course, talking about early nineteenth-century America, a society he admired for its peaceful-

---

[1]   A. de Tocqueville, *Democracy in America* (1835–40), in the Fontana Press edn (London: 1994), trans. George Lawrence.

ness, its community spirit and for its way of settling differences. Nevertheless he did have considerable reservations about some aspects of democratic America, mostly based on its tendency to a form of egalitarian culture. In this he was following in Plato's footsteps, for Plato had also criticised the egalitarian tendencies of democracy, as we have seen, but in one significant respect de Tocqueville departs from the Platonic analysis, and arguably he is more accurate at least as far as modern democracies go. For where Plato sees democracy as characterised by a scandalous diversity of taste, morality and attitude—a sort of Nietzschean pandemonium of free spirits—de Tocqueville emphasises democracy's tendency to conformism beneath any superficial diversity.

Where a society is stratified and men are unalike, the few who are really enlightened and learned may be accepted as such, and so become able to wield great power; whereas 'the nearer men are to a common level of uniformity, the less they are inclined to believe baldly in any man or class. But they are readier to trust the mass, and public opinion becomes more and more the mistress of the world'.[2]

In a democracy, although people hate being thought worse than their neighbour and dislike obeying superiors, because of the general egalitarian spirit each person actually has a low opinion of himself and 'thinks that he is born for nothing but the enjoyment of vulgar pleasures'.[3] Democracy dislikes the idea of high ideals beyond those of material self-interest—which is why democracies tend to be unwilling to go to war—but the obverse of this good quality is that all too easily in a democracy a spirit of cultural and moral mediocrity reigns. So along with the dogma of intellectual equality goes a practice of universal weakness. In democracies individuals are weak and conformist, and expect the whole to do for them what they should be doing for themselves, did they really respect themselves or their freedom.

And this paves the way for what de Tocqueville memorably referred to as democratic despotism, a society ruled over by a schoolmaster rather than a tyrant, but despotic nonetheless in its combination of centralisation and popular sovereignty. Over this society and its people

> stands an immense, protective power which is alone responsible
> for securing their enjoyment and watching over their fate ... It

---

[2] *Ibid.*, p. 435.

[3] *Ibid.*, p. 632.

would resemble parental authority if, fatherlike, it tried to prepare its charges for a man's life, but on the contrary it only tries to
keep them in perpetual childhood. It likes to see its citizens enjoy
themselves, provided that they think of nothing but enjoyment.
It gladly works for their happiness but wants to be the sole agent
and judge of it ... Thus it daily makes the exercise of free choice
less useful and rarer, restricts the activity of free will within a
narrower compass, and little by little robs each citizen of the
proper use of his own faculties ... It covers the whole of social life
with a network of petty, complicated rules that are both minute
and uniform, through which even men of the greatest originality
and most vigorous temperament cannot force their heads above
the crowd. It does not break men's will, but softens, bends and
guides it; it seldom enjoins, but often inhibits action; it does not
destroy anything, but prevents much being born; it is not at all
tyrannical, but it hinders, restrains, enervates, stifles, and stulti-
fies so much that in the end each nation is no more than a flock of
timid and hardworking animals with the government as its
shepherd.[4]

De Tocqueville is, of course, sketching an ideal type here, the way
he thinks that a certain type of egalitarian democracy is likely to go.
Much of what he says has come to pass in Western Europe, with its
social chapters, its universal provision of state welfare, its incessant
regulation of more and more tracts of our lives and its obsessive
paternalism masquerading as health and safety. Despotism may be a
strong description of our form of life, surely too strong if one thinks
of Saddam Hussein's Iraq, say, and it is certainly not a tyranny. But
that there is a servile spirit in our commonly held assumption that
the state will look after, regulate, determine and protect our lives
and behaviour in ever increasing detail is less easy to deny. We
might also recall that as long ago as 1859, in chapter five of *On
Liberty*, John Stuart Mill had warned that a universal state education
would be little more than a device for moulding all men alike, inherently mediocre, essentially conformist, and fundamentally illiberal.
Yet in many of our societies and for many of our citizens, universal
state education (or at least a heavy preponderance of free state provision in a mixed system) has come to seem a cornerstone of civilised
existence (along with analogous state health and welfare schemes).
Deaf to the warnings of nineteenth century commentators like de
Tocqueville and Mill, we are then surprised when the results of state

---

[4]   *Ibid.*, p. 691.

education and other forms of welfare are dire throughout Europe and the USA.

Critical as he is of some tendencies of democracy, it seems to be that in one respect de Tocqueville is not critical enough. He clearly thinks that, as part of its general softening effect, democracy will actually make people more humane and gentle, with their passions 'naturally restrained, imagination limited and pleasures simple'.[5] He may be right in his expectation that public policy in a democracy is likely to pay lip service at least to values of humanity and even gentleness, but unlike Plato he clearly did not foresee the extent to which egalitarian assumptions in the populace at large, unchecked by standards of the right way to behave might well issue in individual and group behaviour infused with anger, aggression and resentment; and he paid little attention to the role the mass media, that quintessentially democratic phenomenon, might play in undermining standards of behaviour and conduct. And neither Plato nor de Tocqueville spent much time considering the effect egalitarian assumptions about value might have in a society in which there is not just one, but many so-called cultures jostling for position in a confined social space — maybe because neither would have thought such a society possible, let alone actual.

Democracy, freedom and openness

Our initial examples suggested that democracy is not in itself sufficient for good government. Majority rule can be used to tyrannise, to quash good government, to restrict freedom and to close down openness in a society. Both Aristotle and Plato show us why this will happen when a majority uses democracy to further its own interests at the expense of the whole.

But, unlike Plato, Aristotle gives us some strong reasons to think that, generally speaking, democracy might be the best form of government, provided that there is openness within the democracy and provided that there is within that society a middle consensus, or a consensus of the middle, about what is or is not tolerable, and provided that such a consensus generally prevails.

One could argue that in our first three examples of disordered democracy (a Sharia ruled Algeria, Zimbabwe, Weimar Germany), there was or would be neither openness nor the sort of middle consensus Aristotle is seeking, and that in our fourth example there was danger of the essential consensus failing, but that Mrs Thatcher, by

---

[5]   *Ibid.*, p. 690.

her apparently tough and, among substantial sections of the population, deeply unpopular measures, restored it. That may seem a surprising thing to say of a leader who publicly professed to despise consensus and who, according to opinion polls and to what one hears on television, is personally still the most hated British prime minister of recent decades; but it is worth recalling that Tony Blair, initially the most popular of recent prime ministers and with a huge parliamentary majority to boot, felt no impulsion whatsoever to reverse her policies on trade unions, inflation or privatisation. In other words these supposedly controversial measures, despite initial appearance, actually reflected the consensus in British society, but one which had been hidden and distorted by political activity over some two or more decades.

In fact de Tocqueville gives us a useful clue to analysing the apparent paradox of some unpopular reforms actually being more consensual than what they replaced. The democratic state, as depicted by de Tocqueville, has a tendency to take over more and more of the lives of the citizens. But the more the state grows, the more power and money it has at its disposal. This over-weighty state then becomes a prize to be fought over by any and all vested interest groups, by all in fact who seek power, wealth and influence in the society. So far from incarnating or mediating consensus within a society, the state and its institutions become prizes to be fought over and won. Reforms, such as Mrs Thatcher's which weaken the power of the state or the inequitable legal status of bodies representing sectional interests (such as trade unions), then remove a damaging degree of conflict from the political arena, and leave it to the citizens to fight their differences out among themselves; in these circumstances the state becomes more like a referee in the fight, rather than yet another player in the game, whose decisions will be (more or less) accepted in a consensual spirit, provided only they can be seen to embody a degree of impartiality.

This analysis, encouraging as it may seem, however does rest on one assumption: that at a deep level, at a level deeper than day to day politics, there is within a society consensus on basic values, attitudes and behaviour. To what extent does de Tocqueville's conformity of public opinion represent such a consensus? There are two reasons to be cautious here. First, for the reasons already looked at, a bloated de Tocquevillean state is likely by its very existence and nature to promote divisions within society, and so to undermine consensus, at least on the surface. But more profoundly, the public opinion which holds sway in such a state is likely to be both fickle and, ultimately at least, subversive of long-term standards of value. This is because of its egalitarian roots: from this perspective any view is as good as any other, and the only way of deciding between views is majority opinion. Majority opinion is not determined by long-lasting standards and criteria, but is notoriously subject to media manipulation and distortion, as Plato recognised. And in a society which is dominated by majority public opinion, traditional values and standards are likely to come under assault, particularly if they seem to be standing in the way of instant gratification or egalitarian attitudes.

From this point of view and in an egalitarian democracy, public opinion is likely to destroy the roots of a true 'middle' consensus in a society, one which is based on long-held and settled values, which are taken within the society to have the sanction of some hierarchy of value beyond mere majority opinion as manufactured in the mass media. As Aristotle notes, 'the most extreme democracy, in which all share, is something which not every state can tolerate; and it is not likely to last unless it is well held together by its laws and customs' (*Politics*, 1319b) and, he would no doubt add, by the weight of a middle group reasonable in its attitudes and respectful of those laws and customs. I have been reluctant to speak of this middle group as a middle class, not only because there is no guarantee that with a certain sort of education (or mis-education) the middle classes, as defined in socio-economic terms, will not become highly subversive of law and custom; but, even more, because there can be occasions when it is precisely the working classes which have the most solid and unspoken regard for settled law and custom, as conservative politicians from Disraeli to Mrs Thatcher have recognised. But it is just this often unspoken respect for laws and customs, together with a sense of value beyond what we chose for ourselves on the basis of our own decisions which binds a society together which is going to be missing in a society run by public opinion.

This thought takes us on to a further consideration of openness. I have argued that some formally democratic societies fail through lack of openness (as do many undemocratic societies as well, of course). This might be particularly the case when a majority insist on imposing their religion or moral code on minorities and reject any criticism or feedback on the effect of their codes and policies. For all its democracy in a formal sense, such a society might well be as repressive and unfree as other countries which are formally dictatorships.

The question, though, is how we are to secure openness in a society. Some who have followed what I have been saying about openness and democracy will be aware that Aristotle is not its only source. In the background of my remarks about the unintended consequences of policies and about the need for openness to correct their defects is Karl Popper's *The Open Society and Its Enemies*.[6] Popper was also very aware of the possibility of democracies lacking openness, but he was also sceptical of the efficacy of formal ways of securing openness. For openness is a question fundamentally of attitude within a society and among its rulers. For Popper constitutions guaranteeing fundamental freedoms, just as democracy itself, can have a role to play in a tolerant and humane society, but they are certainly not enough to guarantee it, as numerous examples from the apparently liberal Soviet constitution of 1918 to the current wrangling over the European constitution are enough to show. In Popper's own terminology, if you want openness in an institution you need a spirit of openness in those manning it — and, I would add, if you think that spirit is likely to be found among Europe's current commissioners and fonctionaires, who have for decades floated in a culture of secrecy, evasion and unaccountability, whatever the formal constraints on them, then you are likely to be disappointed.

Multiculturalism and democratic consensus

It is, of course, a further question as to whether a spirit of openness on its own is enough to foster a tolerant and humane society, and one which is becoming increasingly relevant because of a further development in democracy. The development to which I refer is institutional multi-culturalism, that is the notion that one can have different groups, with very different values and world views, all accorded equal standing as groups within a single society. Multiculturalism is usually contrasted with mono-culturalism, according to which, while individuals qua individuals have equal rights under the law, it is assumed that the public institutions and values of the society will reflect those of some dominant and homogeneous group. In a mono-cultural society, immigrants from different places and cultures may well be admitted and even welcomed, but in the public sphere they will be expected to conform to the nation's public attitudes and values.

---

[6]   K.R. Popper, *The Open Society and Its Enemies*, 2 vols (London: Routledge and Kegan Paul, 1945, and subsequent editions).

In practice, of course, few, if any, societies are (or have ever been) wholly mono-cultural, but it is only recently that multi-culturalism has begun to be advocated as a positive value in itself. One recent effect of democratic egalitarianism within the liberal democracies of the West has been to weaken assumptions of superiority about any values, including often the public values of one's own society, and this weakening of faith in current values may also include scepticism about liberal individualism itself (often said to be just the value of the dominant culture(s) in the West). At the same time, whether as effect or cause, there has been a growth of identity politics, the belief that individuals are constituted as individuals by the groups with which, by ethnicity or religion they do identify. Mass immigration and a realisation of the extent to which specific groups within apparently mono-cultural societies have been done down in the past have combined to produce a growing clamour in many Western societies for recognition of group rights and exceptions from national norms in fields such as employment, health, welfare and above all education. The multi-cultural position is that group rights and differences should be recognised in law and practice more generally, and, in the jargon, 'diversity celebrated', not just in peripheral and private things like restaurants and clothes shops, but in the public institutions the very heart of our democracies.

How would a multi-cultural society with differences recognised in all its institutions and welcoming even radical differences among its citizens in such things as religion actually hold together? According to Professor Lord Parekh, an influential proponent of such a view, commitment to the political community itself would be enough to hold a society together, where that politics is itself conceived in terms of a commitment to hold dialogue on differences between groups and positions, rather than resorting to violence or to marginalising dissenters or (if one does belong to a dissenting group) retreating into a self-imposed ghetto. This commitment does not presuppose any shared cultural, ethnic, religious or any other characteristic, nor does it 'involve sharing common substantive goals... nor a common view of (the country's) history which they may read differently, nor a particular economic or social system about which they may entertain different views'; and it can go along with criticising 'the prevailing form of government, institutions, policies, values, ethos and dominant self-understanding in the strongest possible terms', but none of this should be regarded as disloyal 'so long as their basic commitment to dialogue is not in doubt'.[7]

That a commitment to a certain form of openness alone might be sufficient to bind a community together is both radical and reductive, and as I argue further in Chapter 14, is in a certain sense, utopian. While a fuller treatment of these points will be found in the later essay, it might be observed here that dialogue alone will not necessarily prevent either sharp divisions or feelings of being marginalized. In all sorts of areas decisions have to be made in a society, and particularly where fundamental moral differences are at issue (e.g., on abortion, women's rights, arranged marriages, euthanasia, and so on), at least some may feel unable to accept them, even after as much dialogue as anyone could want. Perhaps this might seem initially to imply a minimal state, where very few decisions have to be made as matters of public policy, and this would certainly be in line with what I suggested earlier in discussing de Tocqueville, but before one becomes too sanguine about that, remember that a minimal state would itself be morally unacceptable to those who believe in a collectivist conception of social justice and in state directed education, health and welfare.

But leaving aside here the problem of disputes irresolvable by dialogue (which is developed in more detail in Chapter 14) we need to consider whether any human group could function effectively as a society without something more held in common than a shared commitment to the political process. Does this conception itself, as I argue at greater length in Chapter 14, embody a utopian fallacy?

All the societies of which we have knowledge have, to a greater or lesser degree, had shared sentiments, shared allegiances, shared traditions and shared values. Whether a society would be possible which dispensed with all of this — as Parekh and the multiculturalists advocate — might fairly be said by its advocates to be something which we could not know in advance of an experiment along these lines. But that does not, I think, get to the root of the problem.

What the multiculturalists need to consider are the conditions required for the successful operation of the type of politics they advocate. The type of dialogue — and of tolerance and openness — which they see as underpinning the ideal political set-up is not something which comes from nowhere. As our earlier examples of flawed democracies indicate, much more is needed for a successful democ-

---

[7]   Bhikhu Parekh, *Rethinking Multiculturalism* (Houndmills: Macmillan, 2000), pp. 341–2.

racy than a formal commitment to majority rule. And as Aristotle and Plato and de Tocqueville show, democracy itself has certain inherent tendencies which militate against what might be called societies of free and responsible citizens, living in harmony and fruitful dialogue. In order to counter-balance these tendencies, Aristotle's insistence on a secure and stable middle group in society — no doubt appealing to some settled values and sentiments within that society — seems plausible enough.

But the existence and influence within a society of such a group within a liberal democracy itself depends on the sharing of certain values in that society. These values will typically be those of liberal democracy itself, values which will permit a society to be open, flexible, reasonable and tolerant on the one hand, but without compromising its fundamental stability and commitment to certain conceptions of human autonomy and flourishing on the other. These liberal democratic values historically are Western values, deriving from a long history, with its origins in Greece and Rome, in Christianity and in a history of religious wars and persecutions from which emerged ultimately a culture of rights and tolerance. These values are not necessarily so esteemed in other places and traditions, where our stress on autonomy, tolerance and human rights *can* seem like yet another manifestation of Western imperialism.[8] In other words, the form of politics which the multi-culturalists see as potentially bridging the gap between Western and other world-views itself depends on acceptance of a substantive set of values, which in history have emerged most notably within the Western world, and which for that very reason may well be denied by other potential participants in the multi-cultural democracy.

I am not saying that these values cannot be accepted by others and in other traditions. As I happen to think that these values have a more than local validity, and that they are actually justifiable in terms of certain basic requirements for human flourishing in general, I think it patronising to say any such thing, as I said at the start. But we should not expect them, and the political institutions they have given rise to in the West, albeit intermittently and imperfectly, to take root elsewhere or even to flourish in our own societies without certain conditions being fulfilled. And chief among these conditions is a general agreement on what I have been calling liberal democratic values, such as tolerance and respect for individual free-

---

[8] On this point see Samuel P. Huntingdon, *The Clash of Civilisations and the Remaking of World Order* (London: Touchstone, 1998), p. 194.

dom, together with a middle group in society both large enough and confident enough to ensure that these values persist. But it is not possible for such a middle group to flourish unless its members feel an allegiance to and a stake in their country in a more substantive way than the bare commitment to engage in a Parekhian political discussion. Being a multi-cultural 'community of communities' as Parekh advocates, or simply imposing majority rule will not be enough to get the virtues we really want when we advocate democracy as a form of government. We need a population broadly secure economically and also able to identify positively with the history and core values of their community; and, for a successful democracy not prone to the defects of our four initial examples, among those core values will have to be those of tolerance, of openness in the sense discussed earlier, and, within the limits imposed by the need to share what Aristotle calls the common view necessary to bind any community together, of liberal individualism itself. History shows that we would be unwise to expect any of this to appear out of nothing, by fiat or by military intervention, unless there is already in the life of the populations concerned some elements of the traditions necessary to support such values.

Chapter 12

Hayek and Popper

The Road to Serfdom and The Open Society

From the perspective of the first decade of the twenty-first century it is hard to put oneself in the frame of mind which dominated intellectual life in Britain and much of Europe sixty years ago, particularly over the question of socialism and state planning. Sixty years ago most intellectuals seemed to take socialism for granted. Many were or had been communists; many others were fellow travellers, and many of those who were not were, in Lenin's odious terms, 'useful idiots'. We in the West were, after all, allies of Soviet Communism in the fight against Nazism and fascism, Stalin was familiarly known as 'Uncle Joe', and in the British armed forces education officers were vigorously promoting the virtues of leftist approaches to post-war reconstruction. The Spanish Civil War, only a few years earlier, had rallied many European intellectuals to the republican cause. In Britain at least one would have been hard put to find a voice favouring the nationalists outside the small and supposedly benighted ranks of right-wing Catholicism.

We will leave aside the intriguing question as to what might have been the future of post-war Europe had the communists won in Spain. With the Nazi-Soviet pact of 1938, had Spain gone communist, would there even have been a post-war Europe remotely analogous to the one which actually arose? And even if there had been, would a communist regime in Spain have confined its influence and activity to the Iberian peninsula? In 1945, such questions could hardly have been raised at all, and even now this chapter of counter-factual history might be too hot a potato to handle, and would in any case take us too far from our theme.

Back in the mid-1940s, however, there were a few voices, neither Catholic nor reactionary, raised against the political consensus. How influential they were on the audience they were aimed at that time is perhaps hard to judge, given the almost wilful insistence there seemed to be on giving communism an easy ride, and given the uncritical faith there was in central state planning being a key element in reconstruction. But what we can say in retrospect is that Hayek and Popper, along with Arthur Koestler and George Orwell, were telling people all they needed to know about the intellectual weaknesses, the practical difficulties and the moral defects of collectivism. As time went on, no doubt these ideas entered the intellectual body politic (though to what extent they have been fully absorbed is a question to which we will return). But in the 1940s their enunciation and development was bold intellectually and morally, the more so as they did not depend on any standpoint more contentious than that of a secular liberalism.

The Road to Serfdom appeared in 1944 and *The Open Society and Its Enemies* in 1945.[1] Although Popper acknowledges the 'interest and support' of Hayek, which enabled his book to be published, when he wrote *The Open Society* (in New Zealand) he had not read *The Road to Serfdom*, though he had read some of Hayek's earlier writings (see also *The Open Society*, 1, p. 285). In the circumstances, as we would expect, there are significant similarities and also significant differences between the two authors and their respective books. As I will attempt to show, both similarities and differences became more pronounced as time went on. But to begin with, I will present an overview of relevant themes from each of the books.

The Road to Serfdom

In typically combative spirit early on in *The Road to Serfdom*, Hayek asserts that socialism means slavery and that even in the democratic West we are steadily moving in the direction of socialism (p 10). The underlying reason for this apparently extreme view is that under socialism, even democratic socialism, the ability and enterprise of individuals will be continually thwarted by the will of others who take it upon themselves to decide who gets what. Hayek goes on to quote de Tocqueville: 'Democracy and socialism have nothing in common, but one word: equality. But note the difference: while democracy seeks equality in liberty, socialism seeks equality in restraint and servitude.' (p 18) Hayek also says that the true nature of

[1]   F.A. Hayek, *The Road to Serfdom* (London: Routledge and Kegan Paul, 1944), quoted in the 1962 edn. K.R. Popper, *The Open Society and Its Enemies*, 2 vols (London: Routledge and Kegan Paul, 1945), quoted here from the (5th) 1966 edition.

our civilisation has been seen more clearly by its enemies than by its friends. What he calls 'that nineteenth century totalitarian' Auguste Comte spoke of the 'revolt of the individual against the species' as being 'the perennial Western malady' (p 12). For Hayek this revolt is no malady, but the very means by which the West has grown, succeeded and improved socially. It has done so by making as much use as possible of the spontaneous forces of society, creating a system in which competition will work as beneficially as possible, and in which individuals reap the rewards of their successes and pay the cost of their failures. It is just this system that socialists and collectivists are bent on destroying or at least shackling.

Such is the spirit which infuses *The Road to Serfdom*, and for which Hayek is rightly famous, and which permeated his career. As we have already suggested, for many years he was one of a very few voices arguing forcefully and cogently against collectivism and state planning. There is no doubt as to what Hayek's stance would have been on crucial aspects of politics and economics. In view of all this, it is surprising, in reading *The Road to Serfdom* more than sixty years on, to see how nuanced and 'moderate' Hayek's position there actually is in certain crucial respects.

In view of Hayek's reputation as a critic of any sort of planning (as claimed by Oakeshott, for example, and to which we will return), at the outset it is worth underlining his comment early on in *The Road to Serfdom* to the effect that everyone who is not a complete fatalist is a planner. 'Everybody desires that we should handle our common problems as rationally as possible, and that in doing so we should use as much foresight as we can command.' (p 26) The question, of course, is the extent to which we can rationally use foresight, the distinction in other words between good and bad planning. Thus far, what Hayek says would be consistent with complete laissez-faire, a state in which the only planning admitted is that undertaken by individuals, with the state opting out of economic and social arrangements entirely.

No doubt arguments could be mounted for laissez-faire and, more generally, for anarchism. But such is not, and never was Hayek's position. In fact Hayek's specific repudiation of these extreme positions leaves him vulnerable to the criticism that his own position is, contrary to appearance, consistent with quite a high degree of state control and interference (and, as we will also see, Popper's espousal of negative utilitarianism and piecemeal social engineering is open to similar uncertainties). What Hayek says is that while we should not plan for particular goals for society as a whole (such as controlling prices, setting centralised production targets or getting incomes or wealth to conform to some standard), what we should do is to plan for those social conditions which would permit the highest exercise of individual freedom, so that individuals can then best make their own plans. (A similar distinction between what we might call planning for freedom by means of what Popper calls protective institutions, as opposed to planning which interferes with freedom by imposing the designs of the rulers on others is also a cornerstone of Popper's social philosophy—see also *The Open Society*, 2, p. 131, and the later reference to Hayek in Popper's appendix 29 to chapter 17, p. 331.)

Initially this Hayek-approved type of planning is glossed in terms of rules to ensure universal entry to markets (so no cartels), but he immediately goes on to say that there could legitimately be rules to prohibit abuses (of liberty?) such as over-long working hours or the use of certain poisonous substances. It is true that Hayek does say that we will have to look to see whether in specific cases regulation and prohibition impose too high a social cost for the advantages they bring about. But the trouble is, as we see in the recent wrangles over the European working time directive, there is unlikely to be agreement on this calculation. What for one man is a matter of ensuring fair competition by means of a level playing field is for another a restriction of competition and its advantages.

But this is not the only uncertainty in Hayek's prescriptions for planning. He immediately goes on to add that the preservation of competition is not incompatible with 'an extensive system of social services', to which an immediate riposte might be what about competition within the social services themselves. In fact, as we see later in *The Road to Serfdom* (p 76), Hayek thinks that there is a strong case for the state to act so as to reduce inequality of opportunity 'as far as congenital differences permit' and so far as doing so does not impede the impersonal system of rules under which all are to operate. He also thinks that the state should ensure certain minimum standards in physical necessities and also to organise 'a comprehensive system of social insurance' (p 90).

One might not object to these proposals on *a priori* grounds (whatever doubts one might have fifty years later about the state's ability actually to provide extensive systems of social services and the rest). The difficulty with all this from Hayek's point of view is that those who set up the post 1945 welfare state in Britain might well have described their ambitions in terms very similar to those of Hayek. Even worse, equality of opportunity — to which we are all these days supposed to adhere as the unobjectionable side of equality — proves to be increasingly difficult to distinguish from equality of outcome, for working towards such equality will inevitably mean attempting to reduce the differences which result from previous unequal outcomes (such as the wealth of one's parents, the education one has received, the character one has been endowed with, and even luck and chance). I suspect that there is not going to be a third way here. Those who believe in freedom and, like Hayek, dislike the prospect (or reality) of groups of politicians and bureaucrats determining who should have what and at what time are simply going to have to drop talk of equality of opportunity (as opposed to talk of opportunity), however inconvenient this may be politically and electorally. And, with fifty years of experience in Britain of monolithic state provision of health and education, at increasingly ever larger cost and ever decreasing satisfaction, we should surely heed Hayek's warning of the treacherousness of the apparently reasonable proposition that there is a 'Middle Way' between 'atomistic' competition and central direction — and this half a century before Professor Giddens and New Labour.

In *The Road to Serfdom*, as in his later writings, Hayek marshals a number of arguments against central planning of the economy. Of these perhaps the most fundamental, but also the least developed, is an epistemological argument to show that rational planning by a central agency is impossible. It is impossible because the type of knowledge it would need to be rational simply cannot be had. The only way a large society can be effectively co-ordinated is to allow the workings of competition. Precisely because a large society is so complex and composed of so many different individuals all making their individual choices, it would be impossible to centralise the information needed for rational planning. Competition works by diffusing the information about the myriad un-coordinated choices and actions of millions of consumers and entrepreneurs throughout the whole of society. In this way labour and capital will be pulled to their most productive uses, entrepreneurs will succeed only if they produce goods and services consumers want, and as a result consumers will be offered the biggest range of goods at the best prices.

Hayek does not pretend that markets are perfect, even if they are circumscribed by good rules; there will inevitably be waste and failure and sheer bad luck in the system, as things are tried and found wanting. Though many will gain, and the system overall will be beneficial, some will lose, even catastrophically for those individuals. But the alternative of a system run by a government or a committee of bureaucrats will be far worse. By its interference it will impede the flow of information, and in its pretension to have knowledge which simply cannot be had, its activity will in fact be tantamount to the arbitrary exercise of power by a few over the many. And Hayek thinks that arbitrary power constraining individual freedom is far worse than all of us submitting to the impersonal forces of the market, forces which are not rational, to be sure, but forces which do not in themselves and by their very nature constrain freedom.

Some may, of course, dispute this last point, particularly if central state planning affords them some security against failure in the market. There is, as both Hayek and Popper say, a yearning deep within many of us for a more organic form of society than that of economic liberalism. To this Hayek would no doubt reply in Tocquevillean vein that in the modern world the only form an organic society could take would be a form of despotism, more or less mild, more or less arbitrary. But is Hayek actually right in his epistemological argument? It surely cannot just be because of the unsurveyability point, for that is purely contingent. The unsurveyability Hayek refers to is not that of the mathematical unsurveyability of infinite sets. Though very large, the numbers we are talking about in the market are not infinite. Maybe with the tremendous power of modern data processing, it would be possible to survey all the choices and purchases consumers make almost instantly and to direct production accordingly. Let us, for the sake of argument, and to see what is really going on in Hayek assume for the moment that market decisions could all be surveyed and processed in some huge data bank, enabling planners to act on the information thus gathered.

What Hayek would clearly need at this point is some argument as to the intrinsic unpredictability of the human world, irrespective of its size. There are well known arguments—which Popper has toyed with at various times—about the inability of a predictor within a system to predict the future states of the system, because of the way its own predictions will interfere with that system, and will do so regressively. The disturbance factor of the predictor will obviously increase to the extent that the predictor is itself an agent within the system, as would certainly be the case were the predictor also the agent who planned the system. Intriguing as these arguments are, though, they may not get to the heart of the matter. They certainly carry some weight in the sort of case which Hayek envisages, for the predictor is undoubtedly, directly or indirectly, going to affect the system. But in themselves the arguments do not produce the link between unpredictability and freedom which we seem to need, because the Tristram Shandy effect, as Popper calls it, would not show that a system was not in fact determined or even that a predictor insulated from the system and observing it from outside could not accurately predict its development. Furthermore the basic reason Hayek is arguing against planning is because of the way it interferes with human freedom. It would be nicely symmetrical if the reason why planning is bound to fail is because human freedom itself makes accurate prediction impossible.

There are indeed good reasons to think that human behaviour is both free and unpredictable, indeed that over and above the interference effect of prediction, human behaviour is unpredictable because free. We can point to the basic fact that before a consumer actually makes a choice, no one will know whether or not he or she will. Until he or she is in the position of choosing, maybe not even the subject him or herself knows what will be done. Given that this basic fact is replicated many times each day by millions of individuals in a given market and by millions of others throughout the world, it is going to be very hard to come up with more than very broad-brush probabilistic predictions of the behaviour of markets. And to what might seem the caprice of individuals acting in markets, we can add the phenomenon noted by Popper in the preface to *The Poverty of Historicism*, that namely of the unpredictability of scientific and technological development.[2] As Popper points out, one reason we cannot know these things in advance is because if we did, we would know them already, and so they would not be future developments. Intriguing as this point is, however, the underlying cause of all this uncertainty is that in the human world developments in any sphere depend on all sorts of uncertain factors, including luck, chance meetings of events and people, and above all human creativity. If anyone doubts this, we have only to consider the amazing developments in computing and the internet, developments which even now we can hardly comprehend or survey, but which stemmed originally from the application of some apparently very rarified and abstract mathe-

---

[2]   K.R. Popper, *The Poverty of Historicism* (London: Routledge and Kegan Paul, 1957).

matics to the needs of code-breakers in military intelligence in World War Two and then from the discovery that mechanical valves in the first computers could be replaced by electronic chips. It was — and is — a story full of all the factors just mentioned, and one which has changed the world in ways which would have defied any attempts to predict in advance.

If the epistemological argument is the cornerstone of Hayek's argument against planning, it is supplemented by a strong protest of a moral nature. Hayek is a pluralist about values. There is no single and complete ethical code. People are individuals and should have the freedom to make their own choices and to follow their own values and preferences without being dictated to by others. In this context, a planner, however 'expert' will be just one more player in the game, with no more right to impose his vision as to the correct distribution of goods, say, than any one else. And democracy is no safeguard here, for it is all too easy in a democracy for a majority to trample on the rights of minorities, a result all too common of economic planning. Fundamentally economic planning is objectionable because it treats individuals and their work as means to some end they have not chosen, and in so doing it deprives them of their freedom, for economic freedom is neither more nor less than the freedom to act.

Freedom depends on the individual being able to plan, and to know probable outcomes of his actions. It is precisely this knowledge which is impeded by the actions of planners who constrain and regulate him according to plans of their own, from the point of view of the individual arbitrarily. On the other hand, planning requires a framework of rules and laws, to provide a firm context for individuals to plan. So, to re-emphasise the point already made, Hayek is not saying that the state should not act and rule, but it should do so in order to create a stable and fair context for individuals to act and pursue their own ends.

Strangely enough in *The Road to Serfdom* Hayek says little about the inefficiency of planning, as opposed to its assaults on the freedom of individuals. But he does take up another theme which has also become prominent in recent years, that of demoralisation. For if the state provides all sorts of services and functions for individuals, which individuals could better provide for themselves, this deprives individuals of responsibility, creating a culture of irresponsibility. Part of the reason the state might do this is because of a yearning for security on the part of citizens, a nostalgia for a more organic form of society. But this is an idle dream. Far from producing real security, the state will undermine individual freedom and responsibility in its provision of 'services', without producing any satisfaction with what it provides. This is because of its inbuilt inefficiency and hostility to the sort of competition which would improve those services or even keep them at a reasonable standard. And unsuspected by the politicians who set up the National Health Service in the 1940s, arguably intending to provide a minimum basic service for genuine emergencies, there is also the insatiable demand on the part of the public for an ever-increasing provision for which it is not directly paying. The result inevitably is a provision which simply becomes thinner and more stretched, and less able to provide even the minimum levels regarded acceptable when it was originally set up.

The Open Society and Its Enemies

Hayek's observations about the desire of people to be freed from the burden of economic care (and hence in practice freed from their own freedom) are a good place from which to start our analysis of *The Open Society*. For an important and prominent theme of *The Open Society* is what Popper refers to as tribalism and the desire to avoid what he calls the strain of civilisation (1, p. 176). While tribal societies are based on organic structures and face to face contact, and are typically small enough to operate in these ways, what Popper calls abstract societies are far too large for any of this. Accordingly personal links are far weaker. Many of the people I deal with and whose actions affect me I do not know at all, and our dealings are through the impersonal mechanisms of trade. For an abstract society to operate effectively what is needed are sets of rules governing these impersonal transactions, which will afford agents expectations of outcomes and allow them to plan in the absence of personal dealings and agreements.

It is surely significant that for Popper as for Hayek the condition of possibility of an abstract or great society is trade, for trade breaks down tribalism and heralds an era in which old boundaries and customs melt away. The abstract society, with its inherent drive to cosmopolitanism and universalism, is for Popper the basis on which an open society can emerge. Old certainties and old taboos will not survive the sense that we are now operating in a much wider arena in which people from all sorts of different backgrounds are inter-mingling and dealing with each other. Popper, of course, had experience of just this sort of effect in New Zealand when he was writing *The Open Society*, and also of what he regarded as the benighted efforts of some to preserve Maori ways as inviolate, benighted apart from anything else because Maori ways had never been inviolate, but had always been changing in response to changing circumstance; as one of these benighted individuals was his own Head of Department, with whom he had appalling relations, it is perhaps surprising that in his discussion of tribalism he never mentions the tribalism on his own doorstep. Fifth century BC Sparta, not twentieth-century Maori, is the focus of his discussion, perhaps unfortunately for the Maoris as the dilemmas Popper explores in *The Open Society* are if anything further from being resolved in New Zealand now than they were in 1945. Nevertheless it can be said that in his writing Popper shows an acuity of awareness of the human dimension of the topics he is discussing which Hayek never approaches.

The strain of civilisation is a strain, and people yearn for an atmosphere of security. But once a society has moved away from tribalism, tribal values can be restored only by re-asserting the differences between the tribe and the rest, by restoring or re-instating hierarchies and taboos within, by the attempt to be independent of trade, and in general by what Popper calls anti-humanitarianism, shutting out all 'equalitarian, democratic and individualistic ideologies'. (*The Open Society*, 1, p. 182). Looked at from this angle, the strain of civilisation is simply the strain of being human, of recognising a world of Kantian universality in which all are, first and foremost, rational agents, in that respect equal, and in which all must bear the responsibility and burden of their own freedom. What is interesting in *The Open Society*, and where Popper perhaps comes closest to Hayek, is the way Popper sees the abstract universalism of Kant, in which humanity is defined in terms of shared rationality pertaining to individuals as individuals, as emerging historically from the development of the abstract and boundary-blind relations of trade and commerce.

However, at the very point at which Popper seems closest to Hayek, is actually the one from which a significant difference emerges. It is Popper's Kantian interpretation of trade and its effects and his Kantian analysis of human individuality which actually distances him from Hayek. Popper is a believer in the logical separation of facts and values; so values cannot simply be derived from any sort of teleology and even less from anything like divine commands. As Kant, so Popper believes that we, as rational agents would still have to make our own judgements as to the validity of the commands or the desirability of the ends proposed by nature. In that sense, humans do, for Popper, create values (which anyone with Platonistic leanings, such as Simone Weil or Iris Murdoch, would find objectionable). But — and this is where Popper is quite different from Hayek — although we choose our values in the sense of having to determine them for ourselves, values are not simply a matter of individual choice or preference. They are not arbitrary or relative.

I do not think that Popper could agree with Hayek's claim in *The Road to Serfdom* (p. 42) that as values exist only in individual minds, nothing but partial and, hence, different and inconsistent sets of values exist. Hayek later criticised what he took to be Popper's excessive rationalism (according to which rationalist thinkers will not submit blindly to any tradition).[3] It was just that which Hayek came to advocate, that we submit to values we do understand and cannot justify, in the hope that doing so might lead to successful results. Even a conservative traditionalist might have difficulties with this notion, if only because of the uncertainty in any concrete case that it was the value we did not fully understand which was actually responsible for the result we liked. For Popper, by contrast, values can always be argued about, in themselves and independently, one assumes, of dubious inferences concerning their effects. And without ever being sure we are absolutely right at any given time, these discussions are (or should be) rational, and progress can be made, and in Popper's view has been made (see also *The Open Society*, 1, pp. 64–5, and the 1961 Appendix to volume 2, especially pp. 384–6). In other words, Popper is not a subjectivist about value. In this respect, as in his cosmopolitanism, he is a Kantian, sharing none of the sense of the Austrian economic school of the ultimate undecidability of values which we find in Hayek. He is a rationalist, albeit a critical rationalist here, and this is inconsistent with any form of subjectivism or relativism, even with the rather attenuated and roundabout form we find in Hayek.

Popper's open society is premised on the assumption that its citizens are Kantian rational individuals, free to conduct their own lives and to work out their own systems of value, and also, it emerges, liberated from the typically conservative bonds of nation or roots, and prepared to take the strain of civilisation without lapsing into the warmth and comfort of tribalism. They are also fallibilists. That is, they are prepared to admit that they might be wrong and ready, as

---

[3] F.A. Hayek, *The Fatal Conceit* (London: Routledge, 1988), p. 61.

Popper put it, to listen to the other fellow's point of view. For this reason, too, they will typically be democracies, societies best adapted to discussion of this sort. But discussion as Popper envisages it is something which can make progress. Without having a blueprint for a good society, any more that scientists have criteria for the truth of their theories, in both science and politics progress can be made. We can, through attending closely to the consequences of theories and to the effects of policies, especially to the effects on those they impinge on, get nearer the truth, nearer to what is good. Or so Popper, like Mill, believed (see also *The Open Society*, 2, p. 386).

Popper is as hostile to central planning as Hayek, but his hostility derives from no *a priori* dislike of state activity or of policies designed to do more than simply set up the rules within which individuals and groups will compete. Indeed it has often been pointed out that, while Popper himself may have become more opposed to state activity in his later years, there is little or nothing in *The Open Society and Its Enemies* which is inconsistent with the sort of social democracy of the socialist parties of Western Europe — so long as their activity was conceived in terms of piecemeal social engineering, their policies open to criticism and development, and the government itself dismissable at regular intervals by electorates. Indeed one could argue that the open society itself might require a degree of state activity quite repellent to Hayek in order to bring disaadvantaged and marginalized groups up to the level at which they could effectively participate in its deliberations and discussions. In more general terms, as we have already seen, Popper is quite happy in *The Open Society* to advocate what he calls 'equalitarianism', and he also speaks of the moral demands for equality and for helping the weak as being moral demands (*The Open Society*, 1, p. 65). There is nothing in any of this to rule out state activity in these areas, any more than in the case of what we earlier called Hayek's more nuanced description of the state. And with Popper, there is a further difficulty over 'piecemeal' social engineering. When is a policy a piecemeal one (and hence, for Popper, permissible)? As with so much else in this area, what for some would be an absolutely essential step to removing a manifest evil or to securing participation in the open society or the economy, might for others be a piece of objectionable large-scale planning and interference with essential freedoms. While we might know (or think we know) where Popper or indeed Hayek might have stood on such issues, it is not so clear that their arguments alone secure their conclusions.

Popper's hostility to large scale central planning derives jointly from his fallibilism and his individualism, but it is fallibilism which seems to be more fundamental. Although he is a rationalist, he is a critical rationalist. That is he does not believe that we can ever justify our beliefs. Rationality consists in criticism, and central planners, irrationally convinced of the rightness of their visions, tend to suppress or, more commonly in democracies, simply ignore criticisms of them. They tend, in other words, not to take a fallibilist attitude to their plans. At the extreme they may be totalitarians, so convinced of the rightness of their ideals, that criticism can come only from those who out of moral or intellectual blindness cannot see the truth (and so must be suppressed), but even in mild democracies there is an unfortunate tendency on the part of politician-planners to question the motives of those who disagree. Furthermore, for Popper, as we cannot foresee the consequences of any policy, policies limited in scope are preferable to grandiose blueprints for the whole of society. Both are likely to have unforeseen and unintended consequences, but correction is easier of limited actions, and the harm they might do less as well.

Although in practice, Popperian openness and Hayekian limited government might look very similar, there is I think a significant difference between the two. Both are indeed convinced that the knowledge required by central planning cannot be had, but for Hayek there is, in addition, ineradicable value pluralism. In fact, Hayek seems more realistic here, for Popper's faith in the efficacy of openness and discussion to solve problems and overcome disagreements with 'the other fellow' can seem shallowly optimistic. Of course, there may be people unprepared to discuss at all, and simply shoot their opponents, but this is not where the problem lies. In this case, Popper can appeal to his Kantian humanitarianism, and simply assert that the terrorist or dictator is acting irrationally and inhumanely. The problem for Popper arises where both parties to a discussion are as well-mannered and as Kantian in spirit as possible. However long and painstaking the discussion, this may not be enough to produce agreement or progress on issues on which there are radical differences of perspective. Consider, for example, the differences which exist on matters such as abortion and stem-cell research. Some people, for perfectly good (and not necessarily religious) reasons believe that these things are wholly wrong and that their legalisation is a step towards the dehumanising of society. Others, also for defensible reasons, believe just the opposite. One could, of course, in a democracy simply accept that there is an impasse here, and legislate permissively; and maybe the objectors will eventually die out. But neither of these outcomes would in any clear sense constitute progress from the rational point of view. Kantian discussion may not be as powerful a tool as Popper hoped.

In his own later reflections of morality (particularly in *The Fatal Conceit*), Hayek does not offer justifications, even of a negative sort, of moral principles. What he gives us is the outline of an account of their genesis, along with a functionalist analysis of their operation. The underlying idea is that societies are held together by their moral codes, which are in turn formed by an invisible hand to respond to circumstances in ways the protagonists may well not understand. Nevertheless, particularly in the case of successful societies the morality on which they are founded is disturbed at our peril. In reconstructing our morality we may well remove the very things which made our society strong and successful, examples being the traditional family and the ethic of work and personal honesty associated with some forms of Christianity. Indeed, though an agnostic himself, Hayek writes in favour of the role religion had and might still have in supporting property and the family. Hayek's whole approach here, in some contrast to *The Road to Serfdom*, is to suggest that value pluralism, if taken too far, can lead to the erosion of a society; but this is not because he is able to argue that some values are more rational (or less criticisable) than others. In that sense he retains the stance of *The Road to Serfdom*. But in contrast to *The Road to Serfdom* and to the optimistic liberalism and Kantianism of Popper in *The Open Society*, he came eventually to appreciate the pitfalls inherent in trying to hold a society together on no more than a shared commitment to reason. Humanly and socially speaking that would be too slender a support, powerless against the fissiparous effects of competing and conflicting sets of values.

In short, in the spheres of morality and values, Hayek, the pluralist convinced of the intellectual unassailability of pluralism, despite his well-known disclaimer, becomes a conservative, unconvinced of the possibility of justifying our values or of knowing their truth, but convinced of their necessity. In this context, it is interesting to record that in the 1950s Popper was privately defending Hayek against some of his left-inclined students: a liberal society, Popper himself urged then, needed a framework of conservative values. Indeed, as I have myself argued, Popper had himself moved some way from the rationalism of *The Open Society and Its Enemies* even as early as 1949, with his essay 'Towards a rational theory of tradition'.[4] There, in rather Burkean terms, as we see in Chapter 13, Popper castigates rationalists — even I surmise of a critical sort — for disparaging tradition and thinking that they can do so on the basis of pure reason, through their own brains, so to speak. It seems to me that there is tension here with the thoroughly untraditional and rootless Kantian cosmopolitan citizen of The Open Society, who is supposed to keep everything under constant review, but unfortunately I cannot see where Popper was able to resolve or even explore this apparent tension. No more than the Hayek of *The Fatal Conceit*, in whose direction Popper may have moved over the years, is Popper able to explain just which traditions and values we need as the framework for our liberal society. Perhaps in neo-conservative fashion they just assumed they would be the ones of Anglo-American society since, say, the eighteenth century; but that might not cut much ice with those unconvinced of the worth of such a society.

In this essay, I have tried to bring out some significant differences between the political and social views of Hayek and Popper, differences which may be the more remarkable, given their similarities on many points, and particularly in their conclusions. Both are politically and methodologically individualists. Both are passionate in arguing against collectivism and totalitarianism, and also in warning against tendencies within liberal democracies which tend in that direction. Both show as clearly as need be shown that socialism in its communistic form is not a good idea which went wrong, but that it was a rotten idea from the start, rotten because in its pretensions to knowledge of a universal blueprint, it could produce nothing but tyranny and tears.

Certainly part of their joint message has got through. At least we will find few now arguing in favour of Marxism or Leninism, and the names of Hayek and Popper will often be cited as prophets in this respect, along with Orwell and Koestler and, among those who know at least, with Aurel Kolnai and Michael Oakeshott. But it remains questionable how far the Popper-Hayek message has really got through, in Western Europe at least and at least as regards freedom and individualism. The dream of an unattainable organic

---

[4]   K.R. Popper, 'Towards a rational theory of tradition', included in his *Conjectures and Refutations* (London: Routledge and Kegan Paul, 1963). My article is '*The Open Society* revisited', originally published in *Karl Popper, Critical Appraisals*, eds Philip Catton and Graham MacDonald (London: Routledge, 2004), pp. 189–202, a revised version of which appears here as Chapter 14 .

security combined with freedom remains; where the state has given up direct ownership of resources, it doubles its hold through regulation; welfarism remains an intractable problem holding its clients in penury and demoralising them at the same time; and the state commandeers forty per cent of GDP, wasting considerable amounts of it in the process. All this is dressed up in talk of Third Ways, compassionate conservatism, 'New' Labour and the rest. The upshot is that *The Open Society and Its Enemies* and (above all) *The Road to Serfdom*, for all their obvious faults and lacunae, some of which we have examined here, are as worth pondering now as they were in the 1940s. Faced with the angst of globalisation and the problems of those who cannot cope in modern societies, we may feel that freedom and individualism are not what we want. But we should at least know what it is we are rejecting, and the likely cost.

Chapter 13

Criticism and Tradition in Popper, Oakeshott and Hayek

Sir Karl Popper is unusual among self-proclaimed rationalists in extolling the virtues of tradition and, indeed, in emphasising the need for tradition. His main sustained piece of writing on the subject dates from 1949 and is entitled 'Towards a rational theory of tradition'.[1] In that essay he speaks of the weakness of the normal attitude of rationalists to tradition, an attitude he characterises in the following way: 'I am not interested in tradition. I want to judge everything on its own merits ... quite independently of any tradition. I want to judge it with my own brain, and not with the brains of other people who lived long ago.'[2] The thought, if not the language, is not a hundred miles from what Euripides says in Aristophanes's *The Frogs:* that in his plays he is teaching the audience to use their brains, unfettered by meaningless traditions and uncowed by authoritarian windbags repeating out-dated myths. This is not the view taken by Aristophanes himself, for whom 'using one's brains' can lead all too easily to a kind of ignorant and self-satisfied scepticism and an impermeable discontent with whatever one had not chosen for oneself. Nor, I think, would Popper be happy with the anti- traditionalist 'babbling and prating' with which, according to Aristophanes, Athens was filled at the end of the fifth century BC.

For one thing, Popper is quite clear that without a background of knowledge and of problems and of ethos given to us by tradition, the individual (or the community) would be nowhere. He inveighs frequently against the 'canvas-cleaning' procedures advocated by

---

[1] First published 1949; reprinted as chapter 4 of K. R. Popper, *Conjectures and Refutations* (London: Routledge and Kegan Paul, 1963).

[2] *Ibid.*, pp. 120–1.

Plato and his rationalist followers. 'If we start afresh, then, when we die, we shall be about as far as Adam and Eve were when they died ... we must stand on the shoulders of our predecessors.'[3] And this standing on shoulders is not just a matter of content. Without a research tradition, Popper tells us, a young country like New Zealand will find it very hard to make much progress in scientific research (this was in 1949, and Popper had only recently returned from a seven year stint there, during which, of course, he wrote *The Open Society and Its Enemies*). Popper is scathing, too, about an unnamed American recording of Mozart's *Requiem*, and his complaint is not that the conductor and orchestra concerned did not play the right notes, but rather that there was a tradition of classical performance lacking, something which we might characterise as an approach, a spirit.

He also frequently writes about the critical approach itself as a tradition, founded by Thales, and petering out in Hellenistic times after what Popper saw as its great classical flowering. This tradition, clearly, was not a body of knowledge, but an approach to bodies of knowledge and, in a sense, to tradition itself. But the tradition of criticism is a tradition, a set of practices, beliefs, intimations, insights and attitudes, none of which are immune to criticism themselves and which are nonetheless components of a tradition for all that many critical rationalists fail to see the fact. Indeed, one is never more tradition-bound than when one—as so often here—acts under the constraints of a tradition without realising the fact. So all those undergraduates and sixth-formers busily questioning the 'received notions and methodologies' of their subjects, as their teachers and examiners instruct them, are not the global anti-traditionalists they imagine themselves to be. They are, in fact, the uncritical inheritors of just one more tradition (that of today's 'critical thinking'), whose claim to be more rational than other traditions must therefore be based on grounds other than its own alleged non-traditional character.

The character of contemporary uncritical rationalism is memorably captured by Michael Oakeshott in the first section of his essay *Rationalism in Politics*, captured in terms Popper would agree with. Popper would agree with Oakeshott in dissenting from belief in the power of the independent reason to determine for itself the truth and the existence of infallible methods for doing this (compare Popper's own remarks on Bacon and Descartes and on what he sees as the

---

[3]   *Ibid.*, p. 129.

myth of manifest truth).[4] Oakeshott also questions the possibility of acquiring a completely unprejudiced mind (compare Popper's strictures on presuppositionlessness). Further, Oakeshott rejects the supposed necessity for mental slate-cleaning and political utopianism, and also belief in the power of rational minds between them to devise blueprints for perfection (compare Popper's attacks on utopianism, positive utilitarianism, and his insistence on the fact of the unintended consequences of even the best intended and most altruistically motivated policies).

In face of this measure of considerable agreement between Popper and Oakeshott, it may come as a surprise to read in Popper's essay that he 'largely disagrees with' Oakeshott's strictures against rationalism. Even stranger, perhaps, is the fact that in his essay Popper nowhere addresses these strictures, nor even spells out what they are. Instead, he rehearses arguments and positions which were mostly already (in 1949) well enough known to readers of *The Open Society and Its Enemies*. A rational theory of tradition will devote itself to the analysis of institutions, to the exploration of their mode of functioning, and to criticism of institutions and policies in the light of their intended purposes and unintended consequences. Rationality consists not in starting from scratch, but in the readiness to question anything, should the need arise (and it is worth noting that this qualification may be a important gloss on the original, less qualified, position of *The Open Society and Its Enemies*).

Critical rationalism, in Popper's 1949 view, is a tradition unfriendly to taboos, and tolerant of opposing positions and viewpoints. Traditions and institutions mediate between individuals and their social environment, producing order and predictability in the lives both of individuals and of societies. Traditions can be closed—erecting taboos to deflect criticism—or they can be open and rational, like the tradition of modern science. The truly rational attitude is not to reject traditions, but to treat all traditions and criticisms critically. As parts of Popper's rational theory of tradition, as just described, do in fact conflict with Oakeshott's view, it is the more surprising that in his essay he did not address Oakeshott directly in the 1949 essay, rather than re-hashing themes of *The Open Society and Its Enemies*.

Nevertheless, in the essay *Rationalism in Politics* to which Popper refers, Oakeshott makes only two substantial points in addition to those we have so far considered, and it is not clear that Popper would

---

[4] Michael Oakeshott, *Rationalism in Politics and Other Essays* (Indianapolis: Liberty Fund, 1991), pp. 5–42. The essay in question dates from 1947.

disagree with either of them. They are, first, that in the modern age a stress on technique has replaced a realisation of the importance of tacit and traditional knowledge in any field of activity. Oakeshott gives as examples the attempts of Bacon and Descartes to lay out rules for scientific enquiry, attempts Popper also rejects. Oakeshott believes that the unspoken, unarticulated aspect of an activity is at least as important as what has been or can be explicitly encapsulated in words or formulae. For him, principles are always but an abridgement of a practice, and can be quite misleading if not understood against the background of initiation into a practice.

Popper need not disagree with any of this. Not only does he regard the belief that there is a royal road to truth as a dangerous illusion. He also stresses the importance of the unarticulated background of practice in scientific research, as we have seen. Moreover, in 'Towards a rational theory of tradition', he stresses the importance of the scientific tradition over the bare accumulation of knowledge. He goes so far as to imply that the content of scientific knowledge depends for its significance and status as scientific on its embedding in the scientific tradition. (And compare the passage in *The Logic of Scientific Discovery* where Popper says that the scientific approach cannot be encapsulated linguistically or syntactically, because it is a matter of how one *approaches* theories and problems.)[5]

Oakeshott also argues against the tendency of contemporary rationalists to make all procedures and techniques explicit, and to become self-conscious about all our activities. Here, too, there is nothing with which Popper would disagree. He always stresses the impossibility and pointlessness of defining everything, which he sees as part of the obsessive essentialism of modern philosophy; and he is quite content for much of our thought and activity to remain unarticulated, unless some need for articulation arises. He might even assent to Oakeshott's motto *opportet quaedam nescire* if applied in this context; and in certain anti-justificationist moods he might also show sympathy for Oakeshott's general approval of nescience, at least in contrast to the rationalist drive for total knowledge and complete transparency.

Despite the large measure of agreement, overlap even, between the essays *Rationalism in Politics* and 'Towards a rational theory of tradition', Popper's instinct in distinguishing his overall position from Oakesbott's is correct, which makes it the more regrettable that

[5]   K.R. Popper, *The Logic of Scientific Discovery* (London: Hutchinson, 1959), pp. 81–2.

he never, as far as I know, spelled out in any detail his disagreement with or response to Oakeshott. It is not simply that Popper stresses criticism more than Oakeshott. Oakeshott in fact is quite prepared to give criticism a role in any tradition of activity, and would never impose an *a priori* limit to criticism. (That would be far too rationalistic for him—a point we will return to in considering Hayek.) The difference between Popper and Oakeshott is rather in the way they conceive traditions, institutions and criticism, the difference being broadly that while Oakeshott sees many of our traditions and institutions as having no ultimate ulterior purpose external to their own existence, Popper's talk of piecemeal social engineering leads him to adopt a far more rationalistic and utilitarian approach to traditions and institutions than Oakeshott will allow.

For Popper, what constitutes rationality in science is preparedness to submit theories to empirical testing. In like manner, what constitutes rationality in social sciences in particular, and social life in general, is willingness to test what Popper thinks of as experiments in living: i.e., our social policies and actions. 'A social technology is needed', he says, 'whose results can be tested by piecemeal social engineering.'[6]

What, though, makes the method of empirical testing rational? Here Popper's position exposes him to a problem. He speaks of the aim of science as being either the discovery of satisfactory explanations, which in turn involves the discovery of laws of nature or, more generally, the discovery of truth. What would make a method rational would, it seems, be its contribution to the satisfaction of science's aims. But, as is well known, Popper does not believe that the method of falsification necessarily produces truth or elicits laws of nature. At most, it eliminates error, and one can naturally wonder whether the elimination of error is, on its own, such a big deal as to justify all the effort that goes into science. Nevertheless, from the Popperian perspective what seems to make it possible to speak of rationality in science is an easily perceived dualism of goal and method, even if this leaves us a lot of consequent argument about the link between the two.

In like manner, social policies and action are to be judged in terms of the success they have in achieving the aims of those who plan or perform them. Again it is the simple dualism of goal and means which enables us to speak of rationality.

---

[6] K.R. Popper, *The Open Society and Its Enemies*, vol. II (London: Routledge and Kegan Paul, 1945), p. 222.

But it is precisely any such simple dualism which Oakeshott wishes to reject, and precisely because of this rejection that he would be loath to see politics or practice generally in terms of social engineering. I suspect that he would also have been unbothered by any failure to demonstrate that scientific methods lead ineluctably to some explanation or truth or law beyond those regularities and quantities scientists actually come up with in their work. Such a relativising or internalising of scientific rationality to actual scientific practice would on the one hand save us from fruitless heart-searching that epistemologists of science tend to go in for, while on the other hand it would make it harder than it often is to think of science as more than *one* approach to the world, as *the* truth, or anything like that. Certainly the denial of a clear-cut distinction in science between goal and method and the consequent avoidance of the need to hold the findings of science up to judgement in the light of some extra-scientific exemplar of truth would be entirely in accordance with Oakeshott's attitude to politics and to traditions. To this I will now turn.

In one of his writings on education, Oakeshott says:

> Being human is recognizing oneself to be related to others, not as parts of an organism are related, nor as members of a single, all-inclusive society, but in virtue of participation in multiple understood relationships and in the enjoyment of understood, historic languages of feelings, sentiments, imaginings, fancies, desires, recognitions, moral and religious beliefs, intellectual and practical enterprises, customs, conventions, procedures and practices ... a human being is an inhabitant of a world composed, not of 'things' but of meanings: that is, of occurrences in some manner recognized, identified, understood and responded to in terms of this understanding. It is a world of sentiments and beliefs, and it includes also human artefacts (such as books, pictures, musical compositions, tools and utensils) ... To be without this understanding is to be, not a human being, but a stranger to a human condition.[7]

A tradition of activity, then, is for Oakeshott something we participate in, something from which we derive *meaningful* satisfaction (as opposed to the brute satisfaction of animal needs), something

---

[7]   Michael Oakeshott, 'Education: The engagement and its frustration', in his *The Voice of Liberal Learning*, ed. Timothy Fuller (New Haven, CT: Yale University Press, 1989), pp. 63–94, at p. 65.

which is not an end to anything else, although it may give us ends of its own. In a characteristic passage, Oakeshott writes:

> For a child to learn to walk is not like a fledgling taking to the air: do I not remember being told to 'walk properly' and not shamble along as if I were an ape? The March Hare's dance and the song of the blackbird may be attributed to genetic urges, but a waltz and *Dove sono* are historic human inventions which have to be learned and understood if they are to be known, enjoyed or responded to.[8]

So, there is a tradition of 'walking properly', a tradition of waltzing and a tradition of opera. Within these traditions we may indeed set ourselves goals, but the tradition itself cannot be said to aim at anything else. The traditions persist or fail to persist because people find them meaningful or not; but to say that is to say little more than that people do engage in them. Nowadays, one supposes, people don't in Oakeshott's sense set any great store by walking 'properly', and that, I think, is all there is to it.

Many would take issue with this last claim: the reason, they would say, that people don't any more bother about walking properly is that the very notion of walking properly is itself outmoded, inefficient and irrational. But to argue like this is not to show oneself more rational in any significant sense than those who once insisted on deportment. It is, rather, to show that one has no interest in such matters, and that quality of deportment is not going to count as a reason in one's deliberations and decisions. What makes the repudiation of traditional standards *seem* more rational and more critically aware than the holding on to those standards, here as in many other analogous cases, is that the anti-traditionalist approach often goes along with a stress on such notions as efficiency and simplicity. So the notion grows up that it is more efficient to slouch than to march boldly upright, to wear jeans and plimsolls than suits, and so on. What is the point of old-fashioned deportment? of the wearing of suits? etc., etc. is the characteristic anti-traditionalist cry. And this suggests — erroneously — that there is some extrinsic goal (of walking, of dress) against which one could compare the efficiency of slouching, suits and so on. To think like that is to adopt the modernist, anti-traditionalist position, which one is entitled to do. What is objectionable, though, is the thought that in consciously adopting

---

[8] *Ibid.*, p. 66.

that position, one is being more rational or more critically rational than the traditionalist.

What I am trying to say is well captured by Oakeshott himself in his famous discussions of bloomers, the under-trousers for lady cyclists to which Mrs Bloomer gave her name.[9] Bloomers were supposed to be the 'rational dress' for this activity, and were promoted as such. But why did the designers stop where they did, and not go on to invent women's cycling shorts? They were, of course, constrained by considerations of decency; and so failed to develop the truly 'rational' garment (shorts). But in so failing, they were actually being more rational than they would have been had they put shorts on the market at the time, for they were responding to a fuller range of interests and meanings and desires than the purely, narrowly functional. And to hold that the rational is equivalent to that which maximises efficiency of functionality is not to be more rational than one's traditionalist opponent: it is rather to evince a preference for a particular 'functionalist' approach to life, one which may well be encouraged by the Popperian tendency to see critical rationality in terms of social engineering.

Popper characterises social engineering, as an approach to institutions and policies which examines them as means that serve certain ends, and which insists on a dualism of fact and value in determining whether given means serve the stated ends or not. The position Popper adopts is actually not far from the Weberian account of means-end rationality. Its problem as an account of rationality in the social sphere is that it would be quite at a loss in treating of the desirability or otherwise of good deportment, of waltzing or of bloomers. A very great deal of the meaning we as human beings find and the satisfaction we take in our activities and traditions and institutions has little to do with their efficiency or ability to subserve ends aside from what is involved in engaging in the activities: and this is all overlooked in an analysis such as Popper's which sees everything in engineering terms.

Oakeshott is well known if not notorious, for his insistence that political activity is not and should not be seen primarily as a matter of getting things done, but rather (in his words) as the art of knowing where to go next in the exploration of an already existing traditional kind of society.[10] Politics should not be conceived in terms of passing reforms, bills, policies, constitutions, but rather with the custody of a

[9] See also *Rationalism in Politics*, pp. 81–3.
[10] See *ibid.*, pp. 58–63.

manner of living, and particularly with the prevention of coercion against tyrannies of all sorts. Popper would, of course, agree with the warning against tyrannies but, from an Oakeshottian point of view, even a programme of negative utilitarianism suggests too activist a conception of politics, too great a faith in the power of the state to identify and correct problems, and above all too naïve a conception of how problems might be recognised and identified.

Popperians will naturally criticise Oakeshott for his view that the state should be conceived as having no end beyond itself, no end beyond providing its citizens with the means for living together. The state is, in Oakeshott's terminology, a civil association, not an enterprise association, which he sees as an institution devoted to some set of specific, identifiable ends (such as the relief of poverty, or the education of the ignorant). Politics ought to be like a conversation between people united in history and tradition in which they explore the intimations of their tradition. It should not be regarded as a device to achieve predetermined and independently imposed ends. The fact that politics today—of left and right—is characteristically that of the enterprise association would serve to demonstrate the extent to which the activities of politics and the state itself have become (in Oakeshott's view) objectionably rationalistic.

Negative utilitarianism and social engineering are clearly rationalistic in Oakeshott's sense, suggesting as they do the need for or possibility of neutral checklists of abuses and disorders for the politician to solve, and a quasi-mechanical procedure for evaluating the success of policies. As the Popperian view is one which many, if not most, political thinkers would accept without a second thought, it might seem perverse to say anything in favour of Oakeshott's position. Nevertheless, I will say the following: in abstract it is hardly possible to list the abuses which need reforming, or to estimate the costs which might be acceptable in reforming them. Only against a background of some settled conception of what life is and how it should be lived is there any chance of reaching a consensus on anything more than relief of the most obvious emergencies. Utilitarians, even of a negative sort, underestimate the extent to which estimations of happiness and misery, even of pleasure and pain, are constrained and circumscribed by considerations of the sort which weighed—albeit unconsciously, but to that extent more weightily—with Mrs Bloomer.

It is easy to agree with Popper that once a particular policy has been decided upon, it is rational to monitor its effects, but far less easy to estimate in a context-free manner the rationality of aiming at a particular end or the acceptability of a given means. Oakeshott's conception of politics as the drawing out of intimations we or some other group already implicitly have is closer to the reality of politics than the political stance of the rationalist, in which what are imagined (wrongly in Oakeshott's view) to be eternal and universal ends are purposely sought by the best available techniques. As in the case of bloomers, the means by which we seek given political ends are never means merely, nor are the ends ends absolutely speaking. Discomfort we have in experience with the means may often make us revise our notions of ends (as when, to use one of Popper's own examples, the pursuit of equality turns out to cost too much in freedom); but this is another way of saying that means, too, are ends, or rather that in most human affairs there is no clear-cut distinction between the two. And this, in turn, is a reflection of the Oakeshottian fact that human life is lived mainly on the level of intelligibilia, meanings, rather than on the simplistic model of biologically driven desire satisfaction.

Within a particular tradition or particular conception of life, we will engage in various practices and policies, to some considerable degree, I am suggesting, and often despite appearances, for their own sake: they wear their charms (or otherwise) on their sleeves (even if we are often misled by rationalism into thinking that they can be judged in terms of extrinsic and separable ends). The thought I am struggling to express might be put like this. The rationalist, including the negative utilitarian like Popper, thinks of politics in terms of the elimination of abuses, in terms of progress towards some particular goal or goals (such as the minimisation of suffering or the relief of poverty). In science we can, if we like, think of progress towards truth, and perhaps make some sense of it.

But the notion of progress in the political sphere is far more difficult and contestable. It is not just that in the social sphere any political change inevitably has drawbacks and problems, but rather that goals and ends shift continually, and ends and means are inextricably intertwined. Was it progress towards some independently acceptable and justifiable goal, such as the preservation of individual freedom, when Mrs Thatcher curbed the arbitrary power of trade unions, a measure which apparently commanded widespread support in the country? (If it was, we would have to show what I cannot see how to show, that the gain in freedom to the unaffiliated citizen was not made at the expense of the freedoms of individual trade unionists to pursue their ends.) Or was it rather that for one reason and another, people were simply not prepared to go on living as they had been, subject to what had come to be seen as the arbitrary exercise of force by 'free' trade unions and their members?

Here an Oakeshottian analysis in terms of a drawing out of intimations of a tradition of checks and balances and of the dispersal of power which we are all party to might seem more plausible; and it might also explain the widespread resistance to other of Mrs Thatcher's policies on the grounds of unreasonable centralisation (and also incidentally to the poll tax which, however just abstractly and however rational it no doubt was from a genuinely impartial point of view, offended most people's actual, historically given sense of justice). The pursuit of politics, then, becomes more a question of removing friction within the civil association as civility is understood at a particular place and time, rather than an enterprise driven by the pursuit of progress towards independently determinable goals. From this point of view, the political tradition of a country, far from being criticisable in the light of rationally and universally determinable extrinsic goals, itself sets the goals and defines the limits of what citizens of the country in question are prepared to accept or regard as just.

Even if we agree with Oakeshott that traditions of politics, morality and other human practices and institutions should in the main be conceived in terms of internally generated goals, goals not susceptible of critical assessment from an external, neutral-rational point of view, and not susceptible to the negative utilitarian testing advocated by Popper, a question might still be raised as to the reason why some practices, institutions and traditions persist and others die out. It is precisely this question to which Sir Friedrich Hayek has attempted an answer, an answer which is of interest because he has an Oakeshott-like awareness of the limitations of critical reason. In particular, Hayek is wary of the pretensions of reason to criticise well-entrenched practices effectively. Like Oakeshott, Hayek will emphasise the extent to which our forms of life are governed by unarticulated and possibly inarticulable rules. Unlike Popper who (as we have seen) said that the rationalist will never submit blindly to any tradition, Hayek emphasises that social life would be impossible without a background of shared and unquestioned assumptions. He also says that we should submit to many rules and practices, even though we cannot specify their purpose or point in advance, and even though we are unable to assess either their effects or the desirability of their effects. In rejecting the characteristically rationalist demand that we should do more of this—a demand which is implicit in Popper's talk of social engineering and explicit in his 1949 essay—Hayek comments that making such a demand shows no 'awareness that there might be limits to our knowledge and reason in certain areas' or that 'the most important task of science might be to discover what those limits are.'[11]

Hayek's reasoning is in part epistemological. In a great society, no single mind, and no single aggregation of many minds, can comprehend the full effects of any policy or principle. What for many utilitarians is treated as an annoying inconvenience which can in principle be disregarded is seen by Hayek as wrecking the whole rationalist-cum-utilitarian project of judging acts and principles in terms of direct consequences. The difficulty is not just that the effects of any policy or principle are very widely diffused; it is also that the effects include the often unpredictable reactions to those policies and their effect on the people affected by them. The idea that we could possibly comprehend all this, Hayek sees as a throwback to a primitive animism in which a god was taken to be able to survey the whole of a society.

Nevertheless, while we cannot know the effects of our actions or of the principles which govern the conduct of individuals in a great society, the existence of general rules is, for Hayek, a condition of individual spontaneity and freedom. Only against a settled background of principle can a society of free and spontaneous agents function at all. Which principles should prevail? Here, Hayek attempts an answer which goes beyond Oakeshott's talk of developing intimations already present in a tradition. But his answer is not to the question which principles *should* prevail, so much as to the question which principles *will* prevail; those, namely, which are adhered to by groups which succeed where groups with other principles fail.

Hayek's evolutionary account of principles and practices is highly unrationalistic. Principles and practices succeed not because people can see the reason for them nor because they understand their effects. They succeed by means of the invisible hand or the cunning of reason which determines that just this group with just those principles out-performs its competitors. And even here, we should be cautious; our invincible ignorance of their effects means that we cannot know that it is *because* the group has such and such principles

---

[11]   F. A. Hayek, *The Fatal Conceit* (London: Routledge, 1988), p. 62.

that it succeeds; its success might be for quite other reasons, or even despite its principles. Nevertheless, Hayek constantly warns us against changing principles or rules, and particularly against doing so on rationalistic grounds.

Hayek's position amounts to a combination of the familiar (Wittgensteinian) claim that conscious reasoning and explicit rationality are always embedded in a background of unquestioned practice, together with a strong dose of Darwinism regarding specific practices and their associated modes of reasoning. Here it might seem that critical rationalism could, despite appearances, get a purchase. Even though we don't know the precise or direct effects of policies and principles, and even though we cannot justify them in abstract, cannot we — from our point of view of social and economic success, in contrast, say, to state socialism — pick out enough of what contributes to our political freedoms and moral system to be able to reinforce just those principles and institutions which might support the market system Hayek admires? And Hayek himself does argue in this way in his practical policy proposals.

Looked at like this, Hayek's position comes to resemble a two-step rationalism, rather like Hare's critical moral thinking. You identify a certain type of society as being more successful than its competitors, more morally desirable, or whatever. You then insist that its principles be adhered to, come what may, partly because you are unsure of the destructive effect abandoning or criticising them might have, and partly because you want participants in the practice to accept the principles intuitively and automatically. But overall, you rationally justify irrationalism at the first level in terms of the supposed good effects discerned at a higher, more global level of enquiry. One can thus both — as Hayek himself does in effect — follow Hume in believing that the rules of morality are not the conclusions of our reason, but evolutionarily selected principles to which we owe unthinking obedience at the level of practice, and at the same time think we have good reason for opting for unthinking obedience to certain principles of whose genesis and case-by-case effects we are uncertain.

There might, though, be something of a rapprochement at this point between Popper and Hayek. Hayek is, in effect, criticising on plausible grounds the Popperian insistence that it is irrational to submit blindly to any tradition. But in *The Fatal Conceit* Hayek does speak, not wholly ironically I think, of his insight that tradition is in some respects superior to conscious human reason as being something that 'only a *very* critical rationalist could recognise'.[12]

Nevertheless, some might feel that there is something decidedly fishy about a reconciling project which would make Hayek, the exponent of the invisible hand and of the cunning of reason in the evolution of science and morality, and the defender of blindly accepting religious sanctions for the upholding of property-rights, into as much of a rationalist as the Popper who wants everything we believe and do to be open, in principle at least, to critical scrutiny and testing at any time. This, indeed, is the critical tradition, and one to which Hayek clearly does not subscribe; and one which Oakeshott would regard as not nearly as unproblematic or as transparent in application as its proponents imply with their talk of rejecting taboos, advocating rational thinking, the relief of suffering, and the like.

In particular, as we saw in considering social engineering, the critical tradition very naturally encourages a utilitarian and interventionist attitude to social affairs which itself rests on a dubious notion of efficiency and universal progress, and on a distinction between goals and means which is hard to draw, to say nothing of the deployment of a notion of suffering (and its relief) which is in practice very far from being a neutral scale against which to assess institutions, moralities and the rest, the notion of unacceptable suffering being something which is largely given to us by our institutions, moral codes and practices.

Hayek's position, indeed, is not merely hard to defend. Even if his profession of ignorance about the effects of principles is consistent with his rationally defending certain principles as more conducive to market systems, it is hard to know how to apply his strictures against criticism and against planning. How can one make a conscious decision not to appraise a principle rationally or plan not to plan? Isn't some form of critical appraisal or of planning implicit in these very decisions? Moreover, as Oakeshott comments:

> a plan to resist all planning may be better than its opposite, but it belongs to the same style of politics. And only in a society already deeply infected with Rationalism will the conversion of the traditional resources of resistance to the tyranny of Rationalism into a self-conscious ideology be considered a strengthening of those resources. It seems that now, in order to participate in politics and expect a hearing, it is necessary to have, in the strict sense, a

---

[12] *Ibid.*, p 75.

doctrine; not to have a doctrine appears frivolous, even disreputable. And the sanctity, which in some societies was the property of a politics piously attached to traditional ways, has now come to belong exclusively to rationalist politics. [13]

We are all, in one way or another, as Oakeshott says, infected with rationalism and it is very hard even for self-professed conservatives not to think rationalistically about politics. The conservative these days has to write books and articles full of argument if he wants to argue against rationalism, although I have to say that I am not convinced by Hayek's attempt to show that respect for tradition is in itself going to lead to a better or even a materially more prosperous society. Even if such judgements could be made at all, it is not respect for any tradition that would count, and in discussing and evaluating different traditions, including those of critical or even constructive rationalism, we are some distance from that pious attachment to traditional ways of which Oakeshott speaks.

I began by mentioning *The Frogs* of Aristophanes and what Popper said about the critical tradition in classical times, and I will end by making a provocative observation. Popper greatly esteems the critical tradition, and for him Socrates is a model. We can also suspect that in science he values the critical method as much as its results, and that even if science stopped making substantive progress, he would still regard the method as worth pursuing on ethical and cultural grounds. [14] Nevertheless, from Aristophanes's point of view, Socrates) along with Euripides, was the villain of the piece:

> They sit at the feet of Socrates
> Till they can't distinguish the wood from the trees
> And tragedy goes to pot
> They don't care whether their plays are art
> But only whether the words are smart
> They waste our time with quibbles and quarrels
> Destroying our patience as well as our morals
> And teaching us all to talk rot. [15]

Is there anything to be said for Aristophanes's view of the critical approach? Now *that* would be a really interesting question, and one to which an Oakeshottian approach would seem far more promising

[13] Oakeshott, *Rationalism in Politics*, pp. 26–7.

[14] Indeed, Popper says as much at the end of *The Logic of Scientific Discovery*, pp. 278–81.

[15] Aristophanes, *The Frogs*, trans. David Barren (Harmondsworth: Penguin, 1964) ll. 1491–9.

than either Hayek's or Popper's. For Hayek's approach, apart from looking at times like an unacceptable demand that we uncritically accept prejudice, involves an assessment which is not just difficult to make, but one which on Hayek's own grounds is impossible to make, viz. whether it is or is not the presence of the critical (or any other) tradition (or which bits of it) which is responsible for material prosperity in a country. Popper's position amounts in the end to an unsupported hope that, with luck, the critical tradition will lead to scientific truth and the relief of suffering, together with a plumping for it anyway. Oakeshott's position, by contrast, involves neither an uncritical acceptance of the critical tradition nor an uneasy rejection of it. He points to its limitations and to its necessity. (Once the genie is out of the bottle, there is no going back to pious traditionalism.) The critical tradition is part of our form of life, our civility. It is, nevertheless, not the whole of our (or of any other) way of life, and the attempt to make it stand over all other traditions can be destructive of much in our life. Recognising these two facts and their implications together might enable us to avoid both the Scylla of dogmatic traditionalism and the Charybdis of relentless and enervating criticism.

Chapter 14

The Open Society Revisited

In this article, I will consider some of the themes of Karl Popper's *The Open Society and Its Enemies*, which we have not so far considered at any length, as well as developing further some points introduced in Chapter 11.[1] In doing this, I will concentrate first on the respects in which Popper's positive vision of the open society he is advocating strikes me as utopian. Many of the criticisms Popper makes of Marx in particular strike me as devastating, of vital importance in the time in which they were written, and also, eventually, a classic case of philosophy influencing world politics for the good. Nevertheless, as I will argue, Popper's own vision is not just, in a certain sense, utopian: it needs considerable supplementation if it is to contribute positively to politics, theoretically or practically. In the closing sections of the chapter I will attempt to sketch the conditions in which an open society such as Popper advocates might develop and flourish.

Popper's open society is contrasted with closed societies, which are societies marked by what Popper would see as oppression and inhumanity. These closed societies may be tribal societies, dominated by tradition, irrational prejudice, xenophobia and rule by hereditary groups or oligarchies. Or they may be more modern types of dictatorship, run by rulers who claim superior (or even infallible) insights into history and society, and who claim on the basis of this knowledge to be able to produce a good (or better) life for everyone. 'Everyone', of course, simply has to submit to this superior knowledge, so there is considerable dictatorial potential in closed societies, which was very much in Popper's mind when he attacked closed societies in the 1940s.

---

[1]   K.R. Popper, *The Open Society and Its Enemies*, 2 vols (London: Routledge and Kegan Paul, 1945), 5th revised edn 1966.

Open societies, by contrast, are societies in which everything, policies, institutions, traditions, rulers, are open to criticism, and open to criticism from anyone. Anyone may criticise in an open society, especially those directly affected by a given policy or institution. In an open society policies and institutions are modified by continual monitoring of their effects, and in the light of their ability to solve the problems they are supposed to solve. Rulers do not attempt to impose blueprints for the good life on the whole of society. Instead they seek to rectify obvious problems and abuses through piecemeal social engineering, and the continual monitoring of effects.

The open spirit is one which listens, as Popper puts it, to the other fellow's point of view. Differences are resolved and decisions reached through this process of rational discussion, and the spirit of compromise and co-operation. Open societies will probably be democracies, as democracy is the form of social organisation most conducive to the sort of discussion and consultation characteristic of open societies; but democracy is not sufficient for openness, as we have seen in Chapter 11. The majority can tyrannise and sometimes does (as Popper knew all too well from Germany and Austria in the 1930s). For Popper the most important feature of an open society is that in it rulers can be replaced regularly and peacefully — because in such a system the rulers are most likely to be sensitive to the feelings and needs of the ruled.

An initial comment on all this might well be that no actual society is completely open in Popper's sense. Even if the liberal democracies of the West are more open than other forms of society (as they surely are), they may not be wholly open, Popper's own admiration for Britain and the USA notwithstanding. Even in Britain and the USA, it would be said, some voices are systematically unheard, such as the unemployed, immigrants, the old and women. Perhaps, as some have argued, Popper himself should have been more aware than he was of the way that power structures, cognitive interest and control of the mass and other media can stifle discussion and marginalize potentially valuable inputs to discussion. Maybe more social equality than Popper was prepared to admit is necessary to achieve the sort of openness Popper desired.

But criticisms of this sort, even if valid, would not invalidate the idea of the open society. They would show only that Popper had not worked it out sufficiently. Nor would they have any tendency to reduce the significance of his repeated assertion that what is critical in an open society is not just the structural and institutional framework necessary to achieve openness, crucial as this is, but a spirit of openness in those who man those structures and institutions. More damaging for Popper's social philosophy is a doubt as to whether any society could actually operate or even survive, given the degree of openness his proposals advocate. But before addressing this doubt head on, we need to say something about the ideological underpinning of Popper's open society.

Underlying the open society are five basic ideas, the first four of which are firmly within the tradition of Enlightenment rationalism and optimism. The first idea is that of the unity of mankind. That is to say, in the open society anyone may criticise and contribute, regardless of origin, race, religion, class or gender. In this context, it is noteworthy that Popper himself was resolutely anti-nationalistic, even to the extent of criticising the very existence of Israel. He also made himself unpopular in the 1960s by saying that Jews in the Germanic countries should have sought to suppress their differences from Germans and Austrians, so as not to have aroused antagonism (not that Popper had any truck with Pan-Germanism). In this dislike of national differences and distinctions, Popper parallels Kant's views on the topic, though whether, as some have suggested, he was yearning for the palmy days of the structurally multi-cultural post-1848 Austro-Hungarian Empire, is perhaps more doubtful.

The second support to openness is the notion of individualism. Popper had an almost pathological hatred of any form of group rule or collectivism (even to the extent of refusing in his eighties to go round a Portuguese palace in a group or 'collective' as he put it). But his insistence on individualism, ontological, political and methodological, was not just pathological. It was based on a Kantian sense of the rational autonomy of each individual, *qua* individual.

Thirdly, and connected to the first two notions, is that of impartiality. Any view may be worth hearing, whatever its provenance. This is not just an Enlightenment view. For Popper it is also an essential similarity between the open society and the ideal scientific community, in which valid criticism of a scientific theory can come from any quarter. The extent to which a human society, open or not, can actually resemble the community of science is something which will concern us later.

Then, fourthly, there is humanitarianism. Popper was horrified from the time of his encounters with revolutionary socialists after the First World War by the readiness of idealists to sacrifice individual lives to-day in order to hasten the birth of some ideal society in the future. Even if there were a greater chance of the ideal society coming about through revolutionary terrorism than in fact is the case, it could never be justified to treat the lives of others as means to the end, again a striking parallel with Kant.

The fifth strand to Popper's thought is where, to a degree, he departs from the classical Enlightenment position. For Popper does not believe that the unfettered use of reason is bound to produce truth or absence from error. He is in no sense an epistemological optimist; he is, in fact, a fallibilist, one who believes that we can never rule out the possibility of error, even in the best regulated and conducted of enquiries. Neither truth nor desirable social outcomes are the inevitable fruit of the use of reason. It is partly because of this that Popper makes criticism and openness so central to the open society, because criticism and openness are the best ways we know of uncovering error and failure in the social sphere. And, as part of his fallibilism about social outcomes, Popper will stress the reality of human freedom, and the way the free decisions of individual human beings affect what happens in both big and small affairs. Not the least of his objections to Marxism is the arrogant assumption of the Marxists that they know how history is going, and that the rest of us simply have to submit both to history and to their superior knowledge of it. It is this idea that history has a definite direction which Popper characterises as historicism, and he thinks it is nonsense (as we saw in Chapter 2). We are free, and within limits we can act, individually and collectively, sometimes even to change what all the experts confidently assert to be the course of history (as, in their different ways President Reagan and Mrs Thatcher and their followers did both in their own countries and in the Evil Empire, and as the Ayatollah Khomeini and his followers did in Iran).

It is important to note at this point that not all the closed societies attacked by Popper are based on irrationalism, either of a primitive or a modern variety, at least not according to their proponents (though, as we will see, Popper himself may have a different view here). In fact, quite to the contrary, the closed societies Popper spends most time attacking, those of Plato and Marx, both make big claims to be based on reason and science. They both claim that by rational or scientific means it is possible to plan a centrally directed society which will produce more happiness and human flourishing than any other, and this is still the dream of many intellectuals, who would claim no direct allegiance to either Plato or Marx. But for reasons examined in Chapter 12, it is just this sort of knowledge which, according to Popper (and Hayek, with whom Popper has some measure of agreement here) cannot be had.

The open society is presented by Popper as the antidote to the nightmares which arise when totalitarian rulers impose on whole populations their utopian visions based on claims to a degree of knowledge and insight they could not possibly have. Popper's open society, by contrast, is not founded on any plan to be imposed centrally and forcibly on the whole of society, nor on unattainable knowledge, supposedly vested in a few visionaries or some party committee furnished with insight into the course of history or the destiny of mankind. It is, by contrast, pluralist; and its underlying philosophy is negative utilitarianism, rather than some positive vision of heaven on earth.

Without denying these criticisms Popper makes of the closed societies he attacks, there are certain key respects in which the open society, as envisaged by Popper, is itself utopian; that is, it has at its heart an unrealised and unrealisable vision of human society, and one which will actually tend to loosen the bonds which in fact tie societies together.

In the first place, as already mentioned, the open society, like Popper's philosophy more generally, is built on a faith in reason, meaning by that a belief in the power of reasoned discussion to resolve disputes and create social harmony. This faith is combined with a form of cosmopolitan rationalism and Popper's own fallibilism. These are, as noted, characteristically enlightened beliefs, part of the world view bequeathed us by the Enlightenment. As Popper himself observes, what we have been bequeathed intellectually and morally is the need to decide between two competing faiths, no longer between science and religion in a general sense, but now between rationalism and irrationalism (which includes for him not just the irrationalism of tribal taboo and the politics of fascism, but also the mystical philosophy of Plato).[2] We need now to compare these two faiths, as guides to social life.

From the point of view of irrationalists, such as nationalists, fundamentalist religious believers and even Platonic philosophers, Popper's fallibilism and cosmopolitanism will look as partial and tendentious as their beliefs do to the fallibilist Popper. What Popper sees as universal values inherent in Enlightenment rationalism and scepticism might, from the point of view of certain other cultures and faiths, appear as a manifestation of Western imperialism, to

---

[2]   *The Open Society*, 2, p. 246.

these other cultures and faiths, as objectionable and insidious as other more overt manifestations of imperialism.

In this context, Popper's insistence, in line with his general hostility of foundations and justifications, that even a choice in favour of reason is based on an irrational faith is, to put it mildly, disappointing. It leaves him open to the obvious rejoinder that the other faith could be just as true and useful as Popper's, and would determine a rather different attitude to those who disagree—rather more forceful, no doubt, than listening to the other fellow's point of view. So far, my point is that the liberalism espoused by Popper is not merely procedural, nor can it be justified in terms merely of negative utilitarianism. It is actually a substantive politico-ethical position, with its own substantive estimate of the value of (un-Platonic) rationalism, of autonomy and of individuality, just as much as, say, Catholicism or Serbian nationalism or Islam are, with their own rather different evaluations of these matters. What Popper needs at this point is some account of how his (or any other) form of rationalism contributes more to human flourishing and answers more to our needs than these other faiths. What he needs is some positive account of human nature, which will enable us to see the value of critical rationalism as an expression of that nature over its competitor faiths. But it is just this that he fails to offer.

This serious gap aside, have we any reason to think that critical rationalism is actually likely to promote a better form of politics than its competitors? One of its supposed advantages, and the one much emphasised by Popper himself, is that it enables disputes in society to be resolved peacefully, and that by discussions and continual monitoring of policies we may get nearer to the truth. All, of course, hangs on what is meant by 'resolved'.

The methods of science, on the whole, produce a consensus among scientific enquirers. But this is because there is a fairly general agreement within the scientific community about the aims and methods appropriate to science. As Popper himself acknowledged in the original edition of *Logik der Forshung* (*The Logic of Scientific Discovery*), though not subsequently, 'only those sharing the same goal can rationally argue over differences of opinion'.[3] But Popper's open society will precisely not be a community in that sense. In his doctrine of negative utilitarianism he explicitly repudiates the requirement that in an open society there be any general

---

[3] K.R. Popper, *Logik der Forschung: Zur Erkenntnistheorie der modernen Naturwissenschaft* (Vienna: Julius Springer, 1935), p. 10.

consensus about the aims of human life, or about ethics more generally. He hopes to secure enough consensus on policies through insisting that any acceptable policy be guided by the principles of negative utilitarianism, that is that it should be aimed at the removal of obvious suffering and injustice.

But this, too, is dubious. It is hard, if not impossible, to separate the notions of suffering and injustice from some more general conception of what a good life is. What might be the serious oppression of women to one society might be according women their proper role and status in another (or so many Islamists claim about their rules and customs in this area). Is the mere existence of chains of abortion clinics an injustice, as those who see abortion as murder would claim? Or would their absence, and the prevalence of back-street abortions, be unjust and a source of gratuitous and unnecessary suffering? Further, permissible means of removing ills are not always ethically neutral either. We can all agree that the existence of spina bifida and of Huntington's chorea are causes of great suffering to those with the conditions, and their carers, and that getting rid of them would be good. But by any means? By aborting babies with the conditions? Many will think not, and others, perhaps against the majority in the West, will think that even if it could produce a cure for some terrible disease or affliction, research on embryos is not a permissible means either.

In such circumstances, decisions on policy will still have to be made. But given such entrenched disagreement at the level of principle as exists in the cases we have considered, and in other cases too in many areas, policy is not likely to be based on agreement. It is more likely to be based on pragmatism, not to put too fine a point on it, on what the majority will put up with.

On how policies on ethical matters in Western democracies are actually made, see the candid and revealing remarks of Mary Warnock, who has been a legislator as well as a philosopher, in her *An Intelligent Person's Guide to Ethics*. According to Baroness Warnock the morality which rules in legislating in morally contested areas is 'a morality, which though not agreed, is nevertheless broadly *acceptable*', acceptable being just that, what people will in the main accept, something to be distinguished, as she points out, from deciding on the basis of a policy being morally right (or wrong).[4] She says that she came to understand that this notion of 'acceptable' was

---

[4] Mary Warnock, *An Intelligent Person's Guide to Ethics* (London: Duckworth, 1998), pp. 49–50.

not just 'a civil service cop-out', but was actually crucial to making an important distinction between what she calls private and public (i.e. legislative) morality. We are quite a long way there from any high-minded getting nearer to the truth, and, although of course Warnock does not say this herself, far closer to the stealthy if not actually cynical implementation of a morally progressivist agenda which we have seen in legislation over the past half century or so.

In these circumstances the decision making process is by no means necessarily going to lead to truth. It is certainly not aimed at truth. It is aimed rather at consensus and at a sort of tolerance. But just because a majority concurs or pragmatics dictates it, a decision is not thereby right. If abortion, or its criminalisation, or slavery or torture are wrong, then they are wrong, and wrong whatever a majority might think, and even if the majority view had arisen through as much openness and discussion as one could imagine or wish. Indeed, in some circumstances one could doubt that it would even be right to adopt the methods of critical rationalism. Should we say to someone who wants to torture the innocent or join the SS or rape young children 'I may be wrong and you may be right'? Even entertaining the thought that certain practices could, in certain circumstances be permissible, would be to concede too much, to concede that there might really be doubt in this area, a stance leading to weakening of moral commitment individually and collectively. A society which encourages such debates, particularly among the young, may end up in a state of moral uncertainty and decline, on matters where no whiff of fallibilism should have been admitted in the first place (whatever Mill might have said about the value of putting even the firmest principles into question).

So Popper's faith in reason could lead us to a form of uncertainty where, in some matters, no uncertainty should be admitted, theoretically or practically, and which may actually take us away from the truth. It also evinces an approach to society and to institutions which is excessively instrumental. According to Popper, rationality in social life involves a continual willingness to test what Popper, like Mill, thinks of as experiments in living (that is, our actions, policies, traditions and institutions). According to Popper 'a social technology is needed whose results can be tested by piecemeal social engineering'.[5] In the words of Bryan Magee,

---

the Popperian approach involves subjecting institutions to a permanently critical evaluation in order to monitor how well they are solving the problems they exist to solve—and involves moreover a permanent willingness to change them in the light of changing requirements.[6]

Magee makes this remark in an attempt to enlist Popper in the service of the political left, and he points out that Popper has a radical attitude to institutions and to society more generally which is quite at odds with conservatism.

Magee seems to me to be right about the Popper of *The Open Society and Its Enemies*, but both are wrong about institutions. Not all institutions exist to solve problems, and many institutions will be undermined if they are subjected to the strictures of Popperian social engineering. An institution like a church or an ancient university or the Berlin Philharmonic Orchestra or even the junior section of a rugby club does not exist to 'solve problems'. They may, once they exist, have plenty of problems to solve, such as keeping in existence or dealing with their staff or members, but it misunderstands their nature to think of them principally in terms of problem solving. In so far as they exist for anything at all, they exist to embody and pass on a certain form of life. They are the vessels through which and within which particular traditions are transmitted and developed. They exist because the people who belong to them and support them find that they and the activities they promote are worthwhile in themselves.

To say, as Magee said in response to this point, that the youth sections of rugby clubs exist to solve the problem of getting boys to play rugby is not simply a matter of a somewhat empty use of the term 'problem'; it actually mislocates what a rugby club's focus really is. The club's aim is rugby and its spirit ... and companionship and hospitality, etc., etc., as ends in themselves. It no doubt needs to get members to do this, but to represent this truism by saying that it exists to solve the problem of getting boys to play rugby makes it sound as if it is involved in a kind of social work, a subtle transformation of its character, perhaps, but a transformation nonetheless. It is a transformation somewhat akin to the present British government's insistence that one of the things which what it calls 'cultural services' (i.e. museums, galleries, concert halls) are about is 'social inclusion';

[6] Bryan Magee 'What use is Popper to a politician?' in *Karl Popper: Philosophy and Problems*, ed. A. O'Hear (Cambridge: Cambridge University Press, 1995), pp. 259–74, at p. 266.

and in this case the misunderstanding really matters, as literally thousands of museums and artistic companies dumb themselves down in the name of access and outreach. (Managerialism and instrumentalism regarding institutions are no preserve of the political right.)

And there are many other institutions which, though in a sense existing as means to some ulterior purpose (or for solving problems in Popper's terminology), cannot or should not, once they exist, be reduced to that purpose. They develop their own spirit and traditions and way of life which has a value, both for themselves and for the community of which they are a part, quite apart from their extrinsic aims. In this context, one can think of such institutions as regiments, parliaments, the law, schools, the monarchy, the stock exchange, and even some commercial institutions such as Harrods, say, or Nissan. What happens in such cases is that institutions originally formed to promote activities, such as fighting or selling or ruling, which clearly do have instrumental and problem solving aspects, develop traditions and practices with their own intrinsic value, and which then endow the institutions with a value over and above the instrumental. But not only the institutions. The activities they are for are also thereby invested with a value beyond the instrumental, and, for those involved, have the potential to become forms of life worthwhile in and for themselves. It is for this reason, incomprehensible to bureaucrats or Popperian social engineers, that people feel aggrieved when a famous regiment is 'rationalised' by being amalgamated with another, or a school is forced by a bureaucracy unresponsive to its nature to change its character or status. A whole way of life may thereby be lost, and lamented by those to whom it was dear.

To subject institutions with their own spirit and life to the 'permanently critical evaluation' recommended by Popper is likely to destroy what is most valuable in them, because it will look not at what they are, in and for themselves, but what they do, apart from themselves. As an example of the sort of managerialism I am criticising, consider the phrase 'no management without measurement'. One is tempted to say if that is what management is, institutions with their own — unmeasurable — value and tradition would be better off with no management. But that would be unnecessarily perverse, if only because it was often the very unmeasurable and intrinsically valuable spirit of an institution which made it good at the measurable things too, something that often becomes clear only after an institution has been rationalised by social engineers, and its spirit and tradition stripped away in the name of efficient target setting and attaining. Similarly, an institution forced by Popperian social engineers to declare its aims and objectives and then held accountable against a diet of targets met and problems solved is more than likely to lose morale and to wither and decline, as happened to so many institutions in Britain in the 1980s when they were subjected to radical and 'permanently critical evaluation' under Margaret Thatcher's premiership, Margaret Thatcher being the only sort of conservative Magee sees as sitting happily with he calls 'a Popperian approach to the requirements of institutional change'.[7]

Seeing institutions as simply means to ends, decided on by free and rational individuals, who are thereby enabled to criticise and evaluate those institutions is a symptom of an even more basic difficulty with Popper's open society. Who are these free and rational individuals? Criticising the Enlightenment or Kantian view of man as a rational, autonomous, independent individual, de Maistre says this: 'In the course of my life, I have seen Frenchmen, Italians, Russians ... I know, too, thanks to Montsequieu, that one can be a Persian. But as for man, I declare that I have never met him in my life; if he exists, he is unknown to me.'[8]

The point is that, as Bradley pointed out, the man into whose essence his community with others does not enter, who does not include relation to other in his very being, is a fiction. Popper's rational problem solver is just such a fiction. Like Kant's pure rational agent, abstracted from messy and partial human reality and commitment, it is too thin a conception on which to base an individual life, let alone a community.

Communities are not founded on rational decisions alone or on just the commitment to openness, as Popper himself acknowledges in 'Towards a Rational Theory of Tradition'.[9] For their very existence they require shared sentiment, shared allegiances, shared traditions and shared values. All this takes us far beyond the considerations of 'appropriateness, efficiency and simplicity' which Popper thinks should concern the social engineer, and beyond the judgement of institutions, traditions, policies and the rest in terms of the externally

[7] *Ibid.*, p. 267.

[8] J. de Maistre, *Oeuvres Completes*, 14 vols (Lyons: Vitte, 1884–7), vol. 1, p. 74.

[9] In K.R. Popper, *Conjectures and Refutations* (London: Routledge and Kegan Paul, 1963), pp. 161–82.

and independently specifiable problems they are supposed to be solving.[10] It is of the essence of shared sentiment and shared life that much about it is partial, historical and contingent, and to that extent non-rational. Even though in his post-*The Open Society and Its Enemies* work Popper admits the need for non-rational, historically contingent bonds, these are likely to wither if subjected to the sort of scrutiny in terms of 'reason' and 'problems' which Popper also advocated throughout his career, and which would seem to form the essence of the open society.

Perhaps sometimes they should be subjected to scrutiny, and sometimes be allowed to wither. Not all communities encourage freedom or tolerance or openness, to the extent that openness is desirable. We are here operating in the area of what counter-Enlightenment figures such as Burke and Herder referred to as 'prejudice'. Thus Herder: 'Prejudice is good in its time and place, because it makes a people happy. It takes them back to their centre, attaches them firmly to their roots, lets them flourish in their own way...' By contrast, 'when people dream of emigrating to foreign lands to seek hope and salvation, they reveal the first symptoms of sickness and flatulence, of approaching death.'[11]

One cannot fail to be struck by the fact that this, and kindred passages from Fichte, Herder's follower in this respect, sowed the seeds of German nationalism, a point of which Popper would not have needed reminding. I am not defending any and all traditions, nor am I denying that critical rationalism may not itself be part of a society's traditions. Indeed I think it is part of the Western liberal-democratic tradition here, now, in contrast to, say, Islamic tradition which these days at least appears to be essentially theocratic and uncritical. But the fact that certain types of prejudice and certain types of nationalism are objectionable and should be rationally criticised does not show that a community can exist as such without a degree of Burkean prejudice. Or, as Wittgenstein would have put it, what we need is agreement not in judgement, but in form of life, in acceptance of certain values and institutions as settled, unspoken and uncriticised.

Burke himself insisted that, initially at least, we should cherish prejudices precisely because they are prejudices. Our first reaction

---

[10]　*The Open Society*, 1, p. 24.

[11]　J.G. Herder, 'Yet another philosophy of history concerning the development of mankind', quoted in *J.G. Herder on Social and Political Culture*, ed. F.M. Bernard (Cambridge: Cambridge University Press, 1969), pp. 186–7.

should not be critical. We should always first 'employ (our) sagacity to discover the latent wisdom which prevails in them'. If we find what we seek, we should continue the prejudice, with the reason involved

> because prejudice, with its reason, has a motive to give action to that reason, and an affection which will give it permanence ... (engaging) the mind in a steady course of wisdom and virtue ... (and not leaving) the man hesitating in the moment of decision, sceptical, puzzled and unresolved.[12]

Much of this concerns a difference of attitude between the rationalist and the conservative, as to one's first reaction when confronted with a settled custom or a settled society. But there is also the Aristotelian point that we become virtuous not by reasoning, but by habit. Reason without virtue can as well argue in favour of vice as in favour of virtue, and is only too likely to do so if deployed by people without wisdom, experience of life and habits of virtue. Only if we have virtuous habits to start with can we reason well about morality, which in the individual at least suggest a certain priority of initially unreflective habit over reflection.

In this context the remarks Popper makes about moral education are relevant.[13] Teachers may stimulate interest in values in their pupils, he says, but they must not attempt to impose higher values on them. Nor should they pose as authorities, in science or morals, or anything else. These proposals are doubtless in the spirit of Popperian openness, but they fail completely to address the question raised by Aristotle, of how children and young people are to acquire the relevant habits and virtues, including the intellectual virtues required for the practice of science, unless their teachers pose as authorities, and instil in them habits of virtue. There is certainly a pedagogical case for arguing that, at a certain level, teachers can and should pose as authorities even where they might personally have doubts precisely in order that their pupils should embark on a journey which leads to informed fallibilism in a given area, as opposed to shallow scepticism.

These reflections on education focus on one aspect of the more general problem raised by Popper's open society. The general problem (which is also raised by Parekh's multi-culturalism, as we saw in

---

[12]   Edmund Burke, *Reflections on the Revolution in France* (1790), as in the Penguin edn (Harmondsworth: 1968), p. 183.

[13]   *The Open Society*, 2, p. 276.

Chapter 11) is that a disposition to criticise and engage in rational discussion is not in itself enough to bind a community together, let alone to resolve a dispute between, say, a liberal democrat full of ideals of openness and an Islamic mullah insisting on Sharia law for his co-religionists even in a liberal democracy.

To think that a disposition to criticise might on its own be enough to hold a community together is itself utopian, and it could be as destructively utopian as some of the other utopias Popper correctly criticises. For encouragement of a relentlessly critical cast of mind concerning settled values and institutions may not be neutral regarding social bonds. It may, as we see in certain political projects today, actually loosen the bonds which tie a people together, by eroding the sentiment and prejudice on which a form of life depends. And once these ties are eroded, the impeccably liberal and critical community which emerges may not have within itself enough self-belief to defend itself effectively against an enemy which actually believes in something positive, and does not feel constrained by the niceties of rational discussion and openness.

In 1941, in an article entitled 'Wells, Hitler and the World State' George Orwell asked what had kept England on its feet in the past year:

> In part, no doubt, some vague ideas about a better future, but chiefly the atavistic emotion of patriotism, the ingrained feeling of the English-speaking peoples that they are superior to foreigners. For the last twenty years the main object of English left-wing intellectuals has been to break this feeling down, and if they had succeeded, we might be watching SS men patrolling the London streets at the moment.

By contrast, 'for the common-sense, essentially hedonistic world-view which Mr Wells puts forward, hardly a human creature is willing to shed a pint of blood'.[14]

What about Sir Karl's open society? It is true that much blood was shed in the past, has been quite recently and maybe will be shed in defence of Britain and the USA, and Britain and the USA are, as far as any societies are, open societies. Our values are those Popper admired: tolerance, liberalism, democracy, free speech and the rule of law. No doubt part of what we fight for, when we fight, and for all the complications, failures, compromises and muddying of waters

---

[14]   George Orwell, 'Wells, Hitler and the World State' (1941), in his *Critical Essays* (London: Secker and Warburg, 1946), p. 84.

in conflict, is for the defence of these values. But in all probability values which are not part of their nature as open societies have also been crucial to the willingness of our fellow-countrymen to fight and shed their blood on many occasions in the past one hundred years. With many of these non-liberal aspects, Popper was clearly uncomfortable, so he reconfigures his ideal society as Britain of the USA with the patriotic, atavistic bits airbrushed out.

To that extent, to the extent that it refers to no actual society and not even to the reality of those societies he most admired, Popper's open society is a utopian vision. And neither he, nor anyone else so far knows whether a society which was completely open and relentlessly self-critical in his sense would be possible. Whether, even if it were possible, it would be desirable, or whether it would be a managerial nightmare (of continuous self-scrutiny and endless target setting) is another question altogether.

Having made these basic criticisms of Popper's open society, it is only right to put them in the context of the development of Popper's own thought. The vision of society we have been considering is that to be found in *The Open Society and Its Enemies*. That book was written in New Zealand, in the early 1940s, but very much in response to events occurring in Europe, particularly in the lands dominated by Hitler and Stalin. As a counter-blast to those societies and ideologies, *The Open Society* is *sans pareil*. And, given its oft-repeated message — that any large-scale attempt to re-mould society centrally is bound to lead to tyranny — it is puzzling that in that book there are many statements which can be seen as, up to a point, friendly to Marxism. I would argue that from the perspective of *The Open Society*, communism cannot be a good idea which went wrong. Involving as it does radical and continual intervention by the state in all areas of life, it was always a terrible idea, and Popper shows us exactly why. Nevertheless, its great merits notwithstanding, *The Open Society* remains over-rationalistic and utopian about reason and about the sort of society it is advocating.

However, it is arguable that by the time he wrote 'Towards a rational theory of tradition' in 1949, Popper himself came to distance himself not only from the rationalists he explicitly criticises, but also from his own earlier rationalistic stance. In 1949 he castigated rationalists in rather Burkean terms (see Chapter 13). They think that they have the means to correct and disparage traditions on the basis of pure reason, through their own brains, rather than confining their criticisms to cases where actual problems were apparent — but doesn't this picture apply at least to some degree to the ideal, thorough-goingly untraditional citizen earlier open society?

But by 1949, when he had appeared to qualify his rationalism in favour of a positive role for tradition, Popper had experienced the traditional societies of New Zealand and Britain, and he liked them. He valued many of their traditions, such as their unspoken and unargued for tolerance, their respect for the law, and their concern for the individual and the underdog, things which go up to make up his own 'irrational faith in reason'. At around this time, in conversation at least, he also defended Hayek against critics from the political left. A liberal society, he said, requires a framework of conservative values.

What might that framework consist in? As Popper himself did not attempt to spell this out in any detail, it would not be inappropriate to end this essay by saying something here about the social and historical conditions which obtain in Britain and the United States and which form the context in which liberalism and openness exist and flourish there—to the extent they do. What has already become clear is that more, much more, is required than an abstract commitment to reason or to the political process. As already suggested in discussing Parekh (Chapter 11), a society committed only to engaging in discussion not only has no real means of resolving basic disagreements. It could very easily subside into continually quarrelling factions who may have no basis for agreement on fundamental points, and who feel no sense of community with each other.

This is, of course, what worries people in the West about large scale Islamic immigration, where the newcomers and their descendents see themselves as belonging to political communities defined by their religion, rather than by the nationhood of the societies they are living in. Some of them also have, in accordance with their faith, a long-term aim of bringing the places in which they live under Sharia law, and regard the institutions and customs of the West as decadent and infidel. It is not that what is said by Muslim groups who see themselves in this way is unintelligible or even necessarily wholly wrong; it is rather that having numbers of people within a liberal society who believe such things throws into sharp relief the substantive commitments of liberal societies. It also poses a significant problem for those societies and their institutions (such as schools), which for centuries have been unaccustomed to the presence within them of groups fundamentally at variance with their beliefs, commitments and practices. Popperian openness on its own is not enough, faced with such radically diverging views once those views are held by significant and vocal minorities.

The open society, in these circumstances, will also become increasingly subject to paradoxes brought about by its own commitment to openness, as we see daily in the West. For example, wanting to express in a meaningful way its commitment to freedom of speech — which it was felt was being eroded from within from fear of Islamic responses such as those following the publication of Salman Rushdie's *The Satanic Verses* — in 2006 a Danish newspaper published cartoons mocking the prophet Mohammed, and in the ensuing and predictable outcry, other papers re-published them. Is this what openness required? Some Muslims and some non-Muslims pointed out that in a tolerant and open society deliberately insulting people was at the very least bad form, and hardly conducive to living together peacefully and tolerantly — which are also, of course, virtues of Popperian openness. So what does openness require here: publication of calculatedly insulting material to insist on freedom of speech or restraint in the service of tolerance?

Other Muslims, however, reacted rather more aggressively. Using their right to free speech, which has been given them in the West, and which in abstract all proponents of openness would defend, they protested noisily and vigorously outside the Danish embassy in London. Inflammatory speeches were made, including calling for death to the blasphemers and also for British soldiers fighting in Muslim lands (but only calling for it). For this exercise of free speech some of the noisier protesters have now been sent to prison for a long time. Of course, all this is against the background of Islamic terrorist plots in London, where maybe calling for attacks on blasphemers and British soldiers comes close to plotting or instigating attacks, but there is more than a hint of contradiction about this episode. By imprisoning the protesters, we in the West show that we believe so strongly in freedom of speech that we lock up those who use freedom of speech to protest about freedom of speech (as the *Economist* rather glibly put it in its 21 July 2007 issue).

Popper himself argued that the open society had to defend itself against threats to openness, and that it should take strong measures to deal with those who would exploit the openness they were granted within an open society to undermine it. These measures would include in certain circumstances suppressing intolerant philosophies by force, particularly those philosophies which forbad their followers to listen to rational arguments and to use violence instead.[15] Terrorists and the like would have no right to complain when the open society moves to curb their freedoms, if they are using these freedoms to pursue illiberal ends (though whether this would extend to imprisoning people who simply say they would like other people to die is another question). Practically restraining those who use their freedoms to undermine freedom might be sensible, though I am unclear whether a fundamentalist cleric would fall under the Popperian stricture of forbidding his followers to listen to rational argument. There might also be a very fine line between a leader denouncing argument and encouraging his followers to use more direct means, not a purely theoretical matter as Western democracies strive to rid themselves of the 'extremist' clerics whose teachings they fear are influencing their followers to take up violence.

But raising the question of how to deal with enemies of openness, important as it is, hardly gets to the root of the problem. The problem is that openness is not in itself enough to keep a society together. Openness can flourish and function positively only given fundamental agreement among citizens, particularly, one suspects a fundamental agreement on the restraint we all need to observe for a free society to be possible. The worry about the presence of large numbers of Muslims in a European country is whether this means that there might be significant groups within the country who are not party to such fundamental agreement.

Against the type of individualism and cosmopolitanism advocated by Popper in *The Open Society and Its Enemies*, it is becoming increasingly clear that the freedoms of the individual valued by Popper and other advocates of openness and liberal democracy (to the extent that the two are the same thing) require a political community and a sense among the citizens that they belong to a political community, and that in a sense their freedoms derive from membership of that community.

Though these are not absolutely necessary conditions of the sort of community necessary for grounding an open society, a common language and culture would be a good basis for the sort of general basis of agreement within which liberty, tolerance and openness might flourish. This commonality of language and culture would ground a sense of historical and political identity, as well as a sense of common interest at some profound level, which would transcend political and other differences at a more superficial level. This sense

[15]   *The Open Society*, 1, p. 265.

of common identity would also, rather against Popperian and Kantian cosmopolitanism, give members of that society a sense that they have duties and responsibilities towards the society, and in the final resort, a sense that their society would be worth fighting for and defending, as we saw with Orwell.

It will be obvious that within the modern world the only states which fulfil these conditions are nation states. So the sense of community a nation state engenders may be extremely helpful towards setting up regimes of openness, in which there is enough shared interest among members of that state to use their freedoms in such a way as not to pull the state apart. But it will also be obvious that nation states may not value individual freedom in the way pre-supposed by talk of openness; they could be nationalist and socialist or both, and they could in various ways elevate the collective above the individual. So nationhood is not a sufficient condition for openness and a regime of liberty. We also need a nation founded on what might be called personalism—a sense of the paramount and uncon-ditional value of the individual, and which in Popper is what we have called his humanitarianism and individualism.

We could debate as to whether personalism in this sense requires a religious and specifically a Christian underpinning. Of course there was such an idea in the European Enlightenment and in some, but not all, of the streams of thought stemming from that Enlighten-ment, and in Enlightenment thinking there was a repudiation of anything specifically Christian. It may, though, be that Nietzsche was right in believing that in the absence of its Christian underpin-ning the nineteenth-century liberal sense of the value and sacred-ness of the individual was intellectually and morally vulnerable.

But, for the purposes of this chapter, we do not need to settle this question or even to pursue it further. What we need to observe is simply this: that the type of liberalism advocated by Popper requires for its implementation a tradition of thought and practice in which a community sustains, but does not swamp, a profound sense of the value of the individual, and in which individuals, in the main anyway, retain enough of a commitment to their community to enable the institutions and practices of openness to operate con-structively and positively, and not destructively and negatively. In the terms of Aristotle, to which we alluded in Chapter 11, in such a polity individuals will act as individuals, but there will be enough of a middle section of the society, agreeing in form of life, to allow that society to function cohesively. It should by now be clear that in

Britain and New Zealand and the United States, Popper found societies with the traditions and common cultures in which the openness he valued was able to flourish.

So the implicit contrast of *The Open Society* is wrong. It is not that there are irrational communities, with no commitment to reason, and rational open societies with no basis in tradition. The open society, where and in so far as it exists, exists as part of a given tradition. One may object to this being seen in terms of an 'irrational' faith in reason, and to return to a point made earlier, one might have preferred Popper to have located his ideas about freedom, individualism and openness in a more fully worked-out notion of human flourishing and human nature, so as to give his — and our — views on society and our tradition a more substantial basis than that of one faith confronting other faiths. Maybe he did not want to do this because he resisted talk of human good, rather than of human harm. But, this admittedly crucial point aside, one can also see some positive point of his talk of an irrational faith in reason if it leads us to see what is surely correct: that the open society itself is a substantive tradition, or a part of one. Openness in a society will be undermined if too many people in it do not share its values and traditions, including openness itself, but also values other than openness itself, which permit a society to see itself as a genuine community. This is a problem which concerns many in the West today, and which has no prospect of a solution so long as we think only in terms of the procedures of critical rationalism, and not in terms of the actual traditions and substantive beliefs which sustain those procedures. In this respect Popper's cosmopolitan individualism is not just utopian; it is utopian in exactly the same way as contemporary neo-conservatism in its belief that, for the best of all reasons, a model of life might be best for all, quite irrespective of local traditions and values.

Chapter 15

Britain and Europe

An Oakeshottian Meditation[1]

Commissioner Patten's advice

On breakfast radio on 1 May 2004, Chris Patten, the former Tory party chairman and then a European Commissioner, protested about Britain having a referendum on the European Constitution which was being proposed at the time. He said — and though it was early in the morning, I'm pretty sure that I got it right — that it was inconsistent for people (in Britain) to think that they knew best for others, while not joining in the club. If you want to know why well over half the British people appeared then (and now) to be against the constitution and why, according to some opinion polls in Britain taken in 2004, nearly half actually wanted to leave the EU, you need look no further.

It is precisely because unlike Mr Patten people in Britain do NOT think that they know best for others that they object to ever increasing European integration at least for themselves. People in Britain and elsewhere who are opposed to further European integration (and I count myself among their number) are quite happy for others in the European 'club', as Patten calls it, to do whatever they want. We believe in the rights of sovereign nations to determine their own fates and policies, even if with some of them such determination leads to some sort of federation. So nothing I say here should be taken as any sort of complaint about a federation between some European states — if that is what they decide. But, against Patten, a large majority in Britain do want the right to decide whether others

---

[1]   It may be of interest to record that this paper was originally given at the annual meeting of the Institute of Political Sciences of the Catholic University of Portugal in 2004; hence the references to Portugal and also to José Manuel Barroso, who is a regular participant in these meetings, and who had just become the President of the European Commission.

should have more power over us — which the majority in Britain do not want: and also over whether we should have more power over them — which the majority also do not want.

And why is Chris Patten, along with many other British Eurofederalists, so unhappy about a referendum? Surely not just because they think they might lose it. At a deeper level it is the bureaucrat's fundamental dislike of giving people choices. People might make the wrong choice. To the bureaucratic mind societies are better and more rationally run as collectively administered enterprises, than as associations of free men and autonomous institutions. If this way of putting things reminds you of the political thought of Michael Oakeshott, it is meant to.

Europe as an enterprise association

Fundamental to that thought is a distinction between government as the guardian of civil association and government as itself an enterprise. In the former conception, the government is seen as a sort of umpire, maintaining the fairness of the game which different players play, making their decisions about their own lives and communities, and competing peacefully with each other under the rule of law; in the latter conception government itself is a player in the collective game, binding all the players, whether they like it or not in some sort of collective enterprise of its own, which is represented as the enterprise of the whole group. In Oakeshott's own words,

> the 'enlightened' rulers of the eighteenth century understood themselves to be the guardians of a comprehensive 'national interest' with a mission to harness their subjects' activities to its promotion and to educate them in the parts they should play.[2]

For Frederick, Joseph and Catherine, read the Commissioners of Brussels (who are largely unchecked by national governments or the European 'parliament') and for the national interest, the 'European' interest.

But, as is vividly illustrated in the case of Europe, for example, in the shenanigans surrounding the selection of the President of the European Commission in 2004, in which the then Prime Minister of Portugal emerged as a compromise candidate because the main players could not agree among themselves on a nomination, there can be no such group enterprise. We are fallen men. None of us has a

---

[2] Michael Oakeshott, *Rationalism in Politics*, expanded edn (Indianapolis: Liberty Fund, 1991), p. 452.

monopoly of truth or of good sense. We have competing conceptions of aims and of the good life and we all are subject to sordid self-interest. The upshot is that in any large scale human enterprise, be it national or European, there will always be major disagreements between the contractors. Decision-making, far from being a dialectical discussion between disinterested Platonic philosophers, becomes a disedifying exercise in horse-trading and bullying by the heavy-weights in the 'community'.

I have not heard of this before, but it seems obvious to me that the European Union, as currently constituted, is a classic example of an Oakeshottian enterprise association, and has been ever since 1948 when Jean Monnet, its visionary and first architect declared that 'we must create new common basic economic conditions and set up new authorities accepted by the sovereign nations'; thus far it could perhaps be conceived in terms of Europe as a civil association, in which the new authorities and conditions stand aside from the doings of the participants and simply remove obstacles to their commerce and movement, with the law seen as the guarantor of the new freedoms to be enjoyed. But Monnet went on (amazingly) 'Europe has never existed. It is not the addition of sovereign nations met together in councils that makes an entity of them. We (the fonctionaires) must genuinely create Europe; it must become manifest to itself...'[3]

The enterprise to which the EU is committed is first and foremost the creation of itself, as a supra-governmental authority, a task of Hegelian pretension (self-manifestation) and of Soviet proportion. Of course, this was an enterprise which could not be revealed in its entirety, at least not at first, and not to the general public—who in many countries would have rejected it. The political Europe was initially presented to electors in Britain and elsewhere as a free trade area (the European Economic Community or Common Market, as it was known in Britain), in line with the first part of Monnet's memorandum.

But if not always explicit, the second part was always implicit. So Sir Edward Heath, who in 1971 took Britain into the EEC as it then was, while then saying that British independence and sovereignty would not be sacrificed, was later able to claim that a far tighter union had always been contemplated. Indeed it had been contemplated even in 1971, and that it had been was actually stated in the

[3]   Quoted in Christopher Booker and Richard North, *The Great Deception* (London: Continuum Books, 2004), p. 49.

official communiqué registering agreement between Heath and the French President Georges Pompidou on British entry (though this was not at the time widely remarked). The communique noted the progress to date of the EEC to 'economic and monetary union' and also Britain's readiness to participate 'fully and in a European spirit in this development'.[4] We will come back to 'the European spirit' later, but what Heath should have been asked in 1971, was how you can have economic and monetary union without sacrifice of independence. This point was vividly brought home in Britain when the British economy was nearly wrecked in 1992 by our being unable to act autonomously to defuse our own economic crisis due to our membership of the Exchange Rate Mechanism (the precursor of the Euro), and perhaps even more vividly by the differential rates of progress of the British and the Eurozone economies since Britain withdrew from the ERM.

So the enterprise to which the European Union is committed is, in the first instance, itself; the creation of a European super-state. Much as European officials and governments may deny it, it is hard to make sense otherwise of the rhetoric of speeds, journeys, railway lines, buffers, clubs, pooled sovereignty, keeping the bicycle upright and the rest; and difficult too to see the creation of European currencies, armies, foreign policies, immigration policies, asylum policies, social policies, labour laws, tax legislation, constitutions, parliaments, supreme courts and also of qualified majority voting in any other light.

Of course, there are hiccoughs and set-backs on the road, but — to use the rhetoric — the direction is inevitably 'forward', with each set back or scandal seemingly becoming just the pretext for yet more regulation or for bringing the failed measure back in a different form, as with the re-branding of the rejected constitution as a 'treaty', definitely a case of 'reculer pour mieux sauter'. After all, if you don't control your finances, your money, your foreign policy, your army and defence, your employment law, your energy policy, who can claim asylum in your country and be a citizen of it, and if your government can be out-voted by other governments on matters of internal policy and its laws struck down by a superior court outside your shores or boundaries, and if you are taxed by an outside body as well, what does your sovereignty amount to?

---

[4]   Quoted in Booker and North, *The Great Deception*, p. 141.

Economic diversion

Let us, then, assume, as both history and logic strongly suggest, that the European state is the proximate end of the European Union. The European state itself is also seen and justified largely in terms of two more enterprises, economic power in the world, and, more fundamentally, peace within Europe itself.

I am not really competent to speak about the economic side of things, beyond remarking that a low growth, highly taxed, socialistically regulated trade barrier area — which is what the EU actually is — is hardly likely to compete effectively with the USA or indeed with China or India if and when those vast countries, with their pools of cheap labour, get going economically. Over thirty years, from 1970 to 2000 there had been no net increase in jobs in the Eurozone area, and unemployment in that zone is far higher than in Britain, which is not in the Euro. And just to make a comparison with the USA, the EU as a whole spends sixty-six per cent of the amount the US spends on defence, yet has only a quarter of the deployable fighting strength.

As far as Britain is concerned, British taxpayers spend in excess of £22bn per annum subsidising the EU, yet eighty per cent of our GDP is domestically generated. We do, of course, trade within the EU, but we are in trade deficit with the EU. So it is unclear why it is to our economic benefit to be in, or why, given the trade imbalance, the Europeans would wish to inflict economic penalties on us were we not to be in. And all this is quite apart from what I regard as the immorality of the CAP, which, by protecting European and mainly French agriculture against imports from the developing world not only makes food far more expensive than it need be for people in Europe (in Britain an extra £20 per household per week), but arguably it is responsible for millions of deaths each year in developing countries unable to trade with us. (That the USA does similar things to South and Central America and elsewhere is no excuse at all.)

But, as I say, economics is not my competence, and I have no doubt the figures I have quoted (which date from 2004) could be challenged, qualified and 'put in perspective' by countervailing considerations (and may in any case need updating). Apart from the general point about socialistic regulation and the CAP I don't want to rest my case on economic considerations, because the cost to Britain could be justified by other considerations. But I do want to say something about peace and war.

Peace in Europe

For it is often claimed the real and ultimate justification of the European project is the creation of European peace. Certainly this is how many Europhiles see it or saw it, including both Monnet and Heath, and I am sure sincerely. And it is also notable that Oakeshott himself sees the embattled state as a case where the state will most directly act as enterprise association, and, when war means mobilisation of the whole population, with justification one might feel when one considers the Second World War. It is also true that peace in Europe is a phenomenon often conspicuous by its absence, particularly during the first half of the twentieth century.

What is not so clear, though, in fact is not clear at all, is why peace in Europe requires supra-national union, as opposed to inter-governmental agreements between sovereign nations. The threat, often advanced by Chancellor Kohl of Germany in the 1980s and 1990s, that without supra-governmental arrangements Germany might once more get out of control in Europe seems unworthy of what has become one of Europe's least belligerent nations, and to those suspicious of Eurofederalism, a rather crude sort of blackmail. In any case, NATO, an organisation of independent states, has proved itself far more robust in the Cold War and since than 'Europe' or any common European foreign policy, which still seems to break down at the first hint of trouble. And, of course, both fascism (Second World War) and communism (The Cold War) were defeated not by any supranational federation, but by agreements and alliances between sovereign nations, in which the USA and Britain were especially prominent.

Autobiographical reflections of a 'Little Englander': The European spirit

But before turning to Britain and the Atlantic Alliance, I want to say something about 'the European spirit'. For the most insidious and underhand weapon of the Eurofederalists is to infer that anyone, particularly from Britain, who opposes their project is a 'Europhobe' or 'a little Englander'; and these terms, as used in these discussions, carry with them an implicit, but nonetheless heavy baggage of xenophobia and racism. In polite circles, it is simply not done to express scepticism about the European project (though one can express scepticism about pretty well anything else, about religion, morality and culture).

In order to rebut the charge that I am either a xenophobe or even a 'little Englander', and more generally that what is referred to as Euroscepticism implies Europhobia (or worse) I will now indulge in a little autobiography.

One of my favourite journeys in Europe goes from Munich to Venice over the Brenner Pass. You start with the cool Bavarian neo-classicism of Munich (pausing no doubt to visit its English garden and the matchless collections of archaic Greek sculpture and European painting in its museums). You go through the gothic and the baroque of German villages, up into the mountains with their strange towns neither precisely Germanic nor Italianate (and languages like nothing else in Europe), and down into the valleys, with every so often among the castles and crags a glimpse of Italian roof tiles and of something owing a debt to Alberti, and into the plains of the great rivers and on to Venice itself. The transitions are seamless. There is throughout an underlying unity of spirit. But what diversity from beginning to end, and how differently expressed!

I first made this journey many years ago, as a sort of refugee from dreary little England (as I then thought it). I had been brought up in a London suburb (the same one, in fact, as David Beckham) and attended a very ordinary school in Tottenham. To my eyes, England seemed characterised by Sundays, during which, apart from Church, nothing was permitted; by post-war austerity and rationing; by inefficient smoke-stack industry and heavy, tasteless food; and by the tedium of official respectability. Each year we were afflicted by smogs, a specially English type of particularly noxious fog, green and brown rather than white, and which penetrated our classrooms, making it difficult even to see the blackboard) which afflicted us annually, and from which people died, and this seemed an apt symbol of our condition.

Not surprisingly I and many other of my compatriots looked to what we then called the Continent for enlightenment. And, within the limits of the amount of travel government restrictions allowed, we found it. Like Turner, our greatest artist, and Ruskin, our greatest critic, we travelled to the sun. We discovered the esprit of French life, its food and wine, the clarity of its intellect, and the joyful sensuality and subversiveness of so many of its writers. We sunk ourselves in the fathomless depths of Germany's music, poetry and philosophy, so exhilarating after the shallowness of the native variety. We climbed up into the Alps and the Pyrenees, so much grander and purer than our British crags. We went down into Italy, and found a culture and a landscape, beyond all our imaginings, rich and profligate in its endless fertility. We went to Greece, discovering antiquity and sleeping among its stones and temples, under skies of undreamed of depth and purity. And no doubt, had we been truly Byronic, we would also have gone to Portugal to discover what Childe Harold called 'Cintra's glorious Eden'.

Travel in Europe made us aware of two things. One was the diversity within Europe itself, a diversity of language, culture and history. Under the common umbrella of its Roman and Christian history there are all manner of differences of identity, of custom, of taste. All these differences are interesting, and most are life-enhancing. They ought to be preserved, and not ironed out in the interest of European 'level playing fields' (what a drab, bureaucratic cliché and yet, how revealing in its notion of levelling!).

The second thing I gained from my travels in Europe was a new estimation of my own country and education. For, however drab things might have seemed, it was precisely my upbringing in Chingford and Tottenham which enable me to respond to the countries of Europe with such enthusiasm and feeling. But, more than that, through the prism of European cultures, I began to understand the virtues of my own, which its surface drabness concealed. Other European cultures exhibited other virtues. But few of them exhibited the particularly British virtues of tolerance and fair play, of understatement which masked but which did not suppress feeling, and of an inbred suspicion of government.

Government and Anglo-American attitudes

This inbred suspicion of government derives from our own political history and tradition, one which developed a particular form of liberalism particularly during the seventeenth and eighteenth centuries, and on which the American constitutionalists also drew (which is partly why for some of us the Atlantic alliance is more comfortable and natural than the European project which owes more to the spirit of Rousseau and the Code Napoléon than to that of Thomas Hobbes and John Locke).

According to this tradition men and human institutions are imperfectible; the good life cannot be secured by large scale utopian projects. However admirable they might be on paper, they are bound to have equally large scale unwanted consequences. It is far better and far more humane to allow individuals to pursue their own limited ends under the rule of law. According to this tradition, government's primary role is to secure peace without and security within, in order that citizens (or subjects) may enjoy as much freedom as possible, consistent with others' enjoyment of similar freedoms. Within this framework, individuals and groups are free to pursue their own ends, according to their own conceptions of the ultimate good, and to set up and join their own autonomous institutions under the law. In this conception autonomous institutions (institutions separate from and not controlled by the state) are seen both as goods in themselves, as releasing and expressing individual initiative, and also as checks on the growth of the over mighty state. And the state itself will be multiple balances of power, between monarchy (or president), parliament and people, within parliament between two houses, between central and local government, and crucially, with a judiciary independent of the legislature, and with a professional civil service and army, politically neutral and independent of political interests.

This framework — in Oakeshott's terms, that of civil association — is not impervious to reform and development, nor, as we have seen in the history of Britain over the past few decades (and particularly since 1997), is it fireproof against the growth of the enterprise state or the incursion of utopian reforms based not on practical necessity but on abstract notions of right and justice. In Britain the state itself has taken over the lives of its citizens in fields such as health and education, imposing on them its own particular views of the good (political correctness and the like), in ways unimaginable to liberal thinkers of only a century ago.

Nevertheless, commitment to basic ideals of tolerance and freedom under the law, and the crucial sense that anything not explicitly forbidden by the law is permitted, remain deep within the British (and also, I believe, the American) psyche, as does the Burkean notion of prescription: that is the idea that arrangements which have evolved over time have a prima facie validity and are not to be altered simply to subserve some abstract principle which may make no connection with the way people actually live and think. There is also a keen understanding that liberty is sustained far more by a spirit of liberty among the populace generally, and crucially among legislators and the judiciary, than by written constitutions, charters, bills of rights and the like. Indeed there is a strong feeling that without that spirit such legal instruments are likely in practice to add little to the real liberties of the citizens, but will certainly add a lot to the powers of regulatory bodies, to the growth of bureaucracy and to the earnings of our learned friends.

Against this Anglo-American background, the European project is likely to seem colossally wrong-headed, even leaving aside the degree of corruption at its bureaucratic heart. It is a utopian attempt to impose sets of abstract principles on peoples with different traditions, values, languages and conceptions of the good, an attempt whose net result is to ride rough shod over those differences. Local loyalties will be destroyed, the effect of which is likely to be widespread resentment of 'Europe' or contempt for its laws. Maybe this conception has affinity with the Napoleonic tradition of administrative centralism in France and with the Bismarckian nation-building project in Prussia and later in Germany. Not having lived under either of these dispensations, I cannot really say. But what I do know is that it sits ill with what I have been calling the Anglo-American spirit of liberty and of recognition of peaceful difference which is at its heart.

When people in Britain get so exercised about edicts from Brussels forbidding them to fish on the high seas, to sell their vegetables to each other in pounds and ounces, to dispose of waste as they see fit, and even to call their (often disgusting) food products what they want, it is not just bloody-mindedness or pettiness. Some of these examples and others which are often highlighted in the British press are trivial in themselves (though many are not). But beneath the reaction even to the apparently trivial cases lurks a strong sense of what government should and should not do. Too much of the Brussellian project offends that spirit of Anglo-American liberalism. And when one considers the benefits of the Anglo-American alliance over the past century in its highly effective opposition to tyranny in Europe and throughout the world, attempting to suppress that spirit is no small matter.

Index

St Andrews Studies in
Philosophy and Public Affairs

www.imprint-academic.com/standrews